WOMEN
IN POLICING

A HISTORY THROUGH PERSONAL STORIES

WOMEN
IN POLICING

A HISTORY THROUGH PERSONAL STORIES

A WORK BY THE
POLICE HISTORY SOCIETY,
EDITED BY TOM ANDREWS

The
History
Press

First published 2024

The History Press
97 St George's Place, Cheltenham,
Gloucestershire, GL50 3QB
www.thehistorypress.co.uk

British Library Cataloguing in Publication Data.
A catalogue record for this book is available from the British Library.

ISBN 978 1 80399 249 5

Typesetting and origination by The History Press
Printed and bound in Great Britain by TJ Books Limited, Padstow, Cornwall.

Front cover image: *Winnifred Hooper and Eileen Normington, c.1945 (Courtesy of Eileen Normington).*

Trees for Life

ABOUT THE AUTHORS

TOM ANDREWS (EDITOR)

Tom Andrews is a lecturer in policing at the University of Derby, teaching new police officers on the Police Constable Degree Apprentice (PCDA) programme. He has been lecturing for two years, before which he was a uniformed police sergeant working on emergency response in Nottingham for thirteen years. During this time he researched and co-authored a history of women in policing within that force. He is the editor of the annual *Journal of the Police History Society* since 2020 and has published two books: *The Greatest Policeman? A Biography of Capt. Athelstan Popkess CBE, OStJ: Chief Constable of Nottingham City Police 1930–1959* and *The Sharpe End: Murder, Violence and Knife Crime on Nottingham's Thin Blue Line*. He has also published articles in various academic journals.

PETER FINNIMORE

Peter was a Metropolitan Police officer for thirty years, serving in many roles and reaching the rank of superintendent. After retirement in 1999 he continued to be a lead HMIC staff officer as a civil servant for another eight years. Twice winner of the Queen's Police Gold Medal Essay Competition, he gained a first-class honours degree in History as a Bramshill scholar. In retirement he has had several voluntary jobs, including chairing the Independent Monitoring Board at the Dover Immigration Removal Centre. His main interests are backgammon, reading and trying to keep fit. He lives in Lympne, Kent. He first learned about Margaret Damer Dawson from her grave and memorial in Lympne churchyard.

DEREK OAKENSEN

Dr Derek Oakensen is an independent historian whose research interests are largely focused on local government and criminal justice in nineteenth- and early twentieth-century Sussex. An earlier paper, *Antipathy to Ambivalence: politics and women police in Sussex, 1915–45*, was published in Sussex Archaeological Collections in 2015.

DR DAVID M. SMALE

Dr David M. Smale served in the Royal Marines and as a constable in Lothian and Borders Police, working in both the City of Edinburgh and in the rural Scottish Borders. He studied with the Open University and at the University of Edinburgh and worked as a Postdoctoral Research Fellow at Edinburgh. He has contributed chapters to books and written articles in academic journals and in popular history magazines. He is presently researching various aspects of the history of policing in Scotland.

JOAN LOCK

Joan Lock's first book, *Lady Policeman*, described her six years' service in the Metropolitan Police during the 1950s. Her second, *Reluctant Nightingale*, told of her previous training as nurse. In 1979, she wrote the first history of the British women police – *The British Policewoman: Her Story*. Since then, she has been a regular contributor to the Police Press and Crime Writers Association magazine, written radio plays and documentaries featuring women police, as well as several non-fiction books and novels on Scotland Yard's first detectives.

Joan's late husband Bob served thirty years in the Metropolitan Police as did her brother, Eric Greenslade, in the Cumbria Constabulary, finally as Detective Chief Superintendent.

EDWARD SMITH

Edward Smith is curatorial assistant of the Metropolitan Police Museum at Marlowe House in Sidcup. He assisted in mounting its 2019 West Brompton exhibition to mark the centenary of female officers in the Metropolitan

Police, and in 2020 wrote the first entry on Sofia Stanley in the *Oxford Dictionary of National Biography*.

LISA COX-DAVIES

Lisa Cox-Davies is a former police officer and is now a doctoral student at the University of Worcester. Her research examines the roles and experiences of women in the police forces of the West Midlands area between 1939 and 1990, with a focus on the period of the Second World War and the impact of the Sex Discrimination legislation of the 1970s.

MARK ROTHWELL

Mark Rothwell is a Dartmoor-based author, biographer and historian who has written several books on the history of policing in Devon and Cornwall including *Policing the West Country*. His areas of interest include police deaths in service, the Great War, the history of women constables, airports constabularies and police transportation. His work as a co-author includes a contribution to the charitable work UK Police Roll of Remembrance published by the Police Roll of Honour Trust.

VALERIE REDSHAW

Valerie worked in the Metropolitan Police before emigrating in 1962 to continue policing in New Zealand. After marriage she resigned to have a family. In 1984 she re-joined the New Zealand Police as an education officer with responsibility for training police recruits, youth aid and senior officers as well as designing the curriculum for all police training. She has represented the New Zealand Police on many public sector bodies including the Equal Opportunities Advisory Group, the Public Sector Training Organisation and the Government Committee for Suffrage Centennial Year. Her book *Tact and Tenacity – New Zealand Women in Policing* represents research she undertook for the fifty-year anniversary of women in policing there. In 1993, Valerie, was awarded the Suffrage Centennial Medal for services to policewomen and in 2007 was made a member of the New Zealand Order of Merit for services to education. Her most recent publication is a memoir entitled *The Things We Keep*.

ROB PHILLIPS

Rob Phillips joined Nottinghamshire Police in 2004 and has served in response, neighbourhood and proactive roles. Among his secondary duties, he is an accredited Wildlife Crime Officer. In 2022 he was appointed to the UK Overseas Territories Hurricane Response Cadre which, when activated by the Foreign and Commonwealth Office, deploys overseas to provide essential law enforcement relief and aid to those locations affected by natural disaster. He is passionate about promoting policing history and heritage and in 2012 arranged an event to commemorate National Police Memorial Day which was attended by dignitaries from around the county. He has represented his force twice at the Cenotaph Festival of Remembrance in London, accepted the Ministry of Defence Employer Recognition Scheme Award in Silver on behalf of the force, and provides advice and training within the force for ceremonial events.

ADAM PICKIN

Adam Pickin has been a police officer for over six years and is currently based at Bodmin, Cornwall, as a neighbourhood beat manager. He has always had a keen interest in history and studied Classical History at Swansea University. More recently he's enjoyed reading the history of police forces and saw this as a fantastic opportunity to research some of history's most influential and important figures.

KATE HALPIN QPM

Kate is a retired Metropolitan Police officer. She had a varied career serving primarily in investigative roles across South East London and a number of specialist departments as well as several international postings. In 1999 she became the first British police woman to be awarded a Fulbright Police Scholarship to examine how the police and partner agencies in Los Angeles approached youth and gang crime. She also undertook a number of secondments with the Foreign and Commonwealth Office in Jordan, London and Iraq. She was part of the team that led the Met's celebrations to mark centenary of women joining the Met in 2019. She is the current Vice Chair of the Police History Society. Kate was awarded the Queen's Police Medal for distinguished service in the 2021 New Year's Honours.

DR CLIFFORD WILLIAMS

Dr Clifford Williams is a historian and retired police officer. He studied History and Social Anthropology at SOAS, University of London, from 1980 to 1983 (1st Class Honours) and Criminology at the Universities of Cambridge and Bradford (where he completed his doctorate). After working as a researcher for the Home Office, Clifford served twenty-five years as a police officer in the Hampshire Constabulary and then a further nine years as a volunteer. He has published books and articles on history and criminology, including *A History of Women Policing Hampshire and the Isle of Wight 1915–2016* and *111 Years of Policing Winchester: A History of the Winchester City Police Force 1832–1943*. His current research includes the history of policing gay and bisexual men.

ANTHONY RAE

Anthony Rae is a retired Lancashire and Metropolitan Police officer. He began research on the UK Police Roll of Honour following the deaths in 1983 of three friends and colleagues, attempting a sea rescue at Blackpool, when he found no such national records existed. He established the National Police Officers Roll of Honour research project in 1995 and founded the Police Roll of Honour Trust charity in 2000, leaving in 2012 for academic research study. In 2016 he received an MA degree in History from Lancaster University related to aspects of police history and deaths on duty. Publications include several Rolls of Honour and Books of Remembrance for police forces and national memorial charities, and some fifty articles in police periodicals, including *Police Review* and the *Police History Society Journal*. He joined the Police History Society member since 1985 and became a committee member in 2011.

MARTIN STALLION

Martin Stallion is a retired reference librarian and a former member of the Metropolitan Police Civil Staff. He was awarded life membership of the Police History Society for his twenty years of service as secretary and in other committee posts. His previous publications include several police history bibliographies, a history of Colchester Borough Police and joint authorship of *The British Police: Forces and Chief Officers*.

CONTENTS

FOREWORD

PAULINE CLARE

It's probably safe to assume you have bought this book or are thinking of buying it because you have an interest in policing. I certainly had a great interest in policing during my thirty-six-year career in the Northwest of England. Since coming to the end of my policing career, my exposure to policing has been limited to the media and a significant number of crime novels!

This book has several authors, all of whom are well qualified to research and present their work. The material is offered in an easy-to-read format, so even the busiest of readers will race through this publication. The authors have produced the most complete document available on women in policing.

I felt honoured when asked to write this foreword. My career – spanning the period 1966 to 2002 – saw considerable change, including the merger of women into mainstream policing. As a result, reading this book and writing the foreword both resurrected past memories and gave me new information. I recalled carrying my police issue handbag and the shorter women's truncheon, and being called out at night to deal with female victims and offenders. Initially I was earning 90% of what my male colleagues earned, and my working hours were shorter. However, when there were no specialist women/children's statements and enquiries to deal with, I performed beat work like my male colleagues, which I thoroughly enjoyed. It felt like I had a foot in both the policewoman's specialist role and general policing.

As I reflected on my own career, strong emotions stirred within me. I loved the excitement of dealing with drunks near the Docks in Seaforth, Merseyside. If they were fit to walk, they would invariably run into a nearby pub and then into the male toilets. Undeterred, I would shout out who I was and that I was coming in! I thought about a time when as a constable I refused to cook breakfasts for my male colleagues when the canteen was closed. I wanted to be out patrolling. When I was called to see the superintendent (male) about my behaviour, I felt pleased when my explanation and actions were supported.

I also felt real sadness reading about the women who lost their lives on duty or whilst serving as police officers. I knew several of them and in fact worked with one of them in Kirkby. What a great loss they were to their families and the service, and I'm so delighted they have been recognised in this book.

Like the policewomen in this publication, I saw many developments in the acceptance of women in the service during my career. An incident in the late 1980s therefore made me question this acceptance. Whilst a superintendent, I attended a social event at an RAF establishment. I was in plain clothes and accompanied by my husband. I handed over our invitation card to be read out to the guests and was shocked to hear the announcer say, 'Superintendent Clare and Mrs Clare.' What fun I had making it clear he had got that wrong!

I think the happiest and most difficult time in my service was as chief constable. Being the first woman chief constable was like living my life in a goldfish bowl: I was a bit of a novelty to those whose stereotype of a chief constable was very different from myself, and experienced these stereotypes on many occasions. Calling me 'Sir' within the service was common, and asking me how I was 'coping' happened frequently. However, the most obvious and hurtful example occurred whilst I was in uniform attending a county event. I had introduced myself to a very senior male guest, who first eyed me up and down then – if that wasn't enough – said, 'If I'd caught you on my rod, I would have thrown you back!' I was livid and decided to walk away.

That was some twenty-six years ago. Now, thankfully, there are many more women in senior roles in all aspects of life. It gives me great comfort to see so many women throughout the UK reaching the position of chief constable, demonstrated by the figures in this book.

My new learning came from the sections on misogyny, menopause, misconduct and lesbian police officers. None of these topics were on the policing agenda during my service, though the difficulties around these matters obviously existed. I believe that one of the major issues facing the police service, and indeed many other organisations and companies, is whether the culture that exists is appropriate for what that organisation hopes to achieve. That is why I recommend this book to senior leaders in all organisations. With heightened awareness of the impact these matters have on staff and their performance, leaders can consider whether they need to take action or not.

We are so fortunate that the work of policewomen over many years has been recognised in this valuable historic record. I applaud the bravery and courage of our predecessors who challenged authority during very difficult times in our history. I thoroughly enjoyed my trip down memory lane and hope you draw strength and understanding from your reading.

INTRODUCTION

TOM ANDREWS

I FEEL IT ONLY FITTING to begin with a thank you. Thank you for picking up this book and demonstrating an interest in policing history. Whatever your reasons for being drawn to this volume, it demonstrates some form of at least passing interest in the events of the twentieth and twenty-first centuries that have come to define the state of the British police today. Of course, as with any events in history, getting to the point we are at today has often taken a profound struggle on the part of many who have gone before. In this work we are celebrating the strength and initiative of a select group of women who pioneered the role of women in policing to the point we find ourselves at today, where gender equality within the police service is the best it ever has been:[1] a third of forces are led by a female chief and seven forces in 2021 recruited more women than men.[2] Things, though, are still far from perfect.

We are also celebrating those women who have played crucial roles in the improvement of the police service as a whole, through their transformative efforts to enable this most visible arm of 'the state' to provide the best service it can. We will also be taking time to remember those women who have given their all in the service of protecting the public, giving their very lives in pursuit of the greater societal good.

This book has largely come about at this specific point in time as a result of a national period of celebration. Since 2015, forces across the country have been celebrating centenaries of their first warranted female officers with powers of arrest, all following in the footsteps of Lincolnshire's and the nation's first, Edith Smith. The majority of forces have commissioned some form of commemorative booklet, presentation, display, social media tribute or combination of those. They have necessarily been compiled by those with an interest in policing history who have had both the time and inclination to conduct and compile that research. This has presented perhaps a unique window of opportunity to collate that expertise and present some of those tales to a wider audience. Martin Stallion has done an incredible job of drawing these various new and pre-existing sources together to compile an extensive and unique bibliography of works relating solely to women in policing that presents ample opportunity for casual further reading and researchers alike.

We are not only at a perfect time to compile this volume, but as the Police History Society, we are also in perhaps a perfect position. With international membership and comprehensive national coverage of all British police forces – territorial or otherwise – there is perhaps no other organisation or group that could feasibly compile a collection with such a broad range of both subjects and contributors. Our list of authors is a veritable Who's Who of experts within the discipline of police history. We are extremely privileged to have many of these as members of the Society, and further honoured that some non-members who share our values have also offered to contribute their knowledge to this wider audience. It is particularly humbling and has been self-evident throughout the compilation of this anthology that all those who have contributed have placed the achievements of their subjects above any personal sense of aggrandisement. This is a true testament to the achievements of those women who we are considering through the respect their biographers have come to hold them in.

Several of our featured stories are not unique accounts of the women they describe. Some, such as Margaret Damer Dawson, have had their tales told in a multitude of places and in an array of different styles. The majority of our pioneering women have featured in the aforementioned promotional materials distributed by the various forces. Others crop up in academic works which detail their achievements; whether that be in local or national journals as the subjects of master's or doctoral theses, or even biographies entirely devoted to them. Many of those whose tales feature herein are even sufficiently well known to have their own (often comprehensive) Wikipedia entries. Others are less renowned, but are no less important for that fact. The aim of this book is to compile these diverse and varied accounts into one single volume, looking at the achievements of a handful of select individuals as well as groups of female officers who *combined* have made a significant impact on policing. Several of the accounts herein are those of pioneering women whose efforts were crucial to the development and acceptance of women as police officers. Other tales provide more of an insight into experiences of female officers at a specific time in general, but conveyed through the stories of exemplar individuals.

This is by no means intended to be a definitive work on identifying all the women who have played pioneering roles in the development of the police. To complete such a study would require an entire series of volumes and decades of research spanning every conceivable aspect of policing. To highlight some particularly notable omissions, we are not telling the story of Edith Smith – the very first woman with a power of arrest. In many senses she is, in fact, unremarkable when compared to her contemporaries involved in 'policing' at the time, despite her claim to fame. She was simply in the right place at the right time. Smith does, however, feature in those stories of her peers Margaret Damer Dawson and Katherine Scott. We are also not relaying the stories of the UK's first female firearms officers; trained police driver; detective; or PSU (riot) officer. Special mention should be given here, though, to Alison Halford, ultimately Assistant Chief Constable of Merseyside Police, who championed and revolutionised victims' rights in sexual assault cases, including pioneering rape crisis centres (now sexual assault referral centres) and improving how abused adult and child victims were interviewed. She was not only the first female station commander (at Tottenham Court Road), she was to become the first woman to serve at chief officer rank.[3] We are also not covering Karpal Kaur Sandhu, the first female Asian officer, out of respect for the tragic circumstances in which she lost her life and her surviving family.[4]

Perhaps the most notable omission, by its sheer duration, is that of 'pre-Peelian' (before 1829) era women who had roles in law enforcement, which, surprisingly, and perhaps contrary to general consensus, was seemingly more common than might be expected. If we expand our definition of constable to include its etymological meaning of 'Count de Stable' (or 'keeper of the stable'), a traditional title for the monarch's lieutenant in charge of their castles and therefore by extension the surrounding county, we can find an example of one such influential woman as early as 1191. Nicola de la Haye was constable of Lincoln Castle by hereditary right, undertaking the role herself, and defended it 'like a man' during two sieges in 1191 and 1217;[5] presumably this comment from Henry III was intended to praise her.

Even if we are limiting our definition to purely the law enforcement role to which it is currently associated, we can find examples far earlier than might be traditionally expected. Some of those known about include a record in the Manorial Roles of Northfield (Worcestershire) where it is recorded that, as early as 1451, one Elizabeth Thichnesse was appointed (parish) constable (albeit a man subsequently offered to undertake her duties);[6] or Jane Kitchen, parish constable of Upton, Nottinghamshire, who served in the role throughout 1644 at the height of the Civil War.[7] Research by J. Charles Cox finds three similar examples of women being appointed petty constables at around the same time as Kitchen in nearby parishes of Derbyshire: an Elizabeth Hurd of Osmaston in 1649; Elizabeth Taylor of Linton, also in 1649; and Clare Clay of Sinfin and Arleston in 1683, albeit, as with Thichnesse, the justices of Sinfin refused her appointment and insisted the previous constable continue in office 'till hee present another more fitt person to succeed him'.[8] If these records can be found in Nottinghamshire, Derbyshire and Worcestershire, it can be expected to an almost certainty that similar appointments spanned the length and breadth of the country. Perhaps that is a research proposition for someone to follow up with, possibly supported by the Police History Society? These fascinating snippets of history go to show that while our pioneers have played key roles in developing the role of women as law enforcers in the modern era, they are not the first to have held the title 'constable' – by over 700 years!

We can also see women working as police 'matrons' or supervisors of female and juvenile prisoners, right through until their appointment as sworn constables and beyond. These were often the wives of constables or gaolers, such as Sarah Batcheldor in Liverpool in the 1820s–30s.[9] Women often had an uncredited role in policing too, as the unofficial and unpaid secretaries of rural constables, responsible for the upkeep of police houses, the taking of messages in their husband's absence, and unable under their spouse's terms of employment to take on any other occupation.[10]

That the history of women in policing goes back far beyond 1915 should not serve to detract from modern achievements at all. In fact, conversely it should aggrandise them, showing that women, who for centuries had been considered not 'fitt' enough to serve as constables or needed men to do the duty for them, are actually more than men's equals. It just took several hundred years, and a steady increase in the responsibilities of women in society in general, for more outspoken women to forcibly interject themselves into the visible representation of the state that is its police. It has then taken further courageous individuals over the subsequent century to demonstrate that the abilities of women at least match, and in many cases surpass, those of their male counterparts. The strength of character displayed by all our subjects, perhaps most overwhelmingly by those who have laid down their lives in pursuit of their duty, is a testament not only to all of them, but to all their contemporaries as well.

In compiling this book there is no other real method to the telling of the story than to do so chronologically. To do otherwise would obscure the progressive nature of the advancement of women's roles in the police.

Our timeline spans almost the entire history of women in modern policing, starting with the almost bitter rivalry between several different experiments of women in policing. The Women Patrols, Women Police Service and Women Police Volunteers were all instigated independently by outside organisations with an interest in increasing women's rights during the First World War. These largely self-appointed 'guardians of morals' monitored young British women who were suffering the absence of husbands and partners fighting the war, apparently overly excited by the arrival of young and often terrified soldiers in garrison towns, in what has been colloquially termed 'khaki-fever'. Indeed, it is no coincidence that the first warranted female officer, Edith Smith, was taken on in Grantham, a large garrison town, as we shall discover in the tale of Margaret Damer Dawson. Only one of these organisations received any kind of official sanction above simple tolerance of their presence; the Women Police Service being contracted by the Home Office to provide security at munitions factories. Three of our initial chapters look at these different organisations and their conflicting opinions on how women should be involved in supporting the war effort. Intriguingly, there is little evidence to support the idea that any of the rival organisations saw a role for women as constables, at least initially. Moreover, it even appears that those involved in their establishment could have, in fact, looked down on the police service itself, seeing their calling as different, and much more akin to social work; as we shall see in the cases of Katherine Scott and Mary Adelaide Hare. Tragically, their tenacity and determination to prove themselves resulted in the premature deaths of several of these early pioneers.

In another, perhaps surprising, throwback to more antiquated times, there is here a further similarity in the use of women to maintain the peace during times of war, when the men were otherwise engaged. Contemporaneous to the aforementioned female petty constables, during the height of the English Civil War, women were called upon to keep a night watch on the town of Nottingham. The Parliamentarian commander of the castle's garrison, Colonel Hutchinson, had no spare troops to patrol the neighbouring town. Lacking for men:

> on one occasion a night watch of fifty women was organised against incendiarists and surprise Royalist attacks – 'it being considered that fifty women in a state of terror would create an alarm that would arouse those sleeping in their beds more effectually than any other means which might be devised'.[11]

Their efficacy is not recorded, and the suggestive use of 'one occasion' implies this experiment was not repeated. There is clearly a seismic difference in the fundamental belief about the abilities of the women conscripted into replacing the men between this instance and their later widespread use in the First World War. Nonetheless, it demonstrates that even in a period where women were treated more as property than equals, there was recourse to using them to 'backfill' in times of crisis in a law-and-order context.

As the book continues, we will see the progression of these self-made roles of the various women's organisations into pseudo-officialdom, which in turn encouraged recognition of the benefits to the forces of having women among their number. This progression was slow, and in many cases halting, as budgets were cut and the untested female officers were therefore the most expendable. Early government commissions into the role of women in policing following the conclusion of the war were also somewhat sceptical of their value, which further hindered their expansion. Not least among these were the 1922 National Committee on Expenditure cuts, or 'Geddes Axe', advocating swingeing cuts to public services following the First World War, under which women police suffered heavily, seeing a reduction from 112 to just twenty-four.[12] This was in spite of mostly favourable evidence of their abilities heard at the Committee on Employment of Women on Police Duties, or 'Baird Committee',[13] and evidence heard in Parliament as regards their efficacy.[14] Edward Smith covers this in his chapter 'The Twenty-Three', looking at the first female recruits into the Metropolitan Police Women Patrols. Lisa Cox-Davies carries on this theme by highlighting the differences in the acceptance of women police by examining the experience in three different Staffordshire forces.

Once begun, however, some things are hard to stop, and there can be no doubt that these early pioneers would have been standout officers, driven by a desire to prove their worth and value. The benefits of allowing women to assist with police work – even if it was only one or two per force in some cases, and then to only deal with women or children – had been demonstrated. Annual reports from the Chief Constable of Nottingham City Police, an early adopter of three policewomen in 1919, state: '[the policewomen] are proving very useful and with added experience their work and sphere of usefulness will be enlarged'. That was compounded the following year with the statement: 'The policewomen employed continue to do most useful work'.[15] This seems very much in line with the views of some fifty other chief constables of the time giving evidence to the Baird Committee.[16] The sheer fortitude of some of the early senior officers, such as Sofia Stanley and Dorothy Peto, whose tales herein follow those of the unofficial wartime pioneers, ensured their survival against some tall odds.

Women's position within the police was tentative at best throughout the interwar years, and numbers still significantly limited. As with so many things, the Second World War was to change that forever. The need to once again call up significant numbers of men to arms, as well as the need for increased Home Guard in the face of invasion and air raids, meant that every available hand was required. The government once again turned to the extensive pool of largely untapped resources that women represented, and women's reserve organisations sprang up in various branches of the military and civilian services. The police were no exception, and the Women's Auxiliary Police Corps (WAPC) was born, the Home Office allowing up to 10 per cent of a force's strength to now be the auxiliary women.[17] Mark Rothwell illustrates the trials and tribulations faced by those women who joined the blue by looking specifically at the experiences of two incredibly brave Plymouth WAPC officers.

It is perhaps telling of the still prevailing attitude towards women in society that many chief constables were against the introduction or use of WAPC officers, in spite of increased responsibilities and loss of staff to the military. Nottingham City Police's Chief Constable of the time, Capt. Athelstan Popkess, established air-raid precautions and planning that were hailed as exemplary and a template the rest of the country followed. He had sophisticated underground control centres co-ordinating police, fire, ambulance and local government responses to any bombings or invasion, and divisional substations to relay orders or casualty information.[18] In spite of this, he was adamantly opposed to taking on any WAPC personnel, despite them potentially being volunteers and therefore not incurring him any expense. His force even had a handful of female officers at that time, unlike many others. He wrote to the Home Office at the outbreak of war on 1 September 1939: 'I do not think there is any need for such a body being formed in this city, and I do not wish to bring the matter before the Watch Committee.' Cox-Davies definitively shows that this was far from a unique standpoint.

Popkess was not above admitting his error, though, perhaps in light of the valuable contribution the WAPC officers had made nationally, and in November 1941 the first WAPC officers joined the force.[19] The high number of military casualties from police forces, coupled with the demonstration of their abilities by the WAPC officers, meant that significant numbers from that reserve were retained by forces as full-time sworn officers after the war ended. Interestingly, however, members of the WAPC were not sworn police officers and lacked a power of arrest; and in fact, memorandums of understanding from the Home Office outlining the terms of service of WAPC recruits explicitly stated: 'Members of the Corps will not be Special Constables'.[20]

The abilities of women to work well in the police had been proven during the Second World War, thanks in large part to the efforts of the oft-forgotten WAPC. Others who had been lucky enough to have been one of the very few sworn officers during that time had been able to exemplify the same fortitude shown by their forebears. In the case of Sophie Alloway, her abilities meant she was posted to Germany to help rebuild the country post-war and establish the women police there – very successfully, reaching high rank and significant respect at the same time. It is Valerie Redshaw's privilege to tell her story.

As a result of their proven abilities, even in the face of significant, often prejudiced opposition, forces began to open their doors far more readily to female applicants and numbers increased significantly in the decade following VE Day. They were still limited by the Home Office, though, to comprising no more than 10 per cent of a force's strength, and existed as a separate entity – the Women Police. They were paid only 90 per cent of the salary of their male counterparts (and were accordingly referred to as the 'ninety percenters'), but did not work night shifts. They were also not allocated specific beat duties, often being supernumerary to shifts and used for additional visibility presence, as bait in sting operations or to replace crossing patrol officers who were off on leave or sick.[21] For the most part they were expected to still deal only with offences involving women and children, and for this they could often be summoned from their homes overnight if such an incident occurred when no Women Police were on duty.

Throughout this time female officers were also implicitly barred from marriage, having to either chose a life of devotion to duty akin to a nun or being forced to leave the service if they found a man with whom they wished to start a family. This was not just local policy or practice, but formed part of the national Police Regulations. This has led to some speculation that many of the women who served a full thirty-year career were lesbians, in a time when coming out as such was unimaginable. Clifford Williams touches on this idea in his chapter exploring the history of lesbian officers.

In 1946, the Home Secretary, Chuter Ede, amended the forced resignation on marriage policy, even stating at a Ryton-On-Dunsmore training school passing-out parade that retaining married women might be beneficial in gaining the respect of younger girls with whom the police would interact:

They have to give advice and help to young girls and on occasion I think it is more likely to be received with respect from a married woman than one who is single. A young girl is apt to think that all women are single after about nineteen merely because they have never had any 'fun'. The fact that a lady has been able to get a husband does entitle her to some respect in the eyes of that particular section of the community.[22]

Clearly there was some thought behind the policy alteration, about the improved community relations the action might foster, even if the prevailing misogynistic sentiment of the time is all too evident.

At the same time, recruitment adverts for women to join the police laid bare the expectations of what the Metropolitan Police were looking for in the 1930s, when they declared 'Hefty girls wanted' who could 'withstand a rough and tumble'. It went on to stipulate that 'they must never marry – or their career will end', and that the ideal candidates were 'spinsters and widows, girls in universities and public schools, and girls with training in nursing and social work', who 'must be at least five feet four inches high'. Such an advert would be anathema to any recruitment campaign today and is clearly awful in its tone by modern standards, but it provides an excellent time-capsule to demonstrate half a century's progress.

They Mustn't Marry

HEFTY GIRLS WANTED FOR POLICE FORCE

WOMEN WITH BRAINS PLUS GOOD PHYSIQUE ARE WANTED. THE PAY AND PROSPECTS ARE GOOD, BUT—THEY MUST NEVER MARRY OR THEIR CAREER WILL END!

They are needed as recruits for the Metropolitan Police Force, and Sir Philip Game, Chief Commissioner, and Miss Peto, Chief of the Women's Branch, are making a special appeal to—

Spinsters and widows, girls in universities and public schools, and girls with training in nursing and social work.

Married women need not apply.

THEY MUST BE HEFTY

Good pay is being offered—53s. 3d. a week, with free quarters in special hostels.

But a high standard of intelligence, tact and physique is being demanded.

The recruits must be at least five feet four inches high.

They must be hefty enough to withstand a "rough and tumble," and they must be fairly good looking.

Beauty from your bath..

ebe

Thankfully, the easing of the restrictions around forced severance on marriage was the start of a slope towards acceptance, and it is around this time that we see Women Police officers achieving not only high ranks in provincial forces outside of the Metropolitan Police, but also respect from their male colleagues. It falls to Rob Phillips and Tom Andrews to give an account of female officers smashing these proverbial glass ceilings with the highest-ranking officer in Nottingham City Police, Jessie Alexander, who reached the position of Police Woman Chief Inspector.

The 1975 Sex Discrimination Act finally saw an end to the separation of the Women's Branch from the (Men's) Police and the theoretical abolishing the title of 'WPC' – even if not in popular parlance for several more decades. This was not the end of the fight for equality, though, nor thankfully of the progress towards it. Sue Fish, later to be Chief Constable of Nottinghamshire, recalls that when she started as late on as 1986, only 8 per cent, or 176 officers, of the total strength of that force was to be women, whichever was the fewer, and no more than two women were to be on each shift. The force were seemingly allowed to get away with this flagrant breach of the law both because it *enforced* the law, and because this policy wasn't physically written down anywhere, and thus not 'official'. Female officers were still issued truncheons half the size of their male counterparts, specifically designed to fit in their uniform-issued handbags.

Thankfully, as women formed an increasing percentage of the police workforce, they also had more influence over the policies and practices of the police. Victims of sexual offences had traditionally had a very difficult time with the predominantly male police force, either in having their reports believed, through some misguided sense that the victim had brought their predicament on themselves by dressing provocatively, in what would now be termed 'victim-blaming', or by the invasive and gratuitous nature of the evidence gathering and questioning they were subjected to by the male officers. The attitudes of the detectives towards victims of the 'Yorkshire Ripper' and 'Sussex Strangler', that somehow because they were sex workers they were less deserving of the police's time and more at fault for bringing the offenders' actions on to themselves, is exemplary of this period. Thankfully, as female officers took up more positions of responsibility they were able to drive through wholesale changes in the way victims were dealt with, making the reporting of sexual offences far less of an ordeal and almost second victimisation than it had been before.

Finally, on our chronological journey we hear from Tom Andrews, who charts the career of Sue Fish, not the first female Chief Constable, but possibly the first who stood at the helm of the force in which she spent the

majority of her career. A woman who beat the gender-biased odds of a typically male-dominated aspect of law enforcement to become the Association
of Chief Police Officers' lead on armed policing. She was instrumental in
further enhancing the rights of women both within and without the police
service, responsible for overseeing the introduction of the country's first
menopause policy within a police force, and introducing the idea of misogyny as a hate crime category. The latter proved prescient when it was to
come to the fore some five years later with the rape and murder of Sarah
Everard, a woman walking alone at night across London's Clapham Common.
This tragic incident – conducted by a (male) police officer, no less – prompted
a wave of demonstrations across the country in favour of increased protec-
tions for women and increased awareness of societal misogyny.

Sue's work crucially took place alongside the steady increase of female officers in the police, which studies have shown has a positive impact on the public's
perception of the police (legitimacy). This comes as result of a marked reduction in use of force by and against female officers, as well as them receiving
fewer complaints and instituting organisational change – as epitomised by Sue
Fish.[23] This serves to cement the impact all these pioneers have had in trans-
forming policing for the better throughout the preceding century.

We conclude with chapters examining more specific histories within this
broader historiography. Clifford Williams looks at the fight for the rights of
the lesbian communities within the police service. The struggle of people to be
recognised for who they are and whom they can love has taken place simultaneously with the fight for equality of women, and spans a concurrent timespan;
albeit taking place far more in the shadows until comparatively recently.

Tony Rae concludes our journey with a reflection on all the women
in policing who have made the ultimate sacrifice in service of the public.
Thankfully, the number of women who have given their lives in the line of
duty is relatively small, but their sacrifice is by no means any less significant
for that. The names of female officers who have been murdered on duty are
evocative of some of the most high-profile incidents in policing: Yvonne
Fletcher, gunned down in the street by diplomats she was sworn to protect,
for whom the hunt for justice has taken in excess of thirty-five years and in
whose memory the Police Memorial Trust was founded; Sharon Beshenivsky,
shot and killed by armed robbers; Fiona Bone and Nicola Hughes, killed in
a brutal ambush involving grenades and a gun by an offender who called in a
hoax burglary report. All went to work expecting to return to their families
and loved ones, but experienced brutal, fatal violence, simply because of the
job they chose to perform.

This book looks to serve as a monument to these and every woman's dedication, stubbornness, beliefs and in many cases self-sacrifice to further their cause and that of every woman in policing from the First World War until today. Every female officer serving today and tomorrow in His Majesty's Constabulary owes their position to the hard-won rights of these forebears and their peers. Every female officer today is their legacy. This hopefully serves as their story. In words etched onto the gravestone of Lilian Wyles BEM by the Metropolitan Police Women's Association: 'We stand upon the shoulders of such pioneers.'

MARGARET DAMER DAWSON

THE WOMEN POLICE VOLUNTEERS
AND THE WOMEN POLICE SERVICE

PETER FINNIMORE

Margaret Damer Dawson in her Women Police Service uniform.

THESE DAYS ONLY THE MOST extreme anti-feminist would deny that policing was a suitable job for a woman. Before the First World War, however,
when women (and especially married women) were barred from so many
occupations, it would have been considered the ludicrous proposition of a
few extreme feminists. It has been suggested that Margaret Damer Dawson,
founder of the Women Police Service (WPS) in 1915, 'began the process of

normalising women in the police force, disproving many of the prejudices of the male policing establishment'.[1] In fact, after the war, progress towards overcoming those prejudices was, like many other facets of women's equality, painfully slow until the 1970s. Some would say it is still slow. Margaret Damer Dawson was certainly one of the key figures among those who created and led women police organisations during the war. But did she advance or retard the development of women policing? Or was her Women Police Service an irrelevance? Could she have contributed more to policing if she had not died suddenly of a heart attack in May 1920?

The context within which she was operating included: a male-dominated society and campaigns, notably the suffrage movement, to promote women's equality; the treatment of women within a criminal justice system run by men; the key role of charities run by middle-class philanthropists in caring for and controlling those in 'moral danger', usually women or children, or who were a 'moral danger' to others; and, of course, the social, political and economic upheaval caused by war.

The women's suffrage movement had gathered momentum in the nineteenth century and became increasingly militant after the founding of the Women's Social and Political Union (WSPU) in 1903. With the declaration of war against Germany in August 1914, Suffragette leaders called for an end to militancy for the duration of the conflict. They believed that by supporting the authorities in a national emergency they could win support for women's equality.

Margaret herself had been active in the National Vigilance Association and the Criminal Law Amendment Committee, two bodies that had campaigned for action against white slavery and to promote what was described as 'social purity'. An undercurrent in these campaigns was that the male-dominated criminal justice system was unlikely to tackle these issues effectively until women were represented in key roles such as magistrates and women police. Little progress had been made in these areas, however, before 1914.

For young women, the war brought new freedoms and opportunities for work outside the home, in industry and agriculture and even abroad as nurses and ancillary workers. This enormous social change brought fresh concerns about the 'moral welfare' of young working-class women. In the autumn of 1914 especially, there was growing fear of an epidemic of so-called 'khaki fever'. In Parliament and the press concern, and in some cases moral panic, was spreading. Young women, it was believed, excited by the arrival of soldiers in camps near towns and cities, were behaving dangerously, 'drinking alcohol, running after men in uniform and behaving immodestly'.[2]

In the House of Lords there was a call for legislation to allow the arrest of 'women of notorious bad character who were infesting the neighbourhood of … military camps'.[3] Although the moral panic was probably disproportionate to reality, it has been estimated that over 6,000 women became involved in various forms of policing during the First World War as a result, often with the aim of promoting 'moral welfare' or 'social purity'.[4] Much of this work was more like voluntary social work than policing. The WPS was one of the most prominent women's policing bodies, largely due to the leadership and organisational skills of Margaret Damer Dawson.

The structure, organisation, efficiency and morale of British policing before and during the war is another important element of the context. Between 1910 and 1920 there were over 180 separate police forces in England and Wales, with little central guidance from the Home Office until the outbreak of the war forced some co-ordination. Discontent among police officers was widespread over issues such as the right to confer (i.e. to form a trade union); pay that was less than that of an agricultural labourer, a third that of a munitions worker, and which was not keeping up with wartime inflation; the loss of the recently introduced weekly rest day, meaning they worked seven days a week with no paid overtime; and they were forbidden from resigning during the war![5] However, in her detailed account of the founding and work of the WPS, Margaret's partner and WPS 'Sub-Commandant', Mary Sophia Allen, makes no mention of the poor state of policing that was to lead to the 1918 and 1919 police strikes and the great improvements thereafter. This omission suggests the pair were far more concerned about setting up a separate women's force, than about the problems of the existing men's force.

MARGARET'S EARLY LIFE

Margaret was born in Sussex on 12 June 1873, the daughter of Richard Dawson, a surgeon who died in 1891. Her mother remarried in 1914 into a wealthy aristocratic family, becoming Lady Agnes Walsingham, wife of Thomas de Grey, 6th Baron Walsingham. Most of what is known about her early life is drawn from the memoirs of her friend and partner, Mary Sophia Allen.[6] We are told that she was educated privately and gained the Royal Academy of Music Diploma and Gold Medal. 'She had remarkably diverse and contradictory gifts, was keenly interested in sport … all the arts' and was 'an experienced alpine climber, an expert motorist, an enthusiastic gardener, [and] a passionate lover of animals'. Her activities included 'frequent trips abroad'.[7]

This could only have been the life of a person of independent means, presumably provided by her wealthy family. Another clue to the wealth of her family comes from the census. In 1881, her household in Hove, including two sisters and a brother, also comprised two nurses, a cook, a housekeeper and a housemaid. The 1891 census lists six servants. Although Margaret's father had died in 1891, the family was still well off. While little is known about her sources of income, at the outbreak of war she owned two substantial properties: 10 Cheyne Row in Chelsea, and Danehill, a large house set in 2 acres in Lympne, near Hythe, Kent.

In 1901, Margaret was staying in Balcombe House, a grand estate near the village of Balcombe, Sussex, the home of the Delius family, with an even larger army of staff and servants. She was an accomplished pianist and had become a close friend of Berthe Delius (a cousin of the composer Frederick Delius) while studying at the London School of Music. She shared with Berthe a deep interest in animal welfare, an interest that seems to have been her main activity up until 1912. For several years they also shared a luxury apartment in Maida Vale, west London, with Lizzie Lind af Hageby, founder of the Animal Defence and Anti-Vivisection Society (ADAVS).[8]

In 1906, she was Organising Secretary of the Congress of International Animal Protection Societies. She accompanied Lizzie Lind af Hageby on a lecture tour in the USA in 1909 and they organised an international conference in London for over 850 delegates. As Honorary Secretary of the International Anti-Vivisection Council, she toured Europe to gather evidence of what she believed to be the cruel treatment of animals in medical research and farming; and she wrote passionately, urging public awakening from the 'lethargy of indifference and ignorance … [to] escape the net of medical tyranny which is slowly but surely being thrown over us'.[9] For her animal welfare work she was honoured by Danish and Finnish animal protection societies. She resigned from her ADAVS post in November 1912 to focus on other philanthropic work. Her deeply held convictions about animal rights were certainly extreme, especially her certainty that diseases were spread not by germ carriers but by other environmental causes. The vivisection of animals for medical research was therefore not only cruel, it was unnecessary. She had demonstrated organisational ability and dynamic leadership that would be crucial in establishment of the Women Police Service.

THE WOMEN POLICE VOLUNTEERS

In the months after the declaration of war, the transition to a war economy and the disruption to society was swift. By October 1914, the National Union of Women Workers (NUWW) had begun organising local Women Patrols, prompted by the many army camps rapidly set up near towns and cities throughout the country and concern about the moral welfare of young women. Other local groups also set up voluntary women's patrols. They were, however, seen as a temporary wartime initiative, with non-uniformed volunteers giving up a few hours a week and not connected to existing police forces. As the national NUWW patrols organiser wrote to *The Times*, 'The voluntary patrols are neither police nor rescue workers, but true friends of the girls'.[10]

In the days following the declaration of war, great numbers of Belgian refugees began to arrive in England. Margaret later related how she 'formed a committee of Chelsea people' and that she became head of 'The Transport Department', having managed to get together ten motor cars. The aim was to meet women and child refugees at the railway stations and drive them to the homes of people offering hospitality. She soon realised, however, that the refugees were in danger of being diverted by criminals who sought to lure them into prostitution or other forms of slavery. After only a few days, she came up with the idea that a body of uniformed and trained women might be the way to counter such moral danger.[11]

She then heard that Nina Boyle, Secretary of the Woman's Freedom League (WFL), a breakaway from the WSPU, was considering seizing the opportunity presented by the war to create a women police group. The WFL, in addition to its militant campaigning for women's suffrage, had already actively campaigned for women's involvement in the criminal justice system, including women police. Before the end of August 1914, advertisements in the WFL's weekly paper, *The Vote*, sought applications for volunteer police-women, able to work four hours a day.[12]

Margaret, who had already begun to recruit volunteers for her cause to protect the refugees, heard about the work of Boyle and the WFL. Realising the similarity of their aims, she arranged a meeting between the pair. It was a success: between them they already had forty volunteers and they agreed to combine and form the Women Police Volunteers (WPV), with Margaret becoming Chief Commandant and Nina her deputy. Boyle had been a high-profile militant women's suffrage campaigner and had been imprisoned three times; it is therefore likely that she agreed to Margaret becoming Chief Commandant so as to present as more acceptable to the authorities.

Initial approaches to Sir Edward Henry, the Metropolitan Police Commissioner, were not received favourably, but Margaret, using police instruction books and training materials, put together a plan that eventually helped win his support. She was also helped by Sir Leonard Dunning, HM Inspector of Constabulary, who provided material from Liverpool where he had been Chief Constable. As far back as 1904, Margaret had been in contact with Sir Edward, who had praised her work with the NVA to combat 'white slavery'.[13] He was certainly opposed to Nina Boyle, describing her as 'an intransigeante [sic] and in opposition to constituted authority', thereby demonstrating the soundness of the decision to appoint Margaret as figurehead.[14] Margaret won his support by reminding him that women's suffrage campaigners had agreed to cease militant activity for the duration of the war.

Although Margaret had asked Sir Edward for permission and approval of the uniform, at this stage she was envisaging a group of unpaid volunteers who would be separate from, but cooperating with, the official forces. She was simply seeking recognition as a partner organisation. The WPV 'were from the outset conceived of as a trained body of professional women who were ready to give their whole time to the job'.[15] They would be different from the official police in that they would be self-funded women of independent means; and they would differ from the NUWW Women Patrols by working full-time and being uniformed, disciplined and well trained.

MARGARET MEETS MARY ALLEN

Mary Sophia Allen was another well-educated middle-class woman, four years younger than Margaret, who had become an ardent Suffragette in the decade before the war. As a devoted follower of Mrs Pankhurst and the WSPU, she was imprisoned three times, became a WSPU organiser, and twice went through the ordeal of hunger striking and the resultant force-feeding. With the order to suspend militant WSPU action, full-time activists had to find other ways of promoting women's equality and the war effort. Mary was excited to hear about the WPV initiative led by Margaret, and 'went to her, burning with anxiety to join the projected organisation'.[16]

There can be no doubt that Margaret and Mary were soon in a loving relationship. Mary's language when describing their meeting and partnership is a convincing clue:

> The meeting … struck an immediate spark, and began a period – all too short alas! – of close association and intimate friendship, ending only with the sudden death of the Chief in 1920 … We both were possessed by an unshakable belief in the elemental needs we were out to satisfy.[17]

Within six months Margaret had written a will in which Mary was sole beneficiary and Mary continued to live at Danehill, Lympne, Kent, the house bequeathed to her by Margaret until after the Second World War.

In the mid-1920s, well after Margaret's death, Mary and her new partner, Helen Bourn Tagart, became acquainted with the well-known lesbian author Radclyffe Hall. They visited Hall and her companion, Una Troubridge, for lunch, where their hosts sympathised with their guests regarding antipathy towards Mary (known in this group as Robert) and the WPS. They all agreed that this was based on the fact that she was known to be 'an invert'. They were heartened to find that they shared common beliefs on the subject of homosexuality.[18]

It is difficult to research lesbian life in the WSPU or other feminist organisations since few lesbians left records of their lives where their sexuality is made explicit, owing to the climate hostile to their sexual orientation.[19] But the hostility was suppressed to some degree, enabling women like Margaret and Mary to live together without attracting much comment or suspicion. The Home Office bias against Margaret, Mary and the WPS after the war, as will be shown below, was founded to a greater extent on their links to the Suffragettes; their belief that a 'Women Police Service' should be a separate organisation from the official male police; and on the fact that Margaret, Mary and their organisation were mostly middle-class women. This represented a very different body of staff from the poorly paid working-class men in the 180 English and Welsh police forces.

Margaret Damer Dawson (left) and Mary Allen.

CREATION OF THE WOMEN POLICE SERVICE

Having set up the Women Police Volunteers in the first two months of the war, Margaret and Nina Boyle devoted much of their energy to training, fundraising, press articles, addressing public meetings and lobbying chief constables outside London about the need for women police. Fundraising was an important element of this marketing work since there was no government grant until 1916. Outside London, the response of chief constables and municipal authorities varied greatly, some welcoming and some rejecting the prospect of women police. 'Early in 1915 the chief bar to the employment of policewomen … was the fear that objections will be raised by the Home Office.'[20] To counter this concern of the chief constables, Margaret obtained a statement from the Home Secretary raising no objection. This was an example, Mary Allen claimed, of the important preparatory and political work carried out by Margaret and Nina Boyle in the early days. This statement was crucial in dealing with local authorities and watch committees. The two leaders were soon, however, to fall out.

While Margaret and Nina were publicising the new organisation, training was developed at St Stephen's House, Westminster, the WPV headquarters. Initially assisted by a police sergeant loaned by Sir Edward Henry, it included drill, police court procedure, giving evidence, a knowledge of general police laws, first aid and some self-defence.

The first actual deployment of uniformed women police came in November 1914, when Margaret selected two of her women, one of whom was Mary Allen, and took them to Grantham. A military camp with over 18,000 troops had been set up just outside a town with a population of 20,000. A women's committee, with the agreement of the civil and military authorities, raised a fund to pay for the WPV officers to travel there. Margaret's brother-in-law, a staff captain at the camp, had played a part in the arrangements.

The Defence of the Realm Act, hurriedly enacted in the first week of the war, introduced unprecedented social control mechanisms which were believed necessary to support the war effort and prevent public disorder. Within a few months, it seemed to feminists like Nina Boyle that the new laws and regulations were limiting women's liberty far more severely than the liberty of soldiers and other men. There were soon examples throughout the country of curfews to keep women 'of a certain class' off the streets, and even of women being court martialled and sent to prison for curfew breaches.[21] Margaret continued the work in Grantham in spite of a restriction order on women issued by the military commander, believing it would help her to win the confidence of the military and civil authorities. Nina called for her resignation on the grounds that she was acting against women's rights and liberty. A WPV meeting was called at which a vote was taken, almost all rejecting the resignation demand. Margaret later claimed that by showing that curfews served no useful purpose, she persuaded the authorities to end them. She also later consistently defended women's rights in a criminal justice system that treated them more harshly than men, on one occasion saying that 'in the realm of morals we have not advanced beyond Adam who was tempted by Eve'.[22]

In February 1915, she created a new organisation, the Women Police Service (WPS), a title for which she obtained Sir Edward Henry's permission. Her almost unanimous support from members shows the loyalty that she inspired from her policewomen. She was not a remote Chief Commandant; she spent time working on the front line and won the respect of her subordinates. The word began to spread among chief constables that uniformed women police could perform a useful role, and the authorities in many towns and cities asked the WPS to provide officers over the next three years.

There were now several different types of women police: the Women Patrols, volunteers patrolling for a few hours a week in plainclothes, organised by the NUWW (by 1915 called the National Council of Women (NCW)); the remainder of Nina Boyle's Women Police Volunteers, who focused on providing a presence in courts and matrons in police stations to improve the treatment of women and children; Women Patrols under the auspices of training schools set up in Bristol and later in Liverpool; some local largely independent arrangements that were made, for example, in Birmingham and Lancashire; and now the Women Police Service. Margaret believed that her organisation, based in London, was uniformed, disciplined and well-trained, in contrast to the other groups that were well-meaning but less effective part-timers.

Back in Grantham in 1915, the sudden growth of the military camp had led to an eruption of crime, drunkenness, exploitation of women and children, and various other criminal opportunities. At first, the three policewomen were treated with a mixture of amusement and contempt, and the Chief Constable allowed them to work 'provided they would not get in his way'.[23] The military authorities were somewhat more welcoming, although the guidance was vague. Initially, protecting young women and children and trying to keep them off the streets and away from 'the dangerous neighbourhood of the camp' seem to have been the main activities. 'But ... we were trained not only to deal with the moral niceties but also, if it became necessary, to use ju-jitsu on a bellicose brawler of either sex.'[24]

The accounts of Margaret and Mary show that these educated middle-class women did spend a significant amount of their time lecturing Grantham families about moral and physical risks. It is hard to believe that two novice policewomen (Margaret had to leave after a few days to deal with other matters) could have made much of an impact. But there is some evidence that they did, perhaps through hard work and strength of personality: 'It was no unusual thing for one or both of us to be on duty twelve hours at a stretch.'[25] As early as January 1915, the commanding officer of the camp wrote to Margaret commending the two police women for removing 'sources of trouble to the troops in a manner that the military police could not attempt'.[26]

Later in the year, the *Grantham Journal* wrote that 'the presence of women police is a distinct advantage to the town'.[27] By this time, the two Grantham policewomen had moved on to Hull, following an invitation from the municipal authorities, and were initially led once again by Margaret, their Chief Commandant. They were succeeded in Grantham by two other policewomen, one of whom, Edith Smith, was widely admired for her policing skills. Later in the year she was sworn in, given the full power of arrest and paid from the same funds as male officers. She is generally regarded as the first 'official' British policewoman with warranted arrest powers.

In Hull, four WPS officers were asked to organise and train a band of forty volunteer Women Patrols, an arrangement that seemed to be successful. The uniformed WPS officers worked full time as directed by the Chief Constable; most of the volunteers worked a few hours a week in plain-clothes with armbands, assisting the WPS. The Women Patrols were part of the NCW initiative running throughout the country. Although having aims similar to those of the WPS, the NCW leadership strongly opposed WPS control of their women in Hull.[28] This was yet another example of the contrasting attitudes of various authorities towards Margaret and the WPS. Some disapproved because of WPS's links with militant Suffragettes; some respected the contribution the WPS made to the moral welfare of women and children and keeping the peace; while others simply did not seem to understand the difference between the various groups.

During 1915 and 1916, the WPS continued to recruit and train policewomen in London. They were then sent to towns and cities throughout the country, and in some London districts where local funds had been raised through donations. Once posted to the various forces, they were under the control of the local chief constable. As such, the arrangements for them across the 180 police forces varied enormously with regard to funding, uniforms, pay, hours of duty and whether or not policewomen were sworn in as constables with powers of arrest. Pressure grew for the legal status of women police and Women Patrols to be regularised. Margaret and Mary secured a meeting with the Home Secretary at which they highlighted the anomalies and inconsistencies that needed resolution. At a public meeting organised by the Criminal Law Amendment Committee in March 1916, Margaret shared a platform with many Establishment figures including Mrs Creighton, representing the NCW Women Patrols. They demanded official recognition for women police, suggesting there was some common ground between the two bodies. Margaret described the work of the WPS, stating that the legality of much of it was questionable but they had 'courtesy and cooperation from the police'. She drew laughter from the audience, saying 'they had been received with open arms'.[29]

The Home Office, preparing a bill to be put before Parliament, sought advice from the Commissioner and HM Inspector of Constabulary. Their reports contained praise and criticism of both the WPS and the NCW Women Patrols, but the overall message to government was that the WPS, mostly ex-Suffragettes, were seeking too much, while the NCW had more realistic ambitions. The Police (Miscellaneous Provisions) Act was passed in July 1916, removing many of the difficulties regarding the official employment of women police. A new type of 'special patrols' soon followed in London, employed part-time by the Metropolitan Police. But Margaret did not regard them as proper policewomen like the WPS: they did not have full powers, were not uniformed and they were drawn from the NCW patrols, probably reducing the chances of Margaret's ambition to create a separate official women's police service from being realised. This setback was soon, however, offset by a new opportunity for the WPS to increase its prestige and scope.

POLICING MUNITIONS FACTORIES

Several huge munitions factories were built in 1915 and 1916, most of the workers being women, although there were many male construction workers. The Ministry of Munitions asked the Commissioner to provide a suitable force of women to police these areas. Unable to do so with his own women police, he referred the Ministry to the WPS. Margaret seized the opportunity, and in July 1916 a formal agreement was signed. The record of the WPS between April 1916 and December 1918 shows that this was not an unofficial organisation 'masquerading' as women police officers, as later claimed by Commissioner Sir Nevil Macready.[30] Under Margaret's leadership it was a well-organised body, selecting, training and supplying policewomen under contract with the Home Office in response to demand from municipal authorities throughout Great Britain. The first agreement with the Ministry specified forty policewomen for the Queen's Ferry factory in Cheshire and 100 for the factory at Gretna.

The former Suffragette Isobel Goldingham, with the WPS rank of superintendent, was appointed by Margaret to run the headquarters operation, including finance and purchasing uniforms and equipment. A complex process at any time, this function was even more difficult in the wartime economy, especially given that the WPS was funded by a mixture of local committees raising funds from private donors and money allocated by municipal authorities. For the first six months there was no government funding, the agreement being that women police salaries would only be paid once they were in post. This placed a great strain on WPS finances, which was only overcome by 'a very munificent donor … [who] had lost two sons in the war and devoted to us the fortune that would have come to those two sons'.[31] As the scope of the work expanded to other sites, however, the Ministry agreed to grants of £850 in January 1917 and £1,700 in January 1918 to fund the WPS headquarters operation.

Between April 1916 and December 1918, 1,044 women were accepted for training from 2,085 applicants, and 985 were supplied to twenty-seven munitions factories and other government establishments.[32] They performed a wide range of duties including enforcing factory rules, especially safety rules, maintaining order, controlling entry and searching workers. A second list of duties applied to the townships, including patrolling, receiving complaints, investigations in cases involving women, taking charge of women prisoners and attending court.[33] Once a policewoman had been posted to a constabulary or factory, the WPS did not retain any operational or managerial responsibility for her. Margaret explained that she was employed by the local chief constable, 'still a member, but an honorary one, of the service'.[34]

THE BENEVOLENT DEPARTMENT

From the beginning of the war, a key motivation for Margaret was the protection of the weak, mainly women and children, and action to remove them from danger and prevent them from becoming victims or criminals. She raised public donations for this aspect of WPS work and formed close links with a wide range of charitable organisations to which women and children in danger could be referred. In the spring of 1917, however, a separate benevolent department was set up, with donations from WPS units, the factories and forces to which they were attached, and the general public, one generous donor giving no less than £2,000. A grant was also received from the Ministry of Health. During six months in 1917, over 500 women were 'picked up' on the street and given immediate assistance, together with many young girls and infants.[35]

A 'baby home' was opened in 1917 in Aldington, Kent, near Margaret's house in Lympne. The home was later moved to a large house overlooking the sea in Hythe, and was a refuge for over twenty young women and their babies. A story has been passed down through one family in Hythe of Ada Bradley, an unmarried mother who was employed as housekeeper by the two women who lived at Danehill. The story goes that the two women liked dressing up in uniforms, which is why they founded, with their own money, the women's branch of the Metropolitan Police.[36] We now know that the WPS was not 'a branch of the Metropolitan Police' and that, while they may indeed have enjoyed their uniforms, Margaret and Mary Allen did have more worthy reasons for forming the WPS.

THE WPS AND THE END OF THE WAR

In February 1918, while the war on the Western Front was still raging and its outcome uncertain, both Margaret and Mary Allen were invested by the king as officers of the Order of the British Empire (OBE). Later in the year, as the German armies began their final retreat, there was widespread acknowledgement of the important role played during the war by women police organisations and growing support for women police to be appointed by the Metropolitan Police and provincial forces. A Ministry of Munitions committee considered the establishment of Home Office-controlled 'women's police patrols'. The committee's report records that Margaret and Mary Allen were prepared to merge the WPS in a new organisation as a step towards the sort of women police force they sought, and as a way of ending the confusion between the various women policing bodies.[37] The leaders of the NCW Women Patrols, however, were less conciliatory, strongly and unfairly criticising Margaret and the WPS for opposing the male forces and seeking inappropriate powers, including the power of arrest.

On 30 August 1918, 6,000 Metropolitan Police officers went on strike over pay and the right to form a union. Sir Edward Henry was made a scapegoat and replaced by Sir Nevil Macready, who was no admirer of either the WPS or the sort of women's police service Margaret was seeking. It was announced in October 1918 that, as an experiment, 112 women were to be employed by the Metropolitan Police under the command of Mrs Sofia Stanley, who was to be appointed superintendent. Mrs Stanley had been the organiser of the Women Patrols and the 'special patrols', from whom most of the first recruits were drawn. Margaret and the other senior women in the WPS were ignored, although Sir Nevil overcame his antipathy towards them sufficiently to ask her to suggest WPS women who might be suitable for his 'experiment'. In a private letter, she says she acquiesced and many of the later recruits came from her recommendations.[38] The terms and conditions under which the 'experimental' women would be employed fell far short of what Margaret had hoped for. The pay was poor and not pensionable, they were 'Women Patrols' not 'women police', they were not sworn in as constables, and they had no police powers of arrest.[39]

In contrast to the attitude of Sir Nevil and the Home Office towards Margaret and the WPS, there was much praise for their wartime work from other quarters. Many of the letters of thanks for the work of the WPS received in the months after the Armistice were reproduced by Mary Allen in *The Pioneer Policewoman*. While they are obviously a selection of the most favourable such letters, they remain no less impressive. They hail from senior military officers, chief constables, charities, committees that funded women police and even the Chief Magistrate of London. They relate primarily to the work in and around munitions factories, at many places in London, especially the canteens and recreation facilities for foreign soldiers, and in police force areas throughout the country.

Other recognition of WPS achievements during 1919 included Margaret and other senior WPS officers attending a garden party at Buckingham Palace to celebrate the war effort of women's organisations. Later in the year, a WPS rally was held at the Hyde Park Hotel. Sir Leonard Dunning made a speech praising the organisation, and when Margaret rose to address the audience she was greeted by a rousing chorus of 'for he's a jolly good fellow'. The *Times* reporter wrote that 'he' was not changed to 'she' because WPS senior officers were all addressed as 'sir'.[40]

Many of the WPS women serving in police forces throughout Great Britain continued to be employed through 1919. There were even a small number in London, supported by local philanthropic committees. Indeed, with demobilised soldiers returning to the country after the end-of-war celebrations, societal disruption made the policing workload at least as great as during the war. Margaret still entertained some hope that she and well over 1,000 trained and experienced policewomen in the WPS would become an officially recognised women's police force. In February 1920, over a year after the official Metropolitan Police Women Patrols had been set up, a Home Office Committee on the Employment of Women on Police Duties, known as the Baird Committee, began to hear evidence. Margaret and Mary Allen gave evidence together, although most of the words are Margaret's. The record provides an important source of information about their motivation and aims.

As the munitions factories were closed, the WPS 'demobilised' many of its members but aimed, Margaret said, to 'keep together the best ones, and to try to get chief constables to take them on'.[41] She had some success, although 'supply exceeded demand'. The sort of women's police force Margaret wished to create became clear. When asked by the committee whether the women's policing movement should be taken over by existing police forces, she replied, 'By the State; not by the existing police ... I think it is time there should be a State service of women police in this country.'[42]

This grandiose plan for a national organisation was almost certainly a strategic mistake. In spite of widespread praise for the work of women's policing organisations during the war, opinion on the expansion of their work in peacetime was sharply divided, and policing outside London was hyper-local, divided up as it was between the near 180 distinct forces. A national organisation was therefore out of the question. Sir Leonard Dunning, who believed in the value of women police, could have helped Margaret's cause if she had scaled back her idea 'of the Women Police Service as an independent body', when her aim should have been 'the employment of women by police authorities as an integral part of the police force'.[43]

It soon became clear why Sir Nevil Macready had not incorporated the WPS into his force. Before the committee had been set up, he wrote to the Home Secretary: 'I hope ... that Miss Damer Dawson or any of her other satellites will not be included thereon, otherwise there will be considerable trouble.' He told the committee that 'the moving spirits [of the WPS] had been militant Suffragettes' and that it was difficult enough to get policemen to work with women without taking on those 'who might have been in court for assaulting police'. The strength of his personal antipathy was apparent in a letter to another committee four years later, when he wrote that 'the main point was to eliminate any women of extreme views – the vinegary spinster or blighted middle-aged fanatic'.[44] There can be no doubt that he was referring to Margaret. On the subject of 'a more militant organisation that had grown up during the war, adopting the title of "women police"', he wrote later that he 'had several conversations with the lady at the head of this body', and accused her of 'converting everything ... to her own point of view, which was inclined to be extreme'.[45]

Every conceivable aspect of the employment of women police was covered by the Baird Committee, too many debates to recount herein. Over two months, forty-seven witnesses were asked about the need for them; the nature of the duties they should perform; pay, terms and conditions; powers of arrest; and their ideal age, marital status, education and class. The debate on the last topic provided some insight into attitudes to class and women's place in society at that time. Macready said that he wanted his policewomen to be 'all sorts': 'a proportion of ... ladies ... he could put into evening dress with some diamonds or whatever they wear', and some women 'at the other end of the scale'. When asked how low on the scale he went, he said that he had a number of constables' wives (constables' wives sometimes helped look after women prisoners) who were about the domestic servant class and a number of former bus conductresses; he thought that was about the limit.[46] Margaret told the committee that of the 1,070 women the WPS had trained and found employment, 669 had previous work experience, while 411 had no prior training but had private means. It is unlikely that any male constables 'had private means'. She believed that recruits should be mature and have 'had some experience of human nature'.[47]

After answering the committee's questions, Margaret was asked if she had anything to add. She read a letter from the Metropolitan Police addressed to the 'so-called ... unofficial and unauthorised' Women Police Service. It warned her that she would be breaking the law if the WPS continued to 'masquerade' in police uniform in London. She then read to the committee her reply, in which she asserted that the work of the WPS had been officially approved, much of it being conducted under government contract. She urged the Commissioner to await the outcome of the inquiry, after which 'it will be easier to decide in an amicable spirit how the new forces are to work'.[48]

The Baird Committee report was presented to Parliament on 5 August 1920. It recommended the continued employment of women police but that their employment could be left to local discretion depending on the local need. Better pay and conditions of employment were recommended, together with powers of arrest. The Home Office promptly sent a circular to constabularies advising them to ignore the recommended better pay and powers of arrest.[49]

MARGARET'S DEATH

While awaiting publication of the Baird report, Margaret died suddenly of a heart attack on 18 May 1920. She was buried in the churchyard at Lympne, Kent, where a memorial recognises her as the founder of the Women Police Service. Just before her death she no doubt harboured some hope that the Baird Committee's report would lead to a continuing role for the WPS; or, perhaps, she had heard that was not going to happen. To Mary Allen, her death was 'a shattering blow', 'hastened by her bitter disappointment at the treatment she received after the war'. 'Instead of being appointed … to the task of organising a permanent body of policewomen, she was deliberately overlooked, and actually officially ordered to cease wearing uniform for the carrying out of activities connected with … women police.'[50] Mary immediately took over as Chief Commandant. Margaret's death received considerable press coverage, with glowing obituaries in national newspapers. Another memorial was put up on the embankment near her home in Chelsea.

Metropolitan Police complaints about the work of the WPS led to Mary Allen and senior colleagues being summoned to Westminster Police Court in March 1921 for the offence of wearing uniforms resembling those of the Metropolitan Police. The magistrates who heard the case were full of praise for the work of the WPS. But the issue was resolved by Mary agreeing to modify the uniform and change the organisation's title to the Women's Auxiliary Service (WAS). Margaret's reputation within the Metropolitan Police is apparent from the memoir of Lilian Wyles, one of the first official Metropolitan Policewomen in 1919, who served until 1949. Lilian, who stood in the court in uniform so that the uniforms could be compared, dismisses the WPS as wealthy middle-class women who were 'self-styled', 'without any authority', and who 'enjoyed their moralistic hobby, giving young men and girls corrective advice'. It was 'unthinkable to have two sets of women, both dressed as police, patrolling the same street, doing the same kind of work'.[51]

Under its new title, the WAS continued to operate for a few years, even sending officers under government contract to Ireland and to occupied Germany. But its influence declined, and in the difficult economic conditions of the 1920s, policewomen were often the first to be cut. The memory of Margaret Damer Dawson's achievements as founder and leader of the WPS also faded. It was somewhat tarnished by the activities of Mary Allen, who travelled widely, usually in her police uniform, and was often mistaken in other countries for the official head of the British women police; an error she did not correct. She became increasingly eccentric, meeting Hitler and Goering and becoming a supporter of the British fascist movement.

The mockery of Margaret and her posh friends in the WPS by Sir Nevil Macready and policewomen like Lilian Wyles is understandable. She had an unconventional lifestyle; her extreme position on the anti-vivisection question was wrong-headed; many of her women had been lawbreakers as Suffragettes; she had a penchant for staged publicity stunts as part of her fundraising; and her action on the streets sometimes seemed prudish and excessively moralistic. But the mockery was unfair.

Some of Mary Allen's descriptions of Margaret are excessive hagiographic 'hero-worship', but one in particular seems accurate in light of Margaret's achievements: 'She could not bear the sight of unnecessary suffering; it revolted her sense of the fitness of things.'[52] She devoted her life, and much of her personal wealth, to humanitarian causes. She organised life-changing help for women and children, and for Belgian refugees placed in danger by wartime disruption to society. She inspired loyalty from the many women who supported her causes. Unlike some of her extreme feminist friends, she was willing to compromise; for example, in her dealings with Sir Edward Henry, in order to progress the women police cause. She created an organisation that trained and deployed over 1,000 policewomen, many of whom, as Lilian Wyles herself writes, went on to work for the Metropolitan Police.[53] Her insistence that a Women Police Service should have been a separate national force was probably a strategic mistake, and one that potentially cost her her dream. But her contribution to showing the value of women police in a fairer criminal justice system was immense, even if it was only the start of a long, slow journey towards integration.[54]

MARY ADELAIDE HARE AND THE WOMEN POLICE VOLUNTEERS, 1914–15

DEREK OAKENSEN

IN A BOOK THAT SEEKS to identify pioneering female police officers, the inclusion of Mary Adelaide Hare (1865–1945) might seem a little odd. Mary Hare didn't much like either the police in particular, or the criminal justice system in general; and the last thing she probably wanted was to be a sworn constable. Trained as a teacher of the deaf, she started her own school and then became involved in the women's suffrage movement soon after moving that school to Hove. By 1914, then, not only did she have a deserved reputation for her work as a teacher, but, notwithstanding the issue of universal suffrage, she was also an experienced campaigner over the treatment of women and children in the courts and by the police.[1] Importantly, Mary Hare saw the involvement of women in policing as a means towards an end and, doubtless many years before her time, argued for the widening of the police agenda. Her views, the formation of the Women Police Volunteers (WPV), 'a special constabulary to protect women', and the difficulties that they encountered, not only serve to identify contemporary local political barriers but also how they later influenced the development of women police in Sussex.[2]

Starting in Norwood, Mary Hare first moved her school for the deaf to Brighton in 1895, then in 1901 to Goldsmid Road in Hove, and finally, in 1909, to 8 San Remo on Hove seafront as numbers of pupils grew. During her time at Goldsmid Road, as well as becoming known nationally as a pioneering teacher of the deaf, she was active in the women's suffrage movement. By 1906, she was a subscribing member of the Women's Social and Political Union (WSPU), a year later participated in the 'Mud March', and was a signatory to the Brighton Women's Suffrage Declaration. In 1908, she chaired a meeting in Brighton of the WSPU and attended another meeting in London that openly celebrated the release of suffragist prisoners.[3] By 1911, her allegiance within the suffrage movement had shifted from the WSPU (with its emphasis on the value of direct action) to the Women's Freedom League (WFL). She chaired several meetings in Brighton in support of the WFL's 'Tax Resistance' campaign, participated in the 'women don't count, so will not be counted' campaign to spoil census forms in the same year, and sold off her own belongings to raise funds.[4]

By 1913, she was the secretary of the WFL's Brighton and Hove branch. In that year the local press carried details of an attack on a suffragist head-quarters in St Leonards (they were mistakenly believed to be responsible for an arson attack in the town). Following this, despite the local detective inspector being placed in charge and the identity of the male ringleaders of the attackers being identified in written statements, there was a demonstra-bly superficial investigation by the Hastings Borough Police which came to nothing.[5] In July, the press also reported an attack on a small East Grinstead contingent attending the National Union of Women's Suffrage Societies' march to Hyde Park. Around a dozen suffragist supporters (which included at least two men) were attacked by a crowd estimated by the local press to be 1,500 strong. The *East Grinstead Observer*, which had announced details of the national march the week before and the intention of local supporters to join it, was critical only of the mob. In emphasising that the suffragists were from the 'non-militant section of the advocates of securing women's suffrage', the *Observer*, unusually supportive compared to most of the Sussex press, con-cluded that the crowd had 'disgraced … the main streets of East Grinstead'.[6]

A major concern for the WFL, however, and one of their core campaigns, involved the way in which women were treated unequally by the courts, especially as witnesses and victims.[7] The so-called 'Hammerwood' case at Sussex assizes in March 1914 exemplified Mary Hare's approach to chal-lenging authority to support women in courts. This particular case (which eventually occupied fifteen days of committal hearings at East Grinstead and then over seven days at the assizes) involved allegations of what the press could only bring themselves euphemistically to describe as 'the grossest of all offences' or 'grave offences against his [*sic*] own daughter'. It was incest, the victims were 13 and 20, and the youngest had to give evidence for an aston-ishing nine hours. The evidence was also considered sufficiently disturbing to excuse the male jurors from jury service for twelve years afterwards. The trial was held in camera and Mary Hare, and a Mrs Nicholls from the same WFL branch, were at first refused admittance, but having repeatedly returned and then challenging the judge to expel them on a point of law, were eventually allowed to be in the court. Mary Hare was to attend several other assize and quarter sessional hearings at Lewes during the next two years (often with Mrs Nicholls), and reported later to *The Vote* that 'orders' to leave courts had become 'requests' and then 'suggestions'; she had made her point.

In October 1914, and by now active in the new WPV, she drew the WFL's attention to the Plymouth Watch Committee's proposals to introduce regulations similar to those under the hated Contagious Diseases Acts. These Acts were especially disliked by suffragists, not least because all the legislative sanctions were openly discriminatory. Among other things, they had allowed police to detain women and subject them to forced medical examination for venereal disease. In doing so there was, in practice, little distinction shown between prostitutes and women who just happened to be among the lower classes (men, apparently, weren't considered to be responsible for venereal disease transmission).[8] Though these Acts were repealed in 1886, the Plymouth Watch Committee was planning to use contemporary Defence of the Realm laws to effectively reinstate the powers of the old legislation, and these too would be enforced by the police. In the event, however, a concerted campaign by a number of women's groups put enough pressure on the government and on Plymouth Corporation to ensure the plans were dropped.[9]

On the declaration of war in August 1914, suffrage societies announced a truce and decided to refrain from more militant protests. But others, perhaps sceptical of patriotic fervour, recognised that war conditions might also create new inequalities for women and exacerbate existing ones. These included the WFL's Nina Boyle and Edith Watson, and, if her reported speeches in the first months of the war are anything to go by, Mary Hare. In the same month the Home Secretary announced a recruitment drive for special constables, and on 28 August 1914 the Special Constables Act came into law. This removed the longstanding legal requirement for 'tumult, riot or felony to be apprehended' before special constables could be appointed. Like earlier special constabulary legislation, it also made no mention whatsoever that it applied only to men. So, provided the local chief officer of police agreed and a magistrate would attest them, there was no legislative reason why a woman could not be a police officer, at least for the duration of the war emergency.

Nina Boyle of the WFL saw this recruitment drive as an opportunity to show what women could do, as well as using it as a platform to try to mitigate endemic unfairness in the criminal justice system. An early approach to Ellis Griffith (Undersecretary of State at the Home Office) had resulted in a polite rejection, albeit on the spurious grounds that new legislation would be needed. Her direct approach to Sir Edward Ward, the new Chief Commandant of the Metropolitan Special Constabulary, was peremptorily dismissed; he made it clear that he was only prepared to recruit men in London. Nina Boyle wasn't someone prepared to take no for an answer, and immediately started to form the WPV.[10]

In an appeal for support for the WPV published in *The Vote*, Nina Boyle asked supporters to 'find out whether such a Corps could render service in their own towns, and then proceed to organise it locally if advisable'. By early November 1914, Mary Hare and a small team of supporters were already laying the groundwork for a WPV group in Brighton, and ju-jitsu classes were being advertised there (at 2*s* 6*d* for twelve lessons for WPV recruits). But, before this, Nina Boyle and the 'wealthy and well-connected' Margaret Damer Dawson, having heard that each were trying to recruit women police, had met and agreed to merge their respective organisations under the title of WPV. This helped to mask underlying differences of opinion within the WPV over what women police could and should be doing. In essence, Dawson was prepared to adjust her views to some extent in order to gain official acceptance and support, and then build the women police organisation on the basis of co-operation rather than disagreement. Boyle was not; the WFL were antipathetic towards women being used to selectively control other women, however great the supposed national imperative. Matters came to a head in February 1915, when she forced a vote of no confidence in Dawson's leadership at a special meeting of the WPV and lost. Dawson reformed the group, changing its name to the Women Police Service (WPS), and Boyle and a few allies retained the name (if not much else) of the WPV. In Boyle's view, it was 'regrettable that suffragists, and especially Women Freedom Leaguers, should be so ready to drop their principles for the sake of a little police favour and temporary official countenance'.[11]

Although the lost vote was a watershed, and some studies of women police have suggested that Nina Boyle, Edith Watson and a very small group of supporters then moved to Brighton to re-establish the WPV, this overlooks the work already done there. Though there were not yet any formal patrols, information on places where Women Patrols might be of particular use was being gathered (as Nina Boyle's original plan had suggested). Equally, recruitment was taking place, training being organised, and WPV uniforms were being made at the workshop of the Women's Suffrage National Aid Corps (WSNAC) at 8 North Street Quadrant. The Brighton and Hove branch of the WFL had continued campaigning, especially in support of the welfare work done by the WSNAC, so in one sense it was business as usual. And when Mary Hare addressed an open meeting of the WFL in Brighton on

6 March 1915, that was to be expected, as was the attendance of the local press. Neither policing in general nor the WPV in particular seems to have been discussed at the meeting; this may well have been a deliberate tactic to avoid alerting the authorities locally to the fact that the WPV were ready to launch in Brighton. The WPV would have known about discussions already taking place in the town about the formation of a potential rival group, the Women Patrols; it is possible that there was an undeclared race to see who could get there first and grab the local headlines.[12]

On 18 March, the WPV was launched in Brighton at a public meeting, chaired by Mary Hare and with a main speaker (a Mrs Tanner, as Nina Boyle was ill) from the national Executive Committee of the WFL. Mary Hare described the problems that the WPV had already found in the town, especially public houses staying open after permitted hours and parts of the town 'which are an absolute disgrace to any town where there is any regard for decency or moral behaviour'. She concluded: 'we are certainly going to make some stir about this later on'.[13] The meeting got wide coverage in the local press, but not perhaps the sort of publicity that the WPV had hoped for. The *Brighton Herald*, for instance, after noting their links with the suffrage movement, could not resist being patronising: 'they present a very smart appearance, and they look so attractive that you feel you would not at all mind being arrested by them. But if you don't go quietly look for yourself; for these athletic ladies have learned the noble art of ju-jitsu.'[14]

The Brighton Women Police Volunteers practise Ju-Jitsu. Publicity photo.

The journalist's reference to ju-jitsu was more apposite than he probably realised. Never ones to shun publicity, the WPV had had photographs taken of their training in Brighton, and after their formal launch had supplied them to London newspapers. The *Daily Mail* had published one of them showing a ju-jitsu training session, while the *Daily Mirror* published another, commenting that it showed 'Brighton policewomen doing their daily exercises ... they keep themselves in the peak of condition by a regular course of physical drill'. [15]

Condescension aside, the publication of these photographs would not have endeared either Mary Hare or the WPV to the Brighton Chief Constable and Watch Committee; however, they had gone further. They had suggested that the Chief Constable had witnessed and supported their training. There was just one complication: he hadn't. As Chief Constable William Gentle told the *Herald* when asked about his supposed endorsement of the WPV training, '[he] assures us that this is not so, and he wishes to make it quite clear to the public that the uniformed ones are acting without his authority and entirely at variance from his wishes'. It would have been surprising, then, if the first letter from Mary Hare to the Brighton Watch Committee on 22 March was received enthusiastically. The committee were asked to allow a deputation to speak to them about some of the things going on in the town that the WPV felt the local police should know about, including public houses that were regularly keeping late hours. The Watch Committee considered the letter only very briefly before deciding that they would only communicate via the Chief Constable. When Mary Hare did get to meet the Chief Constable, shortly afterwards, the meeting was short and his message was terse: 'they should cease their work'. In any case, he and the Watch Committee had already decided to actively support another new organisation, the Women Patrols. [16]

The Women Patrols were formed under the auspices of the National Union of Women Workers (NUWW), and were politically untainted through association with the suffrage movement. [17] In Brighton and Hove their success and acceptability was due in no small measure to politically influential organisers and supporters. The meeting to formally launch the patrol was held in the Town Hall Council Chamber on 20 March 1915, and by then it had reportedly attracted over sixty women volunteers. Its acceptability to the Corporation and police was reflected by the main speakers, the Chief Constable, a superintendent from the Brighton Special Constabulary (who also happened to be the registrar at Brighton County Court) and the town clerk. Gentle foresaw an opportunity to use the Women Patrols to deal with 'khaki fever' and unsupervised fraternisation with the military; as he put it, 'young girls ... who had scarcely attained the age of mature judgement

... talk to young men and soldiers, regardless of the unfortunate result that might ensue'. He also used the meeting to make his position clear on the two different organisations. The Women Patrols, he said, 'had full police authority to act and he would personally be glad to give all the help he could'. As a measure of this official support, they were given use of the police court at Brighton Town Hall to use as a headquarters. The WPV, on the other hand, 'were acting without his authority ... in a dangerous way'; he was considering 'what steps he should take ... with people who, without official authority, called themselves "police"', and this could well include having them arrested for impersonating an officer.[18]

Most of the local press moved swiftly to align themselves in support of the Women Patrols, and therefore with the Chief Constable and Watch Committee. The *Brighton Herald*, in an unusually lengthy editorial, drew attention to the Women Patrols as 'a body of ladies acting under official recognition', who were also (and this may be just as relevant) 'ladies of position in the town'. The WPV, on the other hand, were said to be 'an entirely independent and unauthorised body, composed in part, if not entirely, of Suffragettes'. (The *Herald* knew the difference between suffragists and Suffragettes, but obviously wanted to make a point.) If that wasn't enough, readers were reminded that, with the Women Patrols, 'ju jitsu or force of any kind finds no place'. (It is difficult to understand if this was because ju-jitsu was regarded as unladylike, or whether the *Herald* knew about the pictures published in London papers.) A similar line taken by the *Brighton Gazette* (consistently critical of anything involving suffragists since 1908) drew a riposte from 'A resident near York Place', who complained about the 'puffing' of the Women Patrols and said that the only ones who 'have done any work of use' were the WPV.

What the WPV now needed was some supportive publicity, and they got it through the *Brighton Graphic*, whose editor skilfully provided both Mary Hare and the Mayoress of Brighton, Mrs J. L. Otter (on behalf of the Women Patrols) with the opportunity to state the case for each of their respective organisations. Rather than seeking to score cheap political points from each other, what resulted was almost an object lesson in potential co-operative working. Although the WPV had a clear preference for working in uniforms (which Gentle abhorred), and the Women Patrols (at least in Brighton) didn't, the two bodies were probably closer philosophically to each other than, say, the WPV was to the new WPS.[19]

The *Graphic* didn't leave it there. Although the WPV operated in both of the towns of Brighton and Hove, the authorities in Hove had, until now, largely remained outside the debate over women police in whatever form.

The Brighton Women Police Volunteers, April 1915.

When asked by the *Graphic* if he 'condemned' the WPV, the Hove chief constable, William Cocks, replied: 'I do not condemn them because I do not know what they are supposed to do.' It could be interpreted either way and was masterful fence-sitting; it was taken by the WPV as tacit approval. Nevertheless, following her rebuff from the Brighton Chief Constable, Mary Hare again wrote to the Watch Committee on 28 April, this time simply asking 'to submit a statement of facts in regard to the conditions in the town': the committee left it nearly six weeks before simply noting its arrival and then effectively ignoring it. By then the WPV seem to have concentrated most of their efforts in Hove, although the *London Weekly Dispatch* (in an article comparing the Women Patrols with the WPV) suggested that while the largest part of the WPV patrolled London parks, 'a local branch patrols Brighton sea-front and Hove Gardens'. [20]

Six months after its official launch, it is difficult to conclude that the Brighton branch of the WPV was making much progress, especially compared with the Women Patrols. The 1915 National Conference of the NUWW was told that there were members of the Women Patrols working in 106 different places. In Sussex, there were patrols (in order of formation) at Chichester, Worthing, Brighton and Hove, Eastbourne and East Grinstead, with over sixty members in Brighton and forty in Eastbourne. Again, the

Graphic published a lengthy article in support of the WPV, this time apparently written by Mary Hare's deputy, Inspector Clara Redfern. Although the article discussed the sort of work that could be undertaken by women police, it explicitly avoided mentioning 'the local part of our efforts', explaining that this would 'be fully dealt with' at a public meeting on 25 October.

This meeting was to all intents and purposes a relaunch of the WPV in Brighton, and was due to be addressed by the 'Chief of the Women Police Volunteers in London' – Nina Boyle. She nearly didn't make it. She had surrendered to an arrest warrant at Stratford-upon-Avon on 15 October and appeared in court the next day. The case, for not complying with regulations requiring registration at hotels and boarding houses, was dismissed because a warrant for Boyle's arrest had been issued without the magistrates bothering with a summons first. She was awarded 3 guineas costs and both she and Mary Hare (who had gone to Stratford to support her) were late arriving at the WFL's annual conference as a result.

With her overnight experience in police cells ('it would be difficult to exaggerate the hygienic impropriety and indecency of the arrangements') it was unsurprising that the Brighton meeting was given a 'stirring address' by Nina Boyle, according to the *Sussex Daily News*. She emphasised the need for more volunteers in Brighton, not just for the WPV but also to help run the WSNAC workshop, which was in financial difficulty, being entirely funded by donations from WFL members. Mary Hare was equally optimistic, describing the 'courtesy, support and kindness' from magistrates, the Watch Committee, and the Chief Constable in Hove; even to the point where the Watch Committee had agreed to close Hove Lawns at dusk following a WPV report. In Brighton, on the other hand, not much had changed. The Watch Committee still insisted that any contact with the WPV be via the chief constable, and although similar concerns over goings-on in Madeira Drive and Dukes Mound in Brighton had been reported to Gentle, nothing had happened. And despite the 'crowded' meeting passing a resolution urging the Brighton Watch Committee to take action, nothing changed.[21]

Things didn't get any better for the WPV after a meeting on 21 November to generate support for the Brighton WSNAC workshop. Mary Hare chaired the meeting and spoke about the need to financially support the workshop, and about the opportunities for practical work with the WPV. But some ill-advised comments about the need to create paid work for those who needed it, however well intentioned, were taken as direct criticism (the *Herald* called them 'taunts') towards those who, for instance, were undertaking voluntary war work in support of the troops. The fallout from this meeting did little to enhance the local image of the WFL. It may have marked the beginning of the end for the WPV in Brighton, since it was no longer mentioned in Brighton newspapers (even in the reliably supportive *Brighton Graphic*).[22] But it had not disappeared entirely, and Mary Hare remained a tireless advocate.

In London, the WPV were pleased to report in January 1916 that Mrs Edith Watson had finally been allowed access to the Old Bailey in uniform, and intended to campaign for women gaolers for women prisoners in police and court cells; but there is no mention of anything happening in Brighton.[23] Locally, Mary Hare had spoken to a group in Southwick about the role of women police in February, and in March addressed the Theosophical Society in Eastbourne on 'Some Town Problems in the light of Theosophy' in her capacity as 'Head of the Women Volunteer Police for Brighton and Hove'. The *Eastbourne Gazette* reported afterwards that 'the Mayors of both towns have expressed their sympathetic approval of the [WPV] movement and the useful work that is being done', but there was probably more than a little wishful thinking in this assertion, especially as far as Brighton was concerned.[24]

The WPV in Sussex did not, however, last much longer after Mary Hare's address to Eastbourne theosophists in March. It (like the WSNAC workshop in Brighton) had consistently been dependant on funding from its own members, and its demise may simply have been a function of too few members and too little cash. That said, while it was never helped by disputes with the authorities in Brighton, it was also the case that the new WPS in London was making progress that the WPV could never realistically hope to match. In June 1916, the WFL at a national level formally recorded the end of the WPV, but in Brighton it was possibly gone a month or two before.[25] In any case, the two main proponents of the Brighton WPV were both to move away in November 1916, Nina Boyle to do war work in a hospital in Mesopotamia and Mary Hare to open a new and larger school in Burgess Hill; there was no realistic chance of a renaissance.[26]

Across Sussex, as far as women police were concerned the Women Patrols predominated for much of the rest of the Great War, except in Bexhill, where policewomen were employed for the first time in July 1917 by the county police authority, the East Sussex Standing Joint Committee (ESSJC). To get to this stage, however, there had been a great deal of negotiating between the chairman of the ESSJC and the Chief Constable of East Sussex on one hand, and Bexhill Corporation and a local committee (consisting mainly of local church ministers and councillors and chaired by the Rev. Edward Mortlock) on the other. They had, as far as the Bexhill authorities were concerned, reached an agreement over the employment of two members of the WPS.

The council, using private donations, would employ them for a month or two's trial, and if this was felt to be successful, then they would be taken onto the county constabulary's strength and payroll. So, in April 1917, Acting Inspector Gertrude Cooke and Sergeant Braddon of the WPS arrived in the town. The next month the ESSJC voted against funding the arrangement, but the Bexhill authorities decided to continue anyway. By June, the Bexhill council was convinced that the experiment had worked; after a lively debate only one councillor dissented. They had had good reports about their work with women and children, and in their view there 'was an urgent necessity for this form of police work being maintained', so they urged the county authorities to change their mind. It seemed to work. At their July meeting, the ESSJC agreed to take on the cost (£4 weekly) as part of the constabulary budget 'for such time as troops were stationed in the borough'.[27]

For whatever reason, the goodwill from the county authorities didn't last much longer. In early November, a new superintendent at Bexhill submitted a report to the Chief Constable on the work of the women police. Though this report and its contents seem not to have survived, they can be guessed: at the next meeting of the county police authority, a motion to dispense with their services was debated. Though the motion was lost, the damage was done, and in January 1918 Margaret Damer Dawson wrote to the ESSJC complaining of the 'intolerable working conditions' that had forced both women to resign in the meantime. But enthusiasm for women police in the town itself was undiminished. The ad hoc 'Social Services' committee of a year before reinvented itself as the Bexhill League of Social Service (BLSS) in early March 1918, still chaired by the vicar of St Stephen's Church. It was advised, in a voluntary capacity, by Gertrude Cooke, and set about raising funds. By early April the WPS had supplied a sergeant and a constable for Bexhill, this time working from an office in a church hall rather than from the police station.[28] Whereas the two policewomen seem to have spent much of their time the year before on routine patrol (local newspaper reports suggest that they were active in reporting wartime lighting offences), the new emphasis was on the protection of women and child welfare. These were the priorities, very similar to those of the WPV in Brighton, that were cited when funding appeals were made, particularly to church congregations.[29]

In June 1918, the finances of the BLSS looked healthy. Donations from benefactors and fundraising events meant they had a surplus that was sufficient to hire a lodging house room to be used for women who needed emergency accommodation (an early form of refuge), and it was being regularly used. But by December the surplus had become tiny, and though funds were bolstered by additional collections taken at local churches, by June 1919 it was reported that there was barely enough money left in the bank to pay the two women police that month.

The first annual meeting of the Women Patrols in Hastings was given considerable coverage by the *Bexhill Observer*, and some in the town were thinking that perhaps the Hastings Chief Constable was right when he suggested that 'taking into account the needs of the town and the character of the population the work of voluntary patrols was better at present than that of paid policewomen'. In July, with the BLSS now even more dependent on ad hoc donations, the Bexhill council petitioned the ESSJC to take on the funding for the two policewomen. The county committee were in no hurry to decide and deferred the matter until their November meeting, when they rejected it; two policewomen at Bexhill were 'not necessary'. But by then the BLSS had run out of money. It is perhaps not uncoincidental that their income first started to diminish around the time of the Armistice; maybe policewomen were perceived as a solution to wartime problems and not peacetime ones? And perhaps because policewomen weren't considered 'necessary' for the East Sussex force, the Standing Joint Committee only appointed two constables in February 1942, and that in the face of opposition from the Chief Constable, who eventually agreed, provided they were 'not involved in moral welfare work'.[30]

Getting official recognition in Brighton was always going to be problematic for the WPV. Even if the Chief Constable and Watch Committee had not been embarrassed by photographs supplied to London papers and the subsequent need for them to deny the WPV claims of official approval, WPV supporters in the town were all too frequently perceived as suffragists and distrusted accordingly (especially by the chief constable). The Women Patrols were a much safer organisation in that sense, not least because their national policy forbade anyone connected with the suffrage movement from acting as a local patrol organiser. In Hove, however, even if the WPV were not openly supported, they were not actively opposed by the town authorities either, and there is some evidence of active co-operation. The result of this (and the influence of later work of a separate Women Patrols branch in the town) may be seen in subsequent debates within Hove's Watch Committee, which led eventually to an almost unanimous agreement to employ women police as part of the borough force's establishment in May 1918 (though they were not actually recruited until February 1919). In Brighton, considerable lobbying by women's organisations eventually forced the hand of a reluctant Watch Committee and even more reluctant chief constable, and two ex-WPS constables joined the force in July 1918. At one point there were a woman sergeant and two constables in the Brighton force, but the turnover of the women officers was high; few stayed for more than a few months. By September 1921 there were none left, and the new chief constable (Charles Griffin, appointed in 1920) made it clear that he had no intention of appointing any more.[31]

Back in April 1915, *The Vote* reviewed the first few months of the WPV, the split with what became the WPS, and the WPV's administrative realignment with the WFL. The article (unsigned, but seemingly in Nina Boyle's style) presciently summarises the difficulties for the unrepentantly feminist WPV throughout its existence, especially the Brighton and Hove unit which operated at arm's length from the main WPV organisation in London:

> The whole thing was admittedly an experiment, and the lines on which it most usefully could be run had to be searched for and found. No precedents existed, no authority was available; and a thousand claims for police women's work existed on all sides. The appearance of the first volunteers in uniform crystallised public opinion as to the desirability of the innovation and by this piece of direct action the Women Police Volunteers did more to break down the barrier of prejudice against the police women than all the previous propaganda of the various reform societies which have advocated the measure during recent years.

And in that sense, if no other, Mary Hare and the Brighton and Hove WPV left an important legacy.[32]

KATHERINE SCOTT

THE FIRST WORLD WAR AND 'WOMEN PATROLS' IN HAWICK

DR DAVID M. SMALE

'MISS SCOTT ORGANISED AND COMMANDED the Women Police Patrols in this town, a body which did excellent service during the war, when thousands of soldiers were stationed in the town and district.' David Thom, Chief Constable of Hawick Burgh Police.[1]

Mr Thom's quotation succinctly describes much of the substance of this chapter; thousands of soldiers moved into the small burgh in Roxburghshire and this resulted in the formation of Women Patrols. This work, however, will address other questions surrounding the introduction of the patrols, particularly: why it was considered necessary to establish a new form of policing to address a newly perceived problem; why it fell to Katherine Scott to take charge; and how far did the patrols promote the development of full-time policewomen in the border counties?

KATHERINE SCOTT'S EARLY LIFE

The Honourable Katherine Grace Hepburne-Scott was born on 19 October 1884, the daughter of Walter Hepburne-Scott, the 8th Lord Polwarth, and his wife, Lady Mary.[2] They resided at Mertoun House, St Boswells, Roxburghshire, close to the River Tweed in the Scottish Borders. Katherine appears to have had an idyllic childhood roaming the large estate and receiving her education from a Swiss lady tutor, Miss Weinmann. In the equally idyllic story of her life, her biographer remarked that she became a lover of nature and poetry, 'and to these a third and yet stronger influence was added, that of a deeply held evangelical faith'.[3] The writer added a few pages later that Katherine was noted for her sympathy, humanity and an interest in helping others.[4] This is a theme that permeates her life story: working to help and protect others. The family formed part of the county elite, and when Scott's brother married, the service was held in St Giles Cathedral, Edinburgh, and attended by the good and the great from all over Great Britain.[5] Nevertheless, early in 1912, the family had to move out of their grand house following financial difficulties.

In July 1914, Katherine was living near Hawick, and in the early days of the war she was appointed Honorary Secretary of the Hawick Branch of the Soldiers' and Sailors' Families Association. She moved into the town to live with the Reverend Dr David Cathels and his wife, and she remained with them for eight months. Katherine, a woman with a deep religious calling, came under the influence of this well-known clergyman in the burgh, who would in 1924 serve as Moderator of the General Assembly of the Church of Scotland. Cathels was later remembered as a man who maintained a 'lofty ideal', and he would 'look upon all men and women as alike; to know neither high nor low, rich nor poor, and to fear the face of no man'.[6] In this matter he reflected Katherine's ideals. Cathels published extensively, religious tracts with two dominant themes: Christian manhood and the evil of alcohol. In 1887, he published *Ourselves and Our Times*, in which he gave wholesome and healthy advice to young men.[7] In 1903, he wrote an article in a local newspaper asking, 'Are Hawick Young Men Deteriorating?' The deterioration was characterised by the men of the burgh being 'conspicuously absent from the services of the Christian Church'. Cathels was concerned because for every twenty young women attending services and church activities, there was only one young man. He struggled to understand what the men were doing, because 'it was impossible to discover them in any religious, intellectual or educational institution at all'.[8] His bewilderment is somewhat contrived; I suspect he was fully aware that the young men were spending their time in the hostelries of the town and enjoying drink.

In the towns of the Scottish Borders, workers in the textile industries were notorious for their drinking habits. This has been explained as a result of working in damp, airless conditions, but in truth, like many of Victoria's working class, alcohol provided an escape from their grim reality.[9] In the 1830s, temperance arrived in the town, and by the end of the decade almost a third of the population had signed the pledge to abstain from alcohol.[10] Nevertheless, heavy drinking persisted, particularly during the summer celebrations of the Hawick Common Riding.[11] This annual event allowed the locals to let their hair down, and when violence or antisocial behaviour erupted at the festivities, alcohol was usually an important contributory factor. Smout has described alcohol as 'an ubiquitous permeation of Scottish Society'.[12] An important influence on public drunkenness was the establishment of a 'new' police force in Hawick in 1846, patrolling the streets with a remit to impose new standards of order on the population. By 1883, the superintendents of both the burgh and Roxburghshire forces reported that drunken, antisocial behaviour at the Common Ridings had seen a sharp decline.[13] This was a trend that Cathels wished to continue; however, it is important to understand that Hawick had a long and annually renewed relationship with drinking to excess.

Stobs Camp, situated 3½ miles outside of Hawick, was established as an army training camp in 1902. This 3,600-acre site was extensively developed with rifle ranges, training grounds that allowed the large-scale manoeuvre of infantry and cavalry, and a railway siding was built to provide the logistical support the camp required. In 1903, volunteer units began to arrive at Stobs, and in July the numbers peaked at 20,000 men. It is clear that a relationship developed between the army units and the population of Hawick, and this was characterised by socialising with the men as they frequented the public houses of the town, and attending events at the camp. In July 1907, the 1st Lothian Volunteer Brigade (Edinburgh) were training at the camp. They paraded through the streets of Hawick and a sports day was organised and attended by a large number of the town's residents, with the 'ladies predominating'.[14] During the same month, the military organised horse racing at Stobs; a Paisley trooper's horse bolted into the crowd and injured a man and woman from Hawick:[15]

THE FIRST WORLD WAR, THE ARMY AND STOBS CAMP

On the outbreak of the First World War, Stobs was designated as a prisoner-of-war camp, and 100 wooden huts were erected to house the expected large number of captured German soldiers. Many of the towns of the Scottish Borders were obliged to billet large numbers of British soldiers in the course of the war, and in January 1915, men of the Black Watch arrived by train and marched through the burgh with their pipe band 'accompanied by a mascot in the shape of a pet goat'.[16] In that month, over 3,000 men were quartered in various parts of the town, and this rose to 5,000 by the beginning of February 1915.[17] Added to this were the British soldiers training at Stobs Camp. Stobs had been upgraded to the headquarters of the prisoner-of-war camp system in Scotland, and by 1916 there were 5,000 prisoners of war and 2,000 enemy alien internees detained there. This required a large military guard at the camp.[18] In February 1915, a local newspaper reported that the 'general conduct of the men has, on the whole, been exemplary, and the police have made no apprehensions'.[19] The author was writing too soon. The vast majority of all the British soldiers in the Hawick area were young men away from home and many living in poor conditions, including huts and tents. While their training was intensive, there were periods when there was little to do, so many visited the hostelries of the burgh.

The coming of the war allowed Cathels to vent his views on alcohol, particularly when thousands of troops arrived in Hawick and the surrounding area. In January 1915, when Katherine was still living with him, he wrote an article for a local newspaper entitled 'An Appeal to Citizenship. The Coming of the Soldiers.' In this work he addressed the problem of plying the soldiers with alcohol, and the tone of his comments almost reveals a panic as the khaki-clad men poured into Hawick. He warned that his fellow townsfolk should not disregard 'the earnest warnings which were given by Lord Roberts and Lord Kitchener against tempting the soldier to drink'. He emphasised that the 'call of duty, of self-denial, of self-sacrifice, of self-restraint, comes to all of us'.[20]

At this stage in the war, Cathels may have been unaware of the conditions in the trenches and the mincing-machine rate of attrition that these soldiers were going to face on the Western Front; however, later that year, with the casualty rates filling the pages of the local newspapers, he continued his theme with 'Our Soldiers and Drink. Who is to Blame?' He lauded the troops because 'they have laid us under a debt which we can never repay', and observed that soon 'they will be in the fighting line, facing wounds and death for us'. Nevertheless, he made quite plain his perception that the increasing lawlessness which the tiny burgh police force struggled every night to contain was the fault of the people of Hawick for providing drink, and licensees allowing the soldiers to become drunk. Cathels considered that he knew what was best for the young soldiers – he obviously did not ask them if they would prefer attending an improving lecture by him or a night in a hostelry – and he blamed his parishioners for allowing the troops to 'forget their manhood and to revel in drunkenness, bestial and unrestrained'.[21]

In all garrison towns, the army employed their own military police to curb the excesses of young men letting off steam before engaging in the attritional warfare of the Western Front. Nevertheless, the burgh police were often called regarding drunken soldiers causing disturbances in the town. Once the troops were in the town, the relationship between the military and the police authorities can be described as a period of toleration at the beginning, but which quickly spiralled downwards into the imposition of harsh sentences on offending soldiers. One of the first to appear at the police court was a Black Watch private who was convicted of being drunk and behaving in a riotous and disorderly manner. His case was aggravated because he was a member of the military police of the regiment:

> Bailie Lyon said he was very sorry to see a soldier in uniform in such a position ... However as accused was the first soldier he had had before him since the military came recently to Hawick, he was disposed to deal leniently with him ... He dismissed accused with an admonition.[22]

There quickly followed a lengthy catalogue of public order offending by the troops: fighting among themselves; conducting themselves in a disorderly manner; assaulting the police and resisting arrest. The massively outnumbered police constables and specials must have had some sympathy for the young men out in the pubs of the town, possibly drinking their last ever pint. It is certain that many of the young men would echo the words of a soldier on being charged by a constable with a petty offence: 'You civilian police are too officious and ought to be in the trenches. You would then have a sense of humour.'[23] Nevertheless, the police and the specials thought that in undertaking their responsibilities to uphold the law, they too were doing their patriotic duty.

Cathels' worries regarding the soldiers and alcohol were shared by many and not just the troops; a social panic emerged because of the increased spending power of female munition workers and the new phenomenon of their public drinking with a perceived drop in production. The Minister for

Munitions, David Lloyd George, repeatedly spoke of alcohol hindering the war effort. In February 1915, he declared: 'Drink is doing us more damage in the war than all the German submarines put together.'[24] He reiterated this the following month: 'Fighting Germany, Austria and drink, and as far as I can see the greatest of these three deadly foes is drink.'[25] It was in this atmosphere of condemnation of alcohol, both on the national stage and literally at her home that Katherine, the woman whose background and interests centred on sympathy, humanity and a desire to help and protect others, set out to find a role in the war and in her town.

WOMEN PATROLS

The fear of the effects of excessive alcohol consumption by the troops was accompanied by another social panic, that of 'khaki fever'. This term was coined to describe reports of immodesty by women in garrison towns. There was a belief that wartime conditions were leading women and girls into, at best, inappropriate relationships with soldiers, and at worst, sexual promiscuity or prostitution.[26] A local newspaper recognised the problem and offered a solution:

> It is natural that these young girls should be excited and carried away by the stress of the present times, and in the presence of so many soldiers in the neighbourhood. The excitement and foolish behaviour which it causes might be a very real danger, and it is in order to help these girls and to direct their interests and enthusiasm wisely that the Women Patrols have been organised.[27]

The Women Patrols were one of two organisations active in forming a police role for women anxious to do their bit. The other and more radical group was the Women Police Service. In Scotland, its most significant activity was at HM Gretna Munitions Factory, the largest producer of cordite in Britain. In October 1916, the Ministry of Munitions employed members of the Women Police Service as 'policewomen' to search and supervise the 11,000 women working at the factory. They were never an official section of the police; however, the historian Louise Jackson considered that their role at Gretna had symbolic importance: it showed that women could serve in security and regulatory roles.[28]

In December 1914, the Secretary for Scotland authorised the Women Patrols and contacted all of the chief constables, requesting them to give the women facilities to work.[29] The patrols were co-ordinated by the National Union of

Women Workers (NUWW) and initially they disclaimed that their role was 'rescue work' (of the morals of young women), yet it very quickly became clear that this was their main function.[30] A pamphlet issued by the NUWW set out the qualifications for a recruit to the Women Patrols in Scotland:

Tact and Sympathy;
Some previous experience of work among girls;
Good health, and
The ability to give not less than 2 hours a week to the work.
Patrols should be preferably above the age of 27.[31]

This list of requirements omits possibly the most important ones. The women recruits were generally married, socially privileged and well educated. These were not women 'who typically would have engaged in paid work'.[32] Their social, economic and educational backgrounds contrasted starkly with the men of the police. Broadly, the Women Patrols were a middle-class force, formed as an instrument to save British womanhood and to secure the post-war future. The duties of the patrols were explained as:

To patrol on the beat assigned to them by the organiser.
To make friends with the girls and gain their confidence.
To warn girls who have been seen speaking to men on duty or behaving unsuitably.
To put the girls in touch with local societies, clubs or classes.
To observe and note anything bearing on the welfare and good conduct of the girls.
To report anything serious to their organiser or Patrol leader.
To write a brief daily report.[33]

In the Scottish Borders the women were all issued with badges, armlets, guide books and authorisation cards signed by the chief constable. Katherine Scott, armed with her faith and desire to help others, stepped forward to be the leader of the Women Patrols in Hawick and Peebles. It would appear that Scott and her women were trained by 'organisers' Miss Niven and Miss St John, and on 1 January 1915 the patrols, consisting of twenty-one women in Hawick and eleven in Peebles, went to work.[34]

Katherine Scott was also concerned for the welfare of the soldiers and identified that a significant problem for the men was keeping their heavy woollen uniforms clean during their training. She instigated a practical solution to this problem and organised a laundry, providing employment for a number of soldiers' wives.[35] There is a sense that Scott, 'bristling with the time, enthusiasm and evangelical spirit which wealth and patronage bestows', had discovered a real purpose for her life.[36] She threw herself into organising the patrols and brought the voluntary organisations and churches in Hawick together to act vigorously to assist in the war effort. The work of Katherine Scott and the women patrolling in pairs, keeping watch on the streets of the burgh and areas around Stobs camp, was described by her former tutor Miss Weinmann: 'Night after night, on cold winter evenings, she would start out into the dark lanes and side streets to look for girls who were hiding there with soldiers.' When she found women and soldiers together, she would earnestly reason with them and convince the females that associating with the men, particularly under the influence of alcohol, could place them in moral danger. She would then almost invariably escort the girls back to their homes. Scott's patrols usually dealt with cases of naïve girls who they considered required protection from the soldiers; however, sometimes the troops needed protection from 'women of the less reputable type'.[37]

In June 1916, two young women from Edinburgh pled guilty at the police court to loitering in Hawick for the purpose of prostitution. They had been previously warned by the police and sent back to Edinburgh, but they had returned. Both women were fined 12s or fourteen days in jail.[38] It is likely that the few prostitutes prosecuted were the tip of the iceberg, with the women finding a keen market in the young men training at Stobs.

In November 1915, an NUWW's report congratulated the patrols in helping women and men: 'Patrols have been heartily thanked by men for freeing them from undesired attentions on the part of women and girls, and equally heartily thanked by women and girls for a like service in regard to men.'[39]

Across the country there were many reported instances of men handing over females to the patrols: 'In one place four soldiers, quite independently, brought to the "Patrol" girls whom they considered to be in danger, and asked that they might be taken care of.'[40]

The moral panic did not exist solely in the minds of the interfering middle-class women. Women, young girls and men frequented the army camp at Stobs, particularly on Sundays. In May 1915, the extent of these visitors to the army, prisoner-of-war and internee camps reached such large numbers that the military turned to legislation to stop them. Lieutenant General Sir J. Spencer Ewart issued an order under the Defence of the Realm Act, prohibiting members of the public from approaching the camp 'nearer than a distance of a quarter of a mile from any side'.[41] Chief Constable Thom of the burgh police received a copy of the order which stated that special passes were required to go near the camps.[42] Undoubtedly, the Women Patrols would have formed part of Thom's strategy to stop the sightseers.

There were remarkably few prosecutions for contravening the general's order, but when detected the accused attracted a heavy fine. In August 1915, a male labourer from Hawick was found within Stobs Camp. He had entered the lines of the 14th Royal Scots 'for the purpose of idling and loitering'. The man had been warned to leave and he refused to go away. At Hawick Sheriff Court he was fined £2 or ten days' imprisonment.[43]

There was one reason why the locals wanted to frequent the camp, and this activity did not threaten to corrupt women and girls. The German and Austrian prisoners produced a remarkable amount of crafted artwork and other items, made from any materials that were at hand; for example, bones from their cookhouse. The bored prisoners of war produced ornate bone and wooden models, toys, small pieces of furniture and souvenirs from Stobs. Some of these goods were sold to the camp guards; however, there was money to be made from selling-on these goods, and it seems likely that some of those frequenting the camp were there to purchase the prisoners' artwork and furniture. This activity became common knowledge, and one correspondent to *The Scotsman*, styling himself the 'Loyalist', deplored the trade and exposed it:

> Sir, a practice is now at full-swing at Stobs Camp which might very properly be termed 'trading with the enemy'. The Germans are an industrious people when they get well enough paid for it, and in captivity they turn this to account by manufacturing large quantities of models, photo frames, fretwork etc., from materials brought in for that purpose … a considerable profit is made.[44]

Notwithstanding this secretive but flourishing trade between the enemy and the locals, as early as March 1915, the *Hawick Express* expressed the belief that 'women police have been a great success where troops are quartered'.[45] Nevertheless, they were a novelty and not fully appreciated; three months later the same newspaper carried a snippet of information that there were 2,014 Women Patrols in England, within a section of jokes including supposedly humorous observations on women.[46] One of those English women, who had been in 'a patrol for five months', reported that the 'mere presence of a Woman Patrol walking up and down created a healthier atmosphere in the streets'.[47] The NUWW commented that in the first months of a patrol the chief constables often expressed doubts, but were invariably won over 'by the tact and discretion of the Organiser and by the quiet unobtrusive way in which the work is carried on'.[48] This statement describes the relationship between Chief Constable Thom and Katherine Scott.

The patrols quickly discovered that endlessly telling girls wandering around the burgh or frequenting the army camps to go home had little effect; they had to provide an alternative or a distraction for them:

> From the first the patrols had found out that it was practically useless to hope to do much unless they had some counter-attraction to the amusements of the streets, and now many new clubs for the recreation of these girls have sprung up.[49]

Katherine Scott soon discovered that the above statement was correct, and four months after taking to the streets she helped launch the Girls' Patriotic Club in Hawick, which met once a week. This club had a cycling and rambling section, and the girls were taught first aid, sweet making and other crafts.[50] Scott led the girls in prayer and visited them at their homes, which afforded her the opportunity to meet their families. The close relationship she had with the girls was described by Miss Weinmann: 'It was a pretty sight to see her surrounded by the crowd of eager faces, each listening attentively to the teaching of their dear "Lady Katherine" as they called her. Each of these girls seemed to feel that she was loved and helped individually.'[51]

It is clear that Katherine Scott considered the Women Patrols to be just one part of a package to provide social care; in 1914, she'd been appointed secretary of the Soldiers' and Sailors' Families Association, which in 1916 became absorbed into the Hawick Pensions Committee. In 1918, she was elected president of the Hawick branch of the NUWW.[52] She immersed herself in charitable works, of which the following are just a few examples: she organised concerts for 1,300 people, 'Keeping them Cheerful'; conducted campaigns including 'Brick Day', raising funds to help build a cottage for disabled soldiers and sailors; and appealed for money to provide serviceable footwear for the 'Sodger's Bairns'.[53]

Scott did not only assist those who agreed to end their 'inappropriate' liaisons with soldiers or those who attended her club; she also helped women and girls who found themselves in the courtroom having been prosecuted by the police or because they were being neglected or abused and needed urgent help. Her tutor and possibly her biggest fan, Miss Weinmann, wrote that: 'in the police court Katie's influence was most helpful to the women and boys who were brought in'.[54] In June 1915, Scott petitioned Hawick Sheriff

Court regarding a 14-year-old girl. Her mother was an alcoholic living apart from her husband and she was cohabiting with another man. The police had received numerous complaints regarding the number of soldiers who frequented the house, and Sergeant Patrickson of the burgh police gave evidence that 'the woman was of loose morals and drunken habits'. Scott was concerned that the girl was being neglected and could become a victim of abuse. The sheriff agreed, sending her to a Church of Scotland home in Haddington for two years.[55]

As the war carried on into its third year, the NUWW acknowledged that there was less need for the patrols, and it would appear that the work of the Hawick patrols declined in the last two years of the conflict. Despite this, they were still operating with Scott in charge until at least May 1918.[56] Throughout the war years, Scott passed on her experience and knowledge by visiting other towns in Scotland offering advice on establishing Women Patrols.[57]

WOMEN PATROLS, THE END OF THE FIRST WORLD WAR AND FULL-TIME POLICEWOMEN IN THE SCOTTISH BORDERS

It is very difficult to assess how well the Women Patrols worked in Hawick; none of the daily reports have survived and we do not even know the names of the women involved. The historian relies to a large extent on assessments like Chief Constable Thom's at the head of this chapter. Articles in local and national newspapers were wholesome in their praise. In late 1918, the debate concerning employing full-time policewomen typically offered views like Bailie Murray of Glasgow: 'the Women Patrols had saved a good many girls, and he had testimony from Army officers to the good work the patrols had done'.[58] The cities of Scotland broadly welcomed policewomen but there was an important caveat, summarised by a commentator in the *Police Review and Parade Gossip*. This correspondent was of the opinion that women police would be ideal for dealing with women and children; however, 'sending them out at night to tackle the burglar ... thief and poacher; dealing with thousands of soldiers and bad characters' should not be allowed.[59]

In May 1918, the NUWW held a meeting in Hawick during which Edith Smith of Grantham outlined the role of women in the police. The keynote of her speech was that policewomen should work with women and children to prevent crime. At the end of the meeting Katherine Scott proposed a vote of thanks to Chief Constable David Thom. He, in turn, thanked Edith Smith, and the local newspaper recorded his comments: 'Mr Thom said he had been convinced since the commencement of his police career, that the prevention of cruelty to children was work that should be done by women.'[60] In a later meeting in Edinburgh held under the title 'What Policewomen Will Do', Mrs More Nisbett, a former Suffragette and serving as an inspector in the city's Women Police, detailed the general duties that they would perform: 'Policewomen were not out for physical force; they were out for moral force. Policewomen should be the custodians of women and children in the cells and before Magistrates; they should take evidence from women and children in delicate cases.'[61]

Despite Thom's opinion voiced in May 1918, the end of hostilities did not see the burgh police recruiting women. Just after the Armistice, the town council received a communication from the NUWW calling attention to the importance of the Women Patrols; however, they decided to let it 'lie on the table'.[62] This effectively allowed the men of the council to delay any decision on women police for the town. Six months later, the burgh's Provost's Committee made its intentions clear when it responded to an enquiry from the Convention of Royal Burghs regarding the employment of women police; the clerk was instructed to respond that the town council did not consider policewomen necessary in a small burgh like Hawick.[63] In October 1919, the provost stated that Chief Constable Thom saw no need for women police.[64] This apparent cooling to the proposition of permanent women police could be explained by a quirk in the manner in which the police were funded. The police grant from the Scottish Office was 'stereotyped', meaning that funds could only be spent in designated areas, and the employment of policewomen was not one of them. Unlike in England and Wales, where the restriction was loosened in 1916, in Scotland the grant money still could not be spent on women police or patrols.[65] These financial restrictions explain why the patrols remained separate from the police in Scotland, while in England policewomen were appearing on the police payrolls. In August 1919, the problem of stereotyping was alleviated when the Scottish Office sent out a circular stating that policewomen could be charged to police funds. Despite this development, in March 1920 the Chief Constable of the border county forces of Berwick, Roxburgh and Selkirk, John Morren, agreed with Thom's position:

> I am of opinion they [women] should not be employed in all Police Duties, but that generally speaking their work should be strictly confined to the investigation of crimes and offences relating to women and young persons, and to certain branches of Detective work … women could be usefully employed in the Clerical Department of the Police Service … there is no need or scope for the employment of women police in any of the County Forces in Scotland.[66]

This view prevailed, and as late as 1938 there were only thirty-seven police-women in Scotland: fifteen in Glasgow, two in Aberdeen, and the rest dispersed in ones and twos across the cities and towns of central Scotland. There were none in the Scottish Borders.[67] During the Second World War, very small numbers of women joined the Women's Auxiliary Police Corps; in Roxburgh County Police, a total of fourteen women served. However, most appear to have remained in post for a year or less.[68]

Scott's biographer remarked that her work with the Women Patrols 'helped to prepare the way for the permanent establishment of Women Police'.[69] In the border counties and burghs, this radical change would have to wait for a further thirty-five years. In December 1952, John Willison, the new Chief Constable of the recently created police force of Berwick, Roxburgh and Selkirk, which included the burgh of Hawick, hinted at a Rotary Club dinner that there would be 'policewomen soon in the Borders'.[70] In his report for 1953, he noted that two 'policewomen constables had been appointed in that year'.[71] It is difficult to ascertain how many female constables are serving in the Scottish Borders in the second decade of the twenty-first century; however, in the whole of Scotland in 2020 there were 5,702, which constituted 48 per cent of Police Scotland's staffing levels.[72]

KATHERINE SCOTT THE SOCIAL WORKER

After her wartime exertions with the Women Patrols, Scott continued to work for the War Pensions Committee until 1921. At that time, she moved to Edinburgh to take up the post of Assistant Secretary for Women's Work to the Social Work Committee of the Church of Scotland, and also as a police court Sister. This was a direct continuation of the work she had commenced during the war in Hawick, and she again immersed herself in it. The role of police court Sister involved her in trying to help the unfortunate women and children who found themselves charged with crimes and offences. She also had to provide the court with an assessment of the accused's background and problems, with a view to influencing the magistrates and sheriffs into appropriate sentencing. Accounts of Scott's work as a police court Sister typically involved naïve country girls arriving in Edinburgh and getting into various degrees of trouble. In one dramatic incident, Scott is even reported to have charged into a brothel to rescue a girl. This culminated with her and the girl running to escape a violent 'heavy-browed bully'.[73] In another case, a 'stunted girl of fourteen' was saved from a life in crime and sent to a training home for domestic servants run by the Church.[74] A further young woman was brought in from the countryside and dumped on a street in the capital, where she wandered around sobbing bitterly. 'Presently a kind-hearted policeman spied the poor little soul.' He took her to a police station and sent for the police court Sister. The girl was provided with a place at the Home Mission until she was able to secure employment.[75]

In 1926, besides the work at the court, other aspects of her social work compelled Scott and her assistant to make 1,263 visits and to conduct over 2,000 interviews. The strain of working beyond her physical endurance forced her to retire and go abroad, and then to England to regain her strength. Scott's energetic, full-on approach to her role of providing social care to women and children in need had taken a heavy toll. She was hospitalised in London, and following an operation she died on 27 January 1928, aged just 42 years.

It is extremely difficult to assess the effectiveness of Katherine Scott and her Women Patrols in the garrison town of Hawick. Her complement of middle-class women patrolled in pairs with no real powers other than persuasion; no real uniform other than an armlet; and no real way of measuring their success apart from the gratitude of Chief Constable Thom. He acknowledged that although they had been formed to police a single perceived problem, he had found them to be an effective tool in fighting the moral panic caused by the wartime social mix of soldiers and women in a small Scottish burgh.

Katherine Scott was the first leader of the earliest form of policing involving women in the Border counties, and it is clear that she considered her 'police' work as being just one element of her mission to provide social care to those less fortunate than her. In all of her work she followed Cathels' lofty ideal of treating every person, no matter their social status or the crime they were accused of, as an equal. Her work with the Women Patrols and as a police court Sister brought her the same rewards: 'the same sense of satisfaction in endeavouring to help one's fellow-men and the same joy of serving Him'.[76] Scott's religious zeal and certainty of purpose propelled her into years of hard work helping those caught up in the maelstrom of the First World War, and for years afterwards. It is perhaps fitting that the headline of her obituary in *The Scotsman* was 'Social Worker's Death'. It is most likely that she would have been pleased with this description.[77]

THE VERY VARIED POLICE EXPERIENCES OF MISS DOROTHY OLIVIA GEORGIANA PETO OBE KPM BEM

JOAN LOCK

WOMAN POLICE PIONEER DOROTHY PETO was active in both world wars. The first saw her dragging hysterical wives from departing troop trains at Bristol's Temple Mead Station and sobering up soldiers fresh from the trenches so they could catch their train home from Euston; the second, riding her bicycle through a Blitz-torn London to check that her policewomen were safe.

In between, she gained a rare insight into the various factions and forces at work during the early years of women policing. She began in 1914 as a member of the voluntary Women Patrols doing 'no less' than a two-hour tour of duty, 'not less' than twice a week. A patrol organiser was sent by the National Council of Women HQ in London to help launch the scheme.

They were taught to keep an eye open for 'stray girls, begging children, tipsy servicemen and amorous couples in public places', but the 27-year-old Dorothy out on her first patrol in Bath was a country girl looking for the excitement of town life. She hoped that each group of people they passed might turn out to be plotting some nefarious deed and convulsed her companion when, on seeing a long, low van with the doors open at the back, she exclaimed, 'How late the beagles are out tonight!' In fact, it was an undertakers van delivering a coffin!

But soon she was to acquire more experience after being selected, on the strength of some service with the St John Ambulance Association, to be secretary to the Women Patrol organiser Flora Joseph. As such, she was sent to gain some patrol experience down at Southampton docks, where things were tougher.

A key problem in Southampton was a small public garden in the centre of the city, where the behaviour of the girls and servicemen was 'so scandalous' that teachers and children, who normally crossed the garden going to and from school, had to go round by another route. Their Patrol Leader, Miss Payne, decided to ask the teachers, instead of going round, to walk 'through slowly and deliberately' – and it worked. Whether the girls recognised their teachers or the men were embarrassed, they didn't know. But, Peto felt, the value of practical common sense was one of the lessons learned.

Bristol was also growing in importance as a seaport. It offered all the lively activity of such places at all hours, and was a place where the Women Patrols happened upon girls missing from home, drunks out of control, women and couples fighting and others becoming intimate. They did what they could about all this, albeit lacking, as they were, police powers. This necessitated specific advice in their instruction book, that 'if you tell a group of bystanders to move on don't look back to see if you have been obeyed'. One of their notable achievements was opening a club for girls which proved very successful.

Then they were asked to add the railway station to their patrol. Consequently, at weekends their hours stretched to 1.30 a.m. to cope with the noisy throngs who came to see off the midnight leave train. As it drew in, the physically stronger women, of whom Peto was one, moved forward to the edge of the platform, so that when the train departed and hysterical women leaped on the footboards for a last farewell, they could drag them back to safety.

One disaster they could not have predicted was the shooting of one woman by her husband or sweetheart from a departing train, which resulted in the patrols then on duty finding themselves witnesses at his trial for murder.

Local organiser Flora Joseph soon decided to open a training school for Women Patrol Leaders, with a longer training course available for Women Police. In the spirit of co-operation, she invited a representative of Damer Dawson's Women Police Service (WPS) to serve on their school committee, and she and Peto were invited to London to witness the WPS's efforts. This resulted in Peto spending three weeks patrolling in London with a certain Mrs Smith, who was shortly due to go to Grantham. There, Smith was later to make history as the first woman to be sworn in as a police officer and to be given a power of arrest. Peto found her to be a woman of outstanding personality, fearless, motherly and adaptable. She profited from the attachment and was not surprised to hear of Smith 'successfully grappling with the problems of a war-time military centre'.

The connection with the WPS did not continue, Mary Allen later claiming that the senior Bristol women could not take the WPS discipline and that they had gone on to copy their school curriculum. Peto claimed that Damer Dawson expected all the women supplied by her, and the Bristol Training School, to remain members of her own organisation and subject to her ultimate control, while the Women Patrols felt all policewomen should be an integral part of the police service under the sole control of chief constables.

However, to gain more experience, Peto went on to study Liverpool's patrol system, which was led by ex-schoolmistress Mabel Cowlin, who had studied sociology at the London School of Economics and was supported in her work by Liverpool City's Chief Constable Sir Leonard Dunning. 'He gave an instruction that his men should pass on to them particulars of young girls found in grave moral danger in the streets.'

Due to its size and population mix of Chinese, West Indian, African, Irish and Italian, Liverpool presented a far greater challenge than Bristol or Bath. The Irish and Italians particularly, she found, were 'ready to boil over at the least provocation'. Add the seamen's dosshouses and dubious cafés, children accosting sailors on behalf of their mothers and acute poverty. Then there were the thousands of American troops coming to fight who were being unloaded there.

Peto claimed that: 'Patrol duty in the Liverpool streets certainly called for both courage and initiative.'

At the heart of the patrols' work were Mabel Cowlin's weekly case meetings, which much impressed Peto – and others. At these, every person or situation dealt with on the beat was thoroughly examined to find the best solution:

> In the years between the two World Wars I met both policewomen and social workers who told me that they owed their whole conception of constructive work to Mabel Cowlin's teaching; and I know how much I learned myself whenever I had the opportunity of sitting in at one of her case meetings in the Liverpool Patrol Office.

Back in Bristol, Flora Joseph having left, Peto took over the training school, which continued to supply trained Patrol Leaders and policewomen; though the latter were persistently unsworn. In their 1918 report, they drew a portrait of the ideal recruit for the Police Service. In addition to a good education, she should possess:

> a good normal physique, be rather large, rather benign and convey the impression that she sees good in the people she meets, rather than evil. The points to be drawn out in Peto's training included acute and accurate observation, swift decision making and a combination of initiative with discipline, of sympathy with judgment, of ready adaptability and the courage to stand on her own feet!

As she commented, 'Some chicken!'[1]

She was delighted when Major Stanley Clark, the Chief Constable of Gloucestershire, turned up asking for two trained women whom he promised to give full powers and the status of constables by the simple expedient of swearing them in under the Special Constables Act, which spoke of 'fit persons' rather than 'fit men'. She gave him her two most promising women. He kept his promise and, in 1921 made one of them his first woman sergeant and he took on some of the ladies being released from the Munitions Police. Their rural beats could be wide, and the women had to go wherever they were needed so they were soon whizzing around on motorcycles.

Back in the Metropolitan Police, Sofia Stanley was finding her hands full training her newly appointed, semi-official Special Patrols, so she asked for Peto's help in taking over the classroom training while she handled the beat side. Peto took every opportunity to get out with the Special Patrols, which must have made for an odd grouping given that the two patrols were always preceded by a police officer to protect them and handle any male offenders.

However, duty at London's mainline railways station was done without their male escort. The women carried out many sobering-up tasks on exhausted servicemen, enabling them to continue their journeys home with some money left in their pockets, for clearly they were sitting targets for pickpockets and dishonest prostitutes.

In 1918, Miss Peto also became head of the Federated Training Schools, which included Mabel Cowlin's Liverpool school and Glasgow's, led by the Scottish Patrols Leader, Edith Tancred.

In 1919, the Sex Disqualification (Removal) Act was passed, allowing for twenty Metropolitan women to be taken on as well as a number in the other forces – but most of them were not attested. The situation needed sorting out, so the Federated Schools pressed for a Committee of Enquiry on Women Police but with little success, so they closed down their training to concentrate on the fight.

In April 1920, they got their committee, chaired by Major Baird. Giving evidence were six chief constables; two HMI Inspectors, one of whom was Sir Leonard Dunning; Sofia Stanley and Lilian Wyles; six of the provincial policewomen, two of them attested; Police Federation representatives; and various other interested groups including the Federated Training Schools, Margaret Damer Dawson and Mary Allen.

When interviewed, Peto still stuck to her seemingly rather odd lower age limit of 27 for women recruits. She told the committee that women were given responsible duties immediately they entered the force which no male officer would have to tackle, and therefore they should be educated as 'it was to the educated classes came the opportunities of getting real experience and the right kind of knowledge' (though she admitted that an older woman who had educated herself could also do well):

> and she should be of a higher social class than male officers. It is very hard for them to go into the force with men of the same standing. It is easier for a woman of somewhat different class to do it and I think the men in many cases feel that themselves.[2]

She was right – they needed an edge. Class was very potent then.

She had wavered on her previous 'rather large' for height, as some forces with 5ft 8in demand found it excluded too many of the 'right sort', but they must be at least 5ft 4in or they couldn't be seen on the street. She was, however, adamant that they should not be asked to do a full day's patrolling, as women could not stay on their feet for eight hours.

Peto was well pleased with the Baird Committee report, dubbing it 'The Policewoman's Charter', as it agreed to most of their needs and insisted that the need for women police was urgent in thickly populated areas. Meanwhile, she applied to a number of police forces for the post of policewoman, but always received the reply 'no vacancies', so she sought the assistance of 'our good friend', Sir Leonard Dunning, now at the Home Office. When he enquired what she had said in her applications, she explained that, although at the Bristol School she had held a rank equal to that of a police superintendent, she was willing to accept no higher rank than inspector. He laughed and advised her to say nothing about rank and just take whatever she was given.

Her good friend also saved the day by informing her that the Chief Constable of Birmingham wanted a woman for the investigation of sexual offences against women and girls. If she applied, Dunning would write him a line on her behalf. Thus, by November 1920, she was widening her experience yet again as a member of Birmingham Constabulary.

In fact, Peto had been unaware that another matter was being held against her. When Sir Charles Haughton Rafter, the Chief Constable of Birmingham, enquired about her with Bristol's Chief Constable, his reply suggested that, while seeming to be a manageable sort of person and of excellent character, he thought she appeared to be more interested in achieving a position for herself than in the police. He added that she had been mixing with people who, while 'perhaps not out-and-out Suffragettes, have grounded views on women's rights'. One presumes he was referring to the WPS. In fact, Peto had broken off relations with them.

The Bristol chief's final remarks probably revealed more about him and the current male attitudes: 'You can never tell what a woman will do, or is up to, until you try her in the shafts, and if she does kick over the traces, then fire her, that is what I would do here.'[3]

Despite these unpromising signs, Miss Peto was to discover that 'One could hardly have found a better force in which to learn the job of a police officer', and she was probably right there. Although not sworn in, their ten policewomen were treated as part of the force. They trained with the men and were employed on outdoor duties under Woman Sergeant Miles, and the Chief Constable, Charles Haughton Rafter, was a supporter of women police.[4]

Also, instead of having to learn about police duty by 'deduction' from court proceedings and police instruction books, she now attended a probationer's course, a CID course, then later, a course via which, in her fourth year, she passed for sergeant.

Initially, however, she was 'saddled with the appalling title of "lady enquiry officer"'. She soon got rid of this by substituting the word 'detective' for 'lady' when signing reports. Whenever she took a statement from a sexual assault victim, a divisional detective inspector would be at her elbow prompting her as to the material required. The only time she was left to get on with it was when the smell in the living room was too much for the inspector and she blessed her defective sense of smell.

She found the blunt 'Brumagem Tyke' (Birmingham Tyke) very different from the easy-going Bristolians, but learned to value a parting 'Yo' ken com again' over any soft-spoken insincerity. She learned the importance of the manner in which medical examinations of young children took place, but did regret the tendency to disbelieve the victims.

However, she much appreciated the comradeship and helpfulness of her fellow officers, which was probably something new to her. From a wealthy family (her grandfather was Baron Peto), she had been home schooled and her only work experience had been attempts at novel writing, which had not succeeded.

The need for her services as a statement taker were widespread and at all hours, so she needed the use of the public bus or her bicycle. After learning about the Gloucester women's motorcycle patrols, she put in an application for one but the force, who were worried about the cost should she have an accident, turned her down and confined her to foot or bus, 'though at night my bicycle often filled the need'.

Of course, by now, women jurors were allowed, so in theory the situation would no longer occur of a rape victim being left marooned in a sea of often hostile men by the call, 'all women out of court'. But there were ways around this, even when there were women on the jury, as she relates regarding a case 'which did little credit to either the judge or women jurors'.

It was a brutal rape case of a girl of 19 or 20, with a trial which Peto was unable to attend. There *had* been two women on the jury but the judge, before the case opened, advised them that as there might be evidence of an unpleasant nature, they could, if they wished, retire. And they got up and left.

'I did think,' the distressed girl told her later, 'that they might have thought what I would have to go through, all alone with men, in that court. I did wish there was just one woman there – I did think they might have stayed!'

When statement work was slack, she traced the families of servicemen killed in the Great War to whom there were medals to be handed over, or whose dependants were entitled to a war pension. She might also be obliged to walk through 'some big departmental store' on the chance of finding a shoplifter. She was a tall woman and one gets the impression that this was not her forte for, one day, she spotted a woman 'behaving most suspiciously', and kept 'discreet observation' on her movements until, at length, 'she stepped out from behind her ambush, saying, 'It may save your time if I tell you I'm the store detective!'

Towards the end of 1924, Peto's father died, so she had to arrange for work which made it possible for her to be home more often. She left Birmingham and spent the next three years as a travelling organiser for the National Council for Combating Venereal Diseases.

In 1927, Liverpool's Mabel Cowlin retired. Peto felt that her second-in-command, Tidd Pratt, well lived up to Cowlin's training, but she did not wish to take over, so Peto was asked to step in and held the fort. Shortly after, though, she was invited to take charge of the Met's women police, and this time Pratt agreed to assume control. Liverpool Patrols didn't realise it then, but they were to be punished for their efficiency in that the Liverpool Police Watch Committee resisted any moves to take on the hoped-for women police. It wasn't until 1946 that their hands were finally forced.

Meanwhile, Peto was fighting to take the Met women out of the doldrums. Her brief as staff officer was to examine the position of women in the Met and advise on a promised expansion programme.

Peto's appointment was not greeted with total delight in the Met. Lilian Wyles, the first woman into the Met CID, explained that Peto would be usurping Inspector Bertha Clayden, who had been taking care of the women's welfare since the 'Geddes Axe' of austerity savings had fallen on the previous leader, Mrs Stanley, in 1922.[5] Clayden was popular due to her own warm qualities and the fact that she was a member of a large police family – which made her more acceptable to the men.

Also, as Wyles put it, Peto 'was not a woman to sink her own ideas for the sake of making herself an easier passage' and she was 'perhaps a trifle too direct for popularity'. But Wyles still maintained that Peto was the best woman for the job and would be remembered as the one who had built a firm foundation.[6]

To start with, Peto herself was given neither rank nor uniform but she *was* attested, which she had insisted upon, and was given a year's probation. After some changes in the force leadership Lord Trenchard took over as chief, and at the probationary year's end, his aide suggested that the simplest thing would be if they just let her probation run on for another year?

She objected 'with considerable vigour', which paid off. Within a matter of days, she found herself transferred from 'S' (Secretarial) Department to 'A' Women Police Department, with the rank of police superintendent.

It was now the time of the Great Depression and people were flooding into London, looking for work and sleeping rough in the parks, squares, along the embankment and in the doorways. Many young girls came in response to advertisements in local papers for domestic servants and were now adrift and 'ready prey'. As Peto pointed out, before 1933, there was no way of dealing with adolescents in need of care or protection. Police could only do their best to try and help them.

Peto grabbed every task she could for her women. Of course, the advent of the Children and Young Persons Act 1933 was timely, and she took care to make her women the experts on that. But there was also the drive to allow women to do escort duty alone, to come out on night duty, to have them take part in brothel raids and ceremonials, run a juvenile bus service and become appointed court officers, not to mention establishing the well-known 'A4 Index for Missing and Wanted Girls'.

Sometimes, it was just a case of seeing where opportunities arose, such as with the children's bus service which came about after Peto saw no less than eight male constables sitting in a row at an London City Council Remand Home, waiting for individual boys and girls to escort, by bus or underground, to various juvenile courts. Why not one vehicle manned by two constables, one male, one female? She put in a report and the scheme was approved.

She admitted that all innovations had their drawbacks. In the previous system, the officer would have had an opportunity for a straight talk which might influence the child for good; whereas when several boys or girls where together, they were liable to out-boast each other and arrive at court in a defiant frame of mind. On the other hand, when younger children were escorted alongside, they were sometimes too busy being helpful and protective with them – which the author saw happen herself, certainly with young girls.

Some aims were met incidentally. Disappointed that the passage of the Children and Young Persons Act did not include the provision that the attendance of children in court should be under the care of a policewoman as requested, it did confirm the requirement they should be 'under the care of *a* woman' (emphasis added). This helped pave the way for the appointment of women police as juvenile court officers, and later on as adult court officers.

The most difficult aim to achieve turned out to be women police being allowed to play a part in ceremonial occasions. These duties only came in bits and pieces, and on VE Day they were part of a 'female services group' in the procession – the last ceremonial occasion during Peto's service.

The women police strength in the Met when she took over had been two inspectors (one uniform, one CID); five sergeants; and forty-seven constables, including one Special Branch officer. All had been attested and she hated losing them, recalled ex-WPC West. 'She came to Albany Street to say goodbye to me and told me she would kill the next [male] PC who went off with one of them.'[7]

For various reasons their promised rate of increase in numbers failed to live up to expectations, but eventually there were some increases and they had to set about recruiting by first deciding their selection standards. These were determined as needing to be unmarried or a widow; not under 22 nor over 35 years of age; and not less than 5ft 4in in height (or they couldn't be seen on the street). The latter proved the most difficult standard to achieve. Many desirable candidates proved borderline and were encouraged to stretch as far as possible.

When the Second World War began, women police were once again in great demand, but Superintendent Peto had still not yet acquired all her promised establishment of 200. She was therefore pleased when the commissioner gave her permission to take on retired officers as the male side were doing.

Many new demands included welcoming refugees and escorting enemy aliens who normally lived in Great Britain to their detention camp on the Isle of Man, and staying with them during the war.

Peto's severe figure on a sit-up-and-beg bicycle became a familiar sight all over London. She was quickly on the scene when West End Central Police Station received a direct hit from a bomb, and ex-WPC Dorothy West recalled her responding with great alacrity when a landmine struck buildings almost opposite Pembridge women's section house. She rapidly rounded up a rescue party which spent the night helping dig out survivors and bodies before returning exhausted and filthy to wash and change for the day's duty.

Her lack of sense of smell proved to have further advantages in wartime. The then WPC O'Leary visited some of the very early makeshift underground shelters with her and was asked what the smell was like. 'With lavatory facilities at the minimum it was pretty horrible but she was intent on getting all the details.'

She was also intent on getting the details about what O'Leary got up to on clubs observations, and would ring up the male officers in charge to check she wasn't having to indulge in too much alcohol.[8]

Shirley Becke, destined to lead the Met women into equality, remembered Peto on selection boards. 'She demanded very high standards,' Commander Becke told *The Job* in 1974. 'She would not tolerate flippancy either in appearance or attitudes to problems though she herself had a very nice sense of humour.'[9]

Tragedy struck for Peto, however. One morning Inspector Violet Butcher was on her way to visit one of her officers at Rathbone Place Police Station, just north of Oxford Street, when she saw a flying bomb check and swoop over her destination. She reached the scene a few minutes later but could do nothing for Woman Police Sergeant Bertha Gleghorn except hold her hand until she was dug out from the debris. Bertha died the next day in the Middlesex Hospital where she had spent many hours guarding attempted suicides and ailing women prisoners. She was the first woman police officer killed on duty, and was under Peto's command.[10]

In 1944, Peto was awarded the King's Police Medal for distinguished service.[11] Two years later, she handed over the reins to ex-Women's Royal Air Force officer Elizabeth Bather. Shortly afterwards, the pair went on a punishing trip to Germany to visit two Met women inspectors, Hill and Alloway, who were helping organise women police in the British Sector post-war.

That they did so with tact was reflected in the fact that relationships remained warm, and every now and then in the fifties at West End Central, German women police would visit London and patrolled in partnership with their British counterparts.

Among the leaders of the early women police, Peto's experiences were unusually various, having served in London, Bristol, Liverpool and Birmingham and alongside such diverse characters as Mabel Cowlin, Sofia Stanley, Mary Allen, Margaret Damer Dawson and Edith Smith, the first sworn-in policewoman.

The Official Encyclopedia of Scotland Yard acknowledged that it was a common observation that Peto 'lived for the police' but, more pertinently, that 'she did more than anyone else to establish the women police as an indispensable part of Scotland Yard'.[12] She therefore deserves her place among the pioneers of women in policing.

THE TWENTY-THREE

THE METROPOLITAN POLICE'S FIRST INTAKE OF WOMEN POLICE

EDWARD SMITH[1]

Metropolitan Police publicity photo 1919. Supt Sofia Stanley,
front row looking directly at camera.

ON THE AFTERNOON OF 17 February 1919, twenty-one women arrived in the dining hall of a new police accommodation block on Ixworth Place in Chelsea, the only room in the building yet furnished, and painted in dark green and buff, the favoured colours of the Metropolitan Police (Met) surveyor at that time. There they were met and addressed by Sofia Stanley, backed up by her second-in-command Elinor Juliet Robertson.[2]

Stanley appointed the first five sergeants and handed out all the women's identity cards; not warrant cards, since the patrols did not have the power of arrest and were viewed by many – or even most – of the male hierarchy as a temporary experiment in the wake of the wartime voluntary patrols.

Who were these women? From what social backgrounds did they come? Did they see being a patrolwoman as a job for life or simply a spell of temporary security in a difficult post-war labour market as men returned from the armed forces to resume their pre-war jobs? Finally, how many of them were still working as patrolwomen in the difficult months of 1922, when the Women Patrols found themselves fighting for their very existence against the headwinds of post-war government austerity? This chapter draws on sources old and new – particularly the newly released 1921 census and service records held in the Metropolitan Police Museum – to answer these questions as best as can be.[3]

In many ways this is not an easy task. No service records survive for Robertson or Stanley and neither of them wrote a memoir. Only eight service records and one autobiography are known to survive for the other twenty-one women.[4] That autobiography, Lilian Wyles's *A Woman at Scotland Yard*, was written in retirement with the benefit of thirty years' hindsight, drawing a mostly impenetrable veil over its author's key and controversial part in the battles of 1922.[5] Its vivid pen-portraits of key figures and episodes are interspersed with more than a few short but sharp pieces of score-settling, with Stanley swathed in fulsome compliments to her former commanding officer.[6]

The only other memoir writers for that period, Dorothy Peto and Mary Allen, are both outliers. Though Peto would later become head of the Met's A4 (Women's) Branch, she was not active in London police work during the 1920s, literally and figuratively distancing her memoirs' account of 1919–22 from the events in question.[7] Peto's and Sofia Stanley's wartime police work had been with the voluntary Women Patrols, run since October 1914 by the National Union of Women Workers (NUWW), originally formed in 1895 to campaign for better working conditions for women. Largely consisting of women from the non-violent branch of the suffragist movement, the main purpose of these patrols was to police the morals of other (usually working-class) women in major cities and garrison towns and to protect women refugees from Belgium and France from being trafficked into sex work, a role they shared with their only wartime competitor, the Women Police Volunteers (WPV).

By contrast, many in the WPV came from the Suffragette movement, whose campaign of vandalism and violence had been paused on the outbreak of the First World War. Moralists such as Margaret Damer Dawson and militants such as Nina Boyle were initially able to co-exist within the WPV, but Boyle's hopes for their patrols to focus on detection rather than moral policing was soon disappointed, with Damer Dawson taking over the organisation in February 1915 and rebranding it the Women Police Service (WPS), whose patrols continued even after the Armistice.[8]

None of the first twenty-one Met patrolwomen in February 1919 had been in the WPS's patrols, since the commissioner not only suspected the highly educated Suffragette background of many in that organisation, but also feared that such a background could cause problems on the beat. It might even have led to patrolwomen working alongside the very same male officers who had arrested them in the pre-war period. In that regard at least, Stanley and other former NUWW patrolwomen were seen as the safer option. That aversion to taking on ex-WPS women does not seem to have lasted long, however, since some appeared in the second and third intakes in March 1919, and many other subsequent ones in the early 1920s.[9] One of them, Alice Bertha Clayden, joined the Met patrols on 30 March 1919, later becoming Stanley's successor and the Met's first Woman Inspector with the power of arrest. Firmly excluded, however, was the WPS's new leader, Mary Sophia Allen, an ex-Suffragette who succeeded Damer Dawson in May 1920.

In 1925, Allen produced an autobiography modestly entitled *The Pioneer Policewoman*. Even if it benefits from Allen's presence in London for much of 1919–22 and was published closer to that period than Wyles's work, in many ways its account is just as much an outsider's view as Peto's. It is also heavily biased against Stanley and the Met commissioners of the time, Nevil Macready and William Horwood, magnifying Dawson's and Allen's achievements as the root of any and every success of the Met patrols, yet somehow also arguing that the Met completely ignored the WPS's wealth of experience and passed over Damer Dawson in favour of Stanley to lead its own patrols.[10] This is in contrast to the picture most other sources give of the growing tensions between Stanley and Allen, as the Met patrols seemed increasingly likely to eclipse the WPS completely – Wyles, for instance, describes such absurdities as WPS and Met patrolwomen facing off against each other from different sides of the same street!

Both bodies wore very similar uniforms, leading to public complaints as Allen's women were often mistaken for Stanley's; thereby giving their – often intrusive – advice an authority it did not actually possess. This came to a head in March and April 1921, when the commissioner brought a court case against Allen and four of her senior WPS patrolwomen.[11][12] This resulted in a token fine, amendments to the WPS's epaulettes and cap badge, its rebranding as the Women's Auxiliary Service (WAS), and most importantly, a huge boost in celebrity for Allen, who became much in demand to supply advice and volunteers for Ireland and the British occupation force in Germany. Her memoir argued that the WAS's prestige was magnified rather than dented by the court case, but it actually marked the high-water mark of its activities in London.[13] Its funds, recruits and authority all sharply declined soon afterwards in the face of the state-funded Met patrols and Stanley's positive publicity drives on her women's achievements. It is also instructive that not once was the WPS mentioned as a possible alternative to the Met Women Patrols in the heated parliamentary debates over the latter's survival in 1922 – in London at least, the only options were seen as the Met's Women Patrols or nothing.

Stanley herself was born Sofia Annie Croll Dalgairns in Palermo on Sicily, where her Scottish railway engineer father was then working. (Serendipitously, Allen came from a not dissimilar background: her father had been a manager and divisional superintendent on the Great Western Railway.) She grew up there and in south London before leaving her family, converting from Presbyterianism to high church Anglicanism, and becoming a head teacher in Poona (now Pune) in western India. There she married Henry Johnson Stanley, a deputy locomotive superintendent on the Madras Railway and son of a naval captain. They had their only child in India before Henry was paralysed in an accident, forcing them to settle in Portsmouth around 1914, though she would eventually return there to work against animal cruelty and child prostitution after her enforced departure from the Metropolitan Women Patrols.[14]

In Portsmouth, Henry and Sofia were visited by Dick Phillips, a police officer they had known in India. That visit probably proved the immediate catalyst for Stanley to join the NUWW's Women Patrols in Portsmouth. This would inevitably not only have brought her into contact with Portsmouth City Police, but with the Met Division which policed the dockyard from 1860 to 1933, one of six such divisions.[15] Met Commissioner Edward Henry invited her to London in March 1917 to head the Women Patrols there, and within a year she had increased them from thirty-seven to fifty-five and instituted monthly reports to the commissioner on the patrols' work. This won Henry's successor, Macready, round to creating Women Patrols within the Met itself, as announced to the press on 3 October 1918.[16] At this time the Met issued daily internal updates known as Police Orders, and those for 22 November the same year duly carry news of Stanley's appointment as the patrols' 'Superintendent' (not to be confused with the male rank of the same name).[17]

For Stanley's second-in-command, Elinor Juliet Robertson, newspapers provide a particularly rich additional source. Nine years Stanley's junior, she had was born in Kensington to Louisa Aikin and her husband John Millar Thomson, a Glaswegian chemistry professor at King's College London. Her grandfathers were a 'medical practitioner' and an anatomy professor. Losing her mother at the age of 17, in 1904 she married John Gardner Robertson from Ross-shire in northern Scotland. He had been managing a hotel in Dingwall in the Highlands at the time of the marriage, but on census night seven years later both husband and wife stated their occupation as 'Private Means'. The couple were then living in the Essex village of North Benfleet, but trouble was perhaps already brewing, since Elinor gave her surname as 'Robertson or Thomson'.

In 1913, Elinor used her own trust funds to spend a few months alone in Canada and, though the couple lived together in the Highlands for a time after her return to Britain, she had decisively left him that December. Reports of their divorce case in 1921 stated that they had disagreed over business matters but that he had given no cause for her to leave him, though the case was brought by the husband and so this may need to be taken with a pinch of salt. He had begun a short-lived correspondence trying to convince her to return, but this bore no fruit, with one of her replies including the phrase: 'I do wish for absolute freedom, and will never go back to our former life. This is the end, and it is now a closed book.'[18] No hint of this background is given in Wyles's account of Robertson and the newspaper reports of the case do not mention Robertson's role with the Met, either out of discretion or from not thinking it significant enough to report even in such sensationalist circumstances. Wyles limits herself to critiquing Robertson's lack of Stanley's 'magnetism' and mentioning the experience she had gained before 1919 'in the managing and disciplining of women'.[19]

Like Stanley, that experience had been gained in wartime voluntary roles, in Robertson's case as second-in-command of the Women's Forage Corps then commander of the Forage Guard, which both related to feeding the huge number of horses the army required for the war effort – a distant echo, perhaps, of the military background of many early male senior Met officers since 1829. In taking on not only these posts but also the risks of a marital separation, Robertson was able to call on her own wealth and that of her family, a background different from many of the sergeants and patrolwomen she commanded and from the vast majority of the women whom she would police. She had moved back in with her father at 55 Bedford Gardens, near Notting Hill Gate, by 19 June 1921, just six days before the divorce was granted on grounds of desertion. Even then she retained her married name, leaving the Met in May 1922, retiring to Cornwall, and dying in 1979.

On Wyles much has already been written, but what of Florence Martha ('Patty') Alliott, Hilda Grace Russell, Constance Mary Carr and Edith Ridley, the other four sergeants from that fateful February day? The 44-year-old Alliott came from a Congregationalist family, her father being one of the first Nonconformists to be allowed to graduate from the University of Cambridge. He trained as a minister but then settled in Bishop's Stortford to run its Nonconformist grammar school. Florence was born there, and her mother's private means enabled them to continue living in Hertfordshire after his death in 1899. She and her mother were living at a hotel in Bloomsbury on census night in 1911 and – though elusive in the 1921 census – Alliott and her mother had probably moved to London permanently by the time of the latter's death in Bromley in 1916. With a chartered accountant and a medical doctor among her brothers, not to mention private means of her own, Alliott's upper middle-class status matched that of Stanley and Robertson, enabling her to serve one year with the patrols, before retiring to south-west England, where she died unmarried in 1964.

By contrast, Hilda Grace Russell was the daughter of a lieutenant colonel in the Royal Artillery from Clifton, West Yorkshire, and his Tasmania-born wife. Though the purchase of army commissions had ceased in 1871, the travelling and living arrangements then probably still largely limited officer rank to those from a well-off background – Hilda was born in Shoeburyness in Essex and her siblings in the East Indies and Woolwich. By 1891 the family were in Lancashire and able to afford a governess and two other servants. Russell trained to be a governess herself, appearing on the census night of 1901 at the training school housed in Scale How at Ambleside in the Lake District. She may not have found a position, since by census night 1911 she had moved back in with her parents, now in Harpenden in Hertfordshire, giving no occupation and subsequently moving with them to Sidcup in Kent by 1921. She did sail to Algiers in 1912, probably with the Church Mission Society, which is recorded as her employer in the 1921 census. After her fourteen months in the Met, she returned frequently to Algiers between 1921 and 1930 as an assistant secretary and missionary, living there permanently for a time as well as travelling to Surabaya in Indonesia.

Wyles observes that 'Not many [of the first intake] … were to live in Ixworth Place: quite a number had husbands and homes. Others lived with parents or ran a flat of their own.'[20] Edith Ridley would also seem to conform to this observation, living in 1921 at a flat in Southwold Mansions in Maida

Vale. She was then 32 years old and affluent enough to afford a live-in 'Lady Help' born in Bermuda. Ridley's own birthplace and nationality are given as 'At sea / British born', meaning it has so far proved impossible to trace her in earlier censuses, though she is known to have remained with the Met until 31 March 1922. This means she fell prey to the Home Secretary's decision that February to allow all the patrolwomen's rolling annual contracts to lapse as they came up for renewal, with the intention that this would disband the patrols entirely by 31 March, an event we will return to later.

That leaves one more sergeant to discuss: Constance Mary Carr. The 1921 census shows her living at the section house in Ixworth Place, making her our first exception to Wyles's observation on housing arrangements and probably the first patrolwoman discussed to come from a working-class background. Born in Leeds in 1871 to a 'jeweller employing two men' and a music teacher, by 1891 she had moved in with an aunt in Leeds who was 'living on own means'. Carr continued to need to make her own living, however, and by 1901 she had moved to Dewsbury to act as housekeeper for an uncle who was a Roman Catholic priest. She seems to have then moved to London, where on census night in 1911 she was a live-in 'Lady Nurse (Domestic)' in a well-off household in Bayswater. She remained in the Met until 26 June 1921, and appears in the census earlier that month living in the women's section house at Ixworth Place. She died in 1937 in the registration district of Wandsworth.

To move on to the sixteen patrolwomen, seven of them shared Ridley's leaving date of 31 March 1922, while four had already left in 1920 and two in 1921. Of the remainder, Kathleen Mulhall served until 1929 but remains elusive in censuses, Hildreth Margaret Watson had left after less than nine months, and Kate Cornford had, on 29 January 1922, gained Stanley's permission to leave the patrols to get married.[21] A formal marriage bar on patrolwomen would not exist until 1927, but Cornford was moving out of London with her new husband, though she would return for her second marriage in 1937. Brighton-born and Fulham-raised, she was an electrician's daughter and had worked as a dressmaker before joining the NUWW patrols for fifteen months and then the Met patrols. At just under 5ft 4in, her joining paperwork had stated '? Up to height standard / Otherwise fit', though her service record states her time with the Met patrols had led to 'debility' and two cases each of influenza and catarrh, complaints that would have been familiar to her male equivalents ever since the Met's formation in 1829.

All eight of the surviving patrolwomen's service records show previous NUWW experience in or out of London. Mary Byrne, for instance, worked as a cook in Brentwood before joining them on 15 July 1918, but was back living in her native County Kildare when writing her application for the Met patrols.[22] Minnie Kemp had been a housekeeper on Newington Green prior to her time as a patrolwoman, though only with an 'Elementary (Board School)' education as compared to Byrne's 'Secondary' or Lilian Wyles's private school in Margate and finishing school in Paris.[23] (A 1922 set of entry qualifications set no minimum educational level other than being 'able to read well, write legibly … [possessing] a fair knowledge of arithmetic, spelling and composition … [and being] generally intelligent'.) Tram conductor's wife, May Margaret Westlake, had not had another job prior to her time as a Met patrolwoman, though this seems to have been rare, with a particular preference for what even at the time was often called social work and among the support staff of mental health institutions.[24]

Frances Waite, for instance, had worked as an 'industrial trainer' and laundry matron at Epsom College; Trewint Industrial Home in Bexley (designed to train female juvenile offenders for factory work); the Royal Philanthropic Home in Hammersmith; and Brentry Imbecile Reformatory in Bristol. These cumulatively led Stanley to leave a handwritten note on her NUWW application: 'A fine looking woman very superior working class. Has done many years work amongst women (inebriation) & girls.'[25] Lilian Morris similarly had spent time as a nurse at the West Riding Asylum near Sheffield; assisting her brother-in-law and sisters at a Church Army Home; and finally in the canteen of the postal censors' office on Houghton Street in Aldwych. One of Morris's NUWW referees was an inspector at Bow Street police station, where her husband also served as a PC.[26]

That background in social work is instructive in what many or even most saw as the primary role of the early Met Women Patrols; that is, providing a reassuring presence and helping women and children. Many early photographs show Met patrolwomen giving directions, and one American even sent a patrolwoman a photograph he had taken of her while on holiday in London. Stanley even added a Welfare Department for homeless and unemployed women at Ixworth Place, though she did also push for an expansion in the patrolwomen's roles, with one sent undercover in public toilets to observe drug deals and others trained in statement-taking for child-abuse cases. Yet she also tried to ensure the patrols' survival by reassuring male officers that the patrols would not expand into full detective work, and by usually favouring the term 'patrolwoman' over 'policewoman' or 'women police'. However, this gave ammunition to Home Secretary Edward Shortt during the Parliamentary debates on the patrols' survival or extinction in June 1922. He argued that if their work was mainly or solely social work it should not be funded by the Home Office, whereas the patrols' supporters counterargued that – even if it was – it still provided a valuable preventive role.[27]

The only known near-dismissal from among the sixteen patrolwomen was Minnie Harriet Kemp (not to be confused with the previously mentioned Minnie Kemp). Born in Aylesford in Kent but living in South Norwood in London, she had spent two months volunteering with the NUWW patrols in Croydon then six months with them full-time. Croydon's mayor requested in 1918 that some of the NUWW patrolwomen working in Croydon be considered for the Met patrols, but Kemp was the only one to qualify on age and height, serving on A (Whitehall), B (Chelsea) and W (Clapham) Divisions. Kemp's sergeant, Violet Butcher, transferred her to Edith Lattimore on 15 November 1921, with reprimands for (in Superintendent Stanley's words) a 'habit of retailing gossip and continual chattering to the male members of the Force'. (Butcher and Lattimore were both from a July 1919 intake.)[28]

Butcher added that it seemed Kemp had 'no interest whatever in the work' and Stanley agreed, stating that she 'does little but gossip & is a continual nuisance to all Sergeants who have charge of her'. However, Stanley's recommendation on 23 November that year that Kemp's contract be terminated does not seem to have been acted upon by the male hierarchy, since Kemp herself then gave a month's notice to resign on health grounds, namely that an illness had 'left my legs so bad, that I shall not be able to do the walking', with respiratory and joint issues a common feature across all eight of the surviving service records.

Of the twenty-one sergeants and patrolwomen whose ID cards had been issued on 17 February 1919, only nine from that intake remained as 1922 dawned, and only two (Wyles and Mulhall) after 31 March that year. News had reached Stanley on 10 February 1922 of the intended disbandment; part of the so-called 'Geddes Axe' wielded against all government departments' spending by the Committee on National Expenditure appointed the previous August.[29][30] Shortt and Commissioner Horwood were both keen on the disbandment and so Stanley and Robertson immediately began manoeuvring against them, leaking information to Margaret Wintringham and Nancy Astor – the UK's first two women Members of Parliament to take their seats – and cultivating allies, from the NUWW to the Archbishop of Canterbury. Though her actions led to an internal enquiry and Stanley's dismissal, she successfully ensured the retention of Wyles and nineteen other officers, who were all also granted the power of arrest. This and Bertha Clayden's appointment as the women's commander in February 1923 allowed the nucleus to grow to fifty by 1925, thereby serving to ensure the long-term survival of women officers in the Met.

In conclusion, the overall impression of the first sixteen patrolwomen is a largely of being from a working- or lower middle-class background, with Stanley, Robertson and arguably four of the five sergeants the more securely middle-class exceptions to that rule. Some of the twenty-one would have been able to live without their police wage – some would not or would have needed the support of their children's or husband's wages. There seems to have been an even spread between those raised in London, those who had moved there with family or for a previous job, and those who were entirely new to the city. All varieties of marital status were represented, with ages ranging from late twenties to late forties and husbands (where applicable) ranging from male constables to a London and North Western Railway clerk at Broad Street station. Applying after having children or while over 35 both seem to have been discouraged but not rigorously enforced, at least before 1922–23. The demographics of these twenty-three women were a natural product of their roots in the volunteer wartime patrols, Stanley's recruitment criteria and public perceptions (and misperceptions) as to whether their purpose was social work, policing or a mixture of the two. However, those same demographics also provided fertile soil in which the role of patrolwoman could over the following century grow into the profession – indeed, the Job [sic] – of today.

THE RECRUITMENT OF WOMEN INTO THE THREE POLICE FORCES OF STAFFORDSHIRE, 1919–46

LISA COX-DAVIES

AT THE START OF THE twentieth century the county of Staffordshire, situated in the West Midlands region, was policed by three forces. These were the two small borough forces of Newcastle-under-Lyme and Stoke-on-Trent, both situated in the north-west of the county, and the Staffordshire County force, responsible for policing the remainder of the county. This chapter aims to examine the different attitudes of the chief constables on the employment and use of women in their police forces, both as police officers and as members of the Women's Auxiliary Police Corps (WAPC), formed during the Second World War. It will also explore how local campaign groups pursued the use of women in policing and how the Second World War ultimately became the catalyst for their employment.

During the First World War, concerns about the morality and behaviour of girls and young women working in munitions factories or frequenting army camps had seen some police forces, such as the City of Birmingham and Gloucestershire, employ policewomen. In keeping with other areas, the National Council of Women (NCW) conducted voluntary patrols in the county of Staffordshire, including the towns of Burton upon Trent and Stafford.[1] Consequently, when the camps closed down at the end of the war, the patrols also ceased. However, the Home Office had seen the benefit of utilising women, and in February 1919 a circular was sent to police forces suggesting that female auxiliaries could offer great assistance in dealing with matters regarding women and children. It suggested that the policewomen who had been formerly employed in police work in munitions factories were a ready source of potential recruits. Yet these women were not to be sworn in as constables and therefore would have no power of arrest. The standing joint committee of Stafford were in favour of the scheme, and suggested to the Chief Constable of the County force that two women would be useful in dealing with matters connected to the military camps in the area. Chief Constable George Augustus Anson disagreed, stating: 'I cannot find that there is any real use for them in a town of the size of Stafford where the general code of conduct and respectability is so high.'[2]

Similarly, the Chief Constable and the Watch Committee of the Stoke-on-Trent Borough force were also reluctant to employ women. In November 1919, a delegation from the local branch of the NCW had urged the committee to follow the recommendations of the Home Office and employ former policewomen to deal with women and children, but their request was refused.[3] Yet, if the Watch Committee had hoped this would be an end to the matter then they were to be disappointed, as at the end of that year a Councillor Miss Farmer joined the committee. She was an enthusiastic advocate of policewomen, repeatedly raising the matter at meetings, and in June 1920, with a majority of one, the committee voted in support of the appointment of women. Yet despite a binding vote, at the next meeting in July some members were still against the idea, with a Mr H.R. Lloyd arguing that these were 'sentimental appointments', and that ex-servicemen should be considered for positions within the force.[4]

The Chief Constable, Roger Carter, appears to have been resigned to the idea of employing policewomen, as he told the committee that it was his opinion that the government would soon compel forces to do so.[5] Despite this view, almost a year later, in May 1921, Carter sought to defer their employment, citing financial difficulties. However, it would appear from comments made by Councillor Farmer that neither Carter nor the Watch Committee had considered the actual terms of service for policewomen, so were not in a position to state what the cost would be to the force.[6] Finally, on 16 June that year, the Watch Committee resolved to employ two women, one as sergeant and the other as constable.[7] The two women were eventually appointed at the end of 1921, and in his annual report to the Watch Committee, Carter pronounced: 'The women police are an innovation here.'[8] Their duties were reported as street patrol, visiting places of entertainment, general enquiries, taking statements and dealing with female prisoners.[9] Ten years later, in 1931, he professed that he was 'wholeheartedly in favour' of policewomen being appointed to every police force.[10]

Carter's assertation was not shared by the neighbouring chief constables of the two other police forces in Staffordshire. They had remained resistant to employing women despite requests and delegations from groups such as Stafford's Women Citizens Association, Women's Co-operative Guild and the local branch of the NCW. The response was always the same: 'it was not felt necessary at this time'.[11] However, the national emergency of the Second World War would finally challenge these views and the two chief constables would find that, as predicted by Carter in 1920, the government would indeed compel them to employ women.

The first indication that women would be expected to be utilised by police forces came in the summer of 1939, when the Home Office suggested that police forces could recruit women to compensate for losing men who would inevitably volunteer for the forces. This new initiative was called the Women's Auxiliary Police Corps (WAPC) and it was envisaged that women would be utilised on station-based duties, such as switchboard and clerical work. The terms and conditions of their service stated that recruits would not require a power of arrest, as the idea was to replace men and allow them to focus on patrol duties.[12] In August, the Chief Constable of Staffordshire swiftly recruited twenty women as special constables for use as a mobile detachment.[13] These early recruits all had their own cars, placing them as either middle or upper class, and when war broke out the women were transferred to the auxiliary corps.

However, after almost a year into the war, the Home Office felt the need to remind police forces that they needed to utilise the auxiliary corps to release men from station-based duties.[14] In September, the relatively new Chief Constable of the Stoke-on-Trent force, Mr Frank Bunn, asked the Watch Committee to authorise the recruitment of six auxiliaries. Interestingly, these women were not to be used on station-based duties but would perform the duties of temporary policewomen and be sworn in, allowing them powers of arrest.[15] Six women were duly appointed in December 1940, and after three weeks of training covering statement taking, knowledge of the law, first aid and court procedures, they were working from police stations across the borough.[16] The force now had a total of eight women, including a newly promoted woman sergeant and permanent policewoman.[17] However, in August 1941, Bunn responded in the negative to a further request from the Home Office urging the increased use of auxiliaries. While it would appear that Bunn was willing for women to deal with matters involving women and children, he was less willing to see them encroach on male roles, as he insisted there was no other suitable work for women. Roles such as working in his office, the Charge Department and station duties were all discounted, as these were already carried out by police reserve constables. Women could not be telephone operators due to the switchboard room being away from the main buildings, and this room was to be guarded by armed men if necessary and any women would require additional protection. Finally, he argued that the headquarters lacked the appropriate facilities for additional women. Similar arguments were also made against women working at divisional stations.[18]

Despite these protestations, it would appear that His Majesty's Inspectorate of Constabulary was not in agreement. In October, Bunn met with Colonel Coke from the department and consequently had a change of heart. He was now able to find numerous roles for women in the staff office, Charge Department, divisional stations and CID, as well as replacing a number of men in the Transport Department, releasing a total of sixteen constables.[19]

In November, the Home Office approved an establishment of twenty-four auxiliaries for the force, of which eight would be attested.[20] The following month advertisements were placed in local newspapers, requiring applicants to be aged between 18 and 40, 5ft 4in or taller, and physically fit. Motor driving, shorthand writing and office experience were deemed to be advantageous. Wages were set at £2 7s a week.[21] Recruitment of the additional auxiliaries proved difficult due to the competing demands for women workers from war factories in such an industrial area as Stoke-on-Trent. However, by September 1942, suitable women had been found as the WAPC numbered twenty-two auxiliaries.[22]

Despite the drive by the Home Office to use women, the Chief Constable of the Newcastle-under-Lyme Borough Constabulary, Mr Wesley Bate, was particularly resistant. In September 1941, the Watch Committee discussed the Home Office circular. While some committee members were in favour, Bate dismissed the use of auxiliaries, echoing the comments made by the Chief Constable of Stoke-on-Trent. He argued against women being engaged on mobile patrol work, stating the cars were manned only by their drivers and telephone duties were already carried out by eleven ex-policemen who had been recalled and were unfit for outside duties.[23] His arguments had the support of some of the committee, with one member claiming such appointments would be a retrograde step for the town, while another contended that 'police work was essentially that of a man'.[24] Consequently, the matter was deferred for another month.

However, by June 1943 the force had made some progress, as it then employed one female civilian member of staff and three auxiliaries, undertaking clerical duties and telephone switchboard work between 9 a.m. and 6 p.m.

Nevertheless, in a Watch Committee meeting held that month, Bate's successor, Mr G.S. Jackson, was similarly unwilling to employ additional auxiliaries, claiming he could not release any further men. Just as Frank Bunn of Stoke-on-Trent had argued eighteen months earlier, he maintained station officer duties could only be carried out by a policeman who was experienced in all matters, while female drivers were only employed in larger forces and his borough already had two men who were also mechanics.[25] Despite these protestations, and possibly due to intervention from the HMIC, it would appear that the force did eventually recruit a further two auxiliaries, as at the end of 1944 there was a total of five, although there are no details of their exact duties.

In stark contrast to the resistance of the Newcastle-under-Lyme force, the auxiliary corps of the Staffordshire County force numbered 150 in November 1942. It was noted that many auxiliaries provided twenty-four-hour coverage in main stations. Unfortunately, examination of the available records does not make it clear whether these women were employed full- or part-time. Chief Constable Lt Colonel Hunter commented: 'Many of them are highly trained in both special and general police duties. They have replaced and are doing the work previously performed by men who have joined the fighting services.'

Their duties were listed as: traffic, and convoy patrol; working in the Special Branch of the Criminal Investigation Dept, where selected women were carrying out Secret Service work; indoor duties, such as caring for, searching and escorting women and juvenile prisoners; general clerical duties, including wireless, teleprinter, telephone, shorthand and typing.[26]

In the main, it can be seen that most of the duties were station based, with the exception of the women engaged on traffic patrol and, from court reports in local newspapers, it would appear that these women were actively stopping motorists and issuing summonses for offences such as speeding.

The chief constables of the three forces that policed Staffordshire clearly had different views on the usefulness of female police auxiliaries, and this also applied to employing policewomen with powers of arrest. Only the Stoke-on-Trent borough force had employed policewomen before 1939, but the outbreak of war and the increased freedom of teenage girls and women, with new-found work opportunities, led to concerns about female behaviour and morality in the county, echoing those expressed in the First World War. The two chief constables of Newcastle-under-Lyme and Staffordshire County, and their police authority committees, found women's and welfare groups repeatedly requesting that their forces recruit policewomen to patrol the streets to deal with such issues; however, on each occasion the request was refused.

In November 1940, the Newcastle-under-Lyme Watch Committee received petitions from a number of concerned groups and individuals, including the local clergy, the mayoress, the headmistress of Orme Girls School and the North Staffordshire Inner Wheel group, whose members were the wives of Rotarians. All were concerned that young women who were working and living in the area were without parental control and supervision, and frequenting with men in the streets after dark. They asserted that police-women could safeguard women's moral welfare. While some members of the committee agreed, including the mayor, it failed to agree a decision and the matter was deferred for a month.[27] The matter was duly discussed again, and despite receiving further appeals from female magistrates and the town's Trades and Labour Council, Chief Constable Wesley Bate stated that there was no evidence of the need for policewomen. While some committee members accepted that the petitioners had genuine concerns, a majority were more willing to accept Bate's assertion that issues of morality were not police work and therefore did not require the employment of policewomen. The matter was again postponed.[28] Less than a year later, in September 1941, there was further discussion, provoking much argument from Watch Committee members, with one member claiming women preferred policemen as they were 'more discreet and tactful and broadminded', adding that employing women would be a retrograde step for the town. Another claimed that those pressing for policewomen in the borough were 'painting far too black a picture of the conditions in the borough'.[29] Bate was resolute in his resistance to the idea of women in his force, and three months later a resolution on the employment of policewomen was defeated by a majority vote.[30]

In 1942, the arrival of Black American troops in the town of Burton upon Trent led to period-typical concerns about the morality of girls and women fraternising with them. Consequently, the standing joint committee of Staffordshire County Police received numerous requests for the appointment of policewomen. In August, the committee received a letter from Mary Holland, president of the local branch of the NCW and who had patrolled Wolverhampton as a member of the WVS Women Patrols, during the First World War. She wrote: 'There are widespread complaints of soldiers – especially members of the U.S.A contingent – being pestered in the streets by women and quite young girls. Only fully trained policewomen can deal with this deplorable state of things.'[31]

The committee refused the request. Similar complaints followed, particularly from local clergy, who highlighted concerns about the behaviour of girls aged between 14 and 16 who were allegedly accosting Black troops.[32]

Faced with so many demands for policewomen, the committee held a special meeting attended by clergy members and representatives of the US forces, but it was decided that policewomen were not to be the solution to the problem and that policemen would simply take the names of 'any girls behaving in an undesirable fashion'. It also recommended an 11 p.m. curfew for US troops.[33]

Women's groups, including the Women's Co-operative Guild and the Free Church Women's Council, continued to appeal for the appointment of permanent policewomen.[34] In November 1942, Mary Holland, frustrated with the lack of action by the police authority, complained directly to Chief Constable Hunter. She wrote:

> The presence of coloured, as well as white U.S.A troops, in the neighbour-hood has made things very difficult, owing to the regrettable behaviour of women – and worst of all, very young girls – who seem to have completely lost their heads. For their sake, as well as for the protection of the men, from often unwanted attentions of these girls, we deplore the attitude of the Council and my committee wish that you should know the position.[35]

The Chief Constable robustly defended the decisions of the committee, stating:

> This moral salvage of the streets is an urgent, desirable, and imperative thing. But there is nothing in connection with the conduct of the men and women in the streets of Burton that women police could deal with better or as well as male members of the Force. I am not in disagreement with the attitude of Burton Watch Committee. In fact, upon this question, they would look to me for advice. The police machine is not intended by Government, nor does the law provide for it, to carry out this work of moral sanitation in the streets.[36]

In April 1943, there were similar concerns in the cathedral city of Litchfield about 'young girls running wild in the streets'. The city's council approached Hunter, requesting policewomen patrol the streets at night. His reply was again in the negative, citing the difference between welfare work and police work. He suggested that such work would be better undertaken by religious and educational bodies, and voluntary associations.[37]

The claim that the police were not responsible for the moral welfare of citizens was one echoed by several chief constables in England. In June 1943, the Newcastle-under-Lyme Watch Committee met again to discuss the matter. The new Chief Constable, G.S. Jackson, reported that he had contacted sixteen of his peers to establish which forces had policewomen, and the nature of their duties. Eight reported that they had no policewomen, while neighbouring Stoke-on-Trent had eight (including six auxiliaries) and the City of Birmingham force, twenty-six. The Chief Constable of Birmingham had stated that none of his policewomen engaged in welfare work, but carried out patrol duties in connection with women and children, as laid down by the regulations detailing the duties of policewomen.[38] Using this information, Jackson claimed that on these grounds it was not cost-effective to employ policewomen. He argued that in 1942 there had only been 119 incidents involving women or children, and consequently, a policewoman would have been needed once every three days. Clearly in agreement about the financial viability of policewomen, the committee accepted his report.[39]

In February 1944, the Staffordshire standing joint committee received further requests from the Stafford branch of the Conference of Women's Organisations and the Women's Guild of the National Union of Railways for policewomen to patrol the streets. Again, the requests were refused by Hunter, who, in his reply to the committee, noted:

> On general grounds I am not against the employment of policewomen. They are a valuable part of the police service today but there is a great dif-ficulty, even in normal times in finding women with the right qualifications for the police service, the difficulty is greater under war conditions.[40]

Hunter's comments about recruitment difficulties were certainly true, as since February 1942 police forces had been prevented from directly employ-ing women between the ages of 20 and 31, unless approved by the Ministry of Labour and National Service. Any woman who was under the age of 20 also found herself liable for call-up upon reaching that age. Consequently, forces were advised to recruit women aged over 31.[41] Yet, despite Hunter's comments, it does not appear that the county force had taken any steps to recruit women, and he was, perhaps, avoiding recruiting from the available pool of women.

A few weeks later, on 30 March 1944, the Home Office finally removed the discretion of chief constables on whether they employed policewomen. A circular was issued ordering police forces in England and Wales to employ permanent policewomen. It specifically stated that they should be employed in areas where large numbers of Allied or British armed forces were stationed, and crucially, insisted that women should be employed to deal with issues of morality, ending the often-used excuses of chief constables. It stated:

Lax conduct between young women and the troops, may if unchecked, bring in its train breaches of criminal law, the matter is one of increasing importance to the maintenance of good relations between the civil population and Allied troops in this country, and on this ground alone, the Secretary of State feels amply justified in regarding it as one with which the police must be prepared to deal.[42]

The reasons for this change of direction from the Home Office are not clear; however, on 10 March a large conference of national women's organisations had been held to discuss the need for policewomen. It highlighted chief constables' stubborn refusals to employ policewomen, with the Archbishop of Canterbury telling the conference: 'It seems the main obstacle has been sheer, downright stark prejudice.'[43]

The conference passed a motion requesting the Home Secretary take immediate action to appoint an adequate number of policewomen. It can also be argued that the Home Office intervened as it was particularly concerned about morality in the build up to D-Day, when the number of troops in the country had greatly increased. Both the British and American authorities had grown increasingly worried about relationships between US troops and British girls. The Americans were anxious about family life in the US and that undesirable girls would want to marry and settle there, while the British authorities were troubled about the numbers of illegitimate babies and concerned about the morale of their own troops.[44]

The Home Office circular asked chief constables to consider the issue urgently and suggested that policewomen or attested auxiliaries could be employed. It made clear that if forces did not comply, then powers under the Defence Regulations would be utilised and the HMIC would be permitted to impose a quota of women upon forces, thus removing the control of chief constables on the matter. The Staffordshire County force reacted quickly and swore in its first six policewomen on 26 August 1944, all of whom had been auxiliaries. One of these women was Mary Wright, who was immediately promoted to sergeant and posted to Burton upon Trent. The force quickly established a Policewomen's Department of twenty, made up of one inspector, two sergeants and sixteen constables,[45] and indicated how suitable women could be found when a force was under pressure to do so. However, despite the threats made by the Home Office, the Newcastle-under-Lyme Force did not appoint its first two women until 1946, who were again former auxiliaries. That same year, the force was absorbed into the Staffordshire County Force under the Police Act, to reduce the number of small and inefficient forces.

For the two forces of Newcastle-under-Lyme and Staffordshire County, the Second World War was undoubtedly the catalyst for women's greater involvement in policing. The formation of the WAPC had allowed women to gain a foothold in policing, arguably only in what were perceived as gender appropriate roles, working mainly inside police stations. Resistance to women conducting operational street duties had continued throughout the war. Excuses about expenditure, lack of need and morality not being a police matter had all been used over the years, and were underpinned by chauvinistic attitudes about the abilities of women. It cannot be known how long such views would have prevailed without the Home Office's definitive intervention; and twenty-four years after that prediction, Chief Constable Roger Carter of the small Stoke-on-Trent borough force was finally proved right.

A TALE OF TWO 'WAPSIES'

EILEEN NORMINGTON AND WINIFRED HOOPER (PLYMOUTH CITY POLICE)

MARK ROTHWELL

DESPITE THE MEASURABLE CONTRIBUTION MADE by women police officers during the First World War (1914–18), there were no plans set forth by the Home Office to enrol women into the regular or special constabulary during the Second World War (1939–45), and certainly no mention of women in the *National Service Handbook*.[1] As a result of this omission, the National Council of Women of Great Britain (NCW) (formerly the National Union of Women Workers, NUWW) pressured the government into creating the Women's Auxiliary Police Corps (WAPC) in August 1939.[2] This was no doubt based upon their perceived success following their role in instigating the Women Patrols during the First World War and the subsequent introduction of warranted female officers. The size, organisation and presentation of the WAPC was primarily left up to the many English, Welsh and Scottish constabularies in existence at the time, albeit there were some national guidelines. Candidates had to be no younger than 18 years old and no older than 55, and of good education and literacy. The WAPC officers themselves were not to be sworn constables, but were to be assistants in administrative functions, releasing male officers to front-line duties. These duties were to include:

The driving of motor vehicles
Maintenance and repair of motor vehicles and other police equipment
Clerical work, including typing and shorthand
Telephone or wireless work
Canteen work
Members of the Corps will not be Special Constables and will not be called upon to perform duties requiring the possession of police powers.[3]

Eileen Normington (left) and an unknown WAPC, c.1945.
(Courtesy of Eileen Normington)

They were accordingly not issued with handcuffs or truncheons, merely chrome police whistles.

The eleventh-hour creation of the WAPC meant that this important auxiliary force existed only in principle, so when war was declared on 3 September 1939, chief constables hastily set about recruiting. This chapter tells the stories of Eileen Normington and Winifred Hooper, two pioneering women who stepped up to the plate and did their bit for the war effort.

EILEEN NORMINGTON

Eileen Normington (née Milo) was born on 30 July 1917 in Plymouth to John and Lily Milo, and was the youngest of three children.[4] Her father, a labourer, was absent when Eileen was born, being otherwise committed fighting for king and country overseas. The Great War still raged, and women did not yet have the vote. Little was young Eileen to know that the very war she was born into would lead to social changes which propelled women into professions traditionally undertaken by men and to Eileen herself becoming a pioneer in adulthood.

It has been implied in recent years, especially in the newspapers and perpetuated on social media, that Eileen Normington was Plymouth's first ever female police officer. Indeed, Eileen herself speculated she was *probably* the first, and there was a time when the lack of contradictory evidence rendered the claim accurate. We now know this not to be true. It is more correct to say that Eileen was the first fully sworn policewoman to take office in Plymouth immediately after the Second World War, under government rules to create women's police departments in the British constabularies. Others preceded Eileen, notably Police Constable Isobel Taylor and Inspectress Audrey Canney, who were appointed in Plymouth in 1919,[5] but they possessed only quasi-police powers and were stood down in 1921. Agnes Valentine Mead was appointed in 1937 as a detective and matron;[6] she transferred to Oxford City Police during the war and was replaced by Iris Martin. Furthermore, Lilian Daisy Gale was sworn in at Plymouth docks in 1943 with the Great Western Railway Police.[7] Regardless, Eileen was there. She did it. She stepped forward and played her part and has fully earned her place in the history books.

Eileen's journey began on 3 September 1939, the day Britain declared war on Nazi Germany. An appeal on the local radio station called for the attendance of women aged 18 to 55 at Greenbank police station, the headquarters of Plymouth City Police, to register for the new Women's Auxiliary Police Corps. In Eileen's words, she was 'game for anything', and without further ado headed down to the station and left her details with Police Sergeant Thurley Beale. She spent the rest of the afternoon on Plymouth's historic Hoe Promenade with a friend, a place popular for the city's twenty-somethings to socialise. When Eileen returned home later in the evening, her mother told her, with some dismay, that a policeman had been around and had left a message to the effect that the Chief Constable wanted to see her.

There was no cause for concern, however. A mere twenty-four hours later, Eileen, then 22 years old, was in uniform at Greenbank police station, which had been recently sandbagged in anticipation of enemy air raids,[8] interviewing other candidates for the corps. She was given the title 'Leading Auxiliary Policewoman' and wore chevrons on her uniform sleeves, so her authority was clear. She reported directly to a regular member of the city force, an inspector named William Ellis. There were originally twelve WAPCs, and over the course of the war the department grew to over forty members on both full-time and part-time arrangements. Eventually, a second Leading Auxiliary Policewoman, named Mrs Critchley, was appointed, and as the work of the department expanded, overall supervision was given to Superintendent Hutchings.

The work of the Plymouth WAPC, known colloquially as 'wapsies', was largely clerical and involved operating the war room at police headquarters, which had a direct telephone line to Downing Street. It was here that bomb sites and casualties were documented, Home Office returns were submitted and general administrative work in support of the regular police force, the First Police Reserve and the Police War Reserve was carried out. It was important that the WAPC stood ready to serve in times of emergency, and as such, three members of the corps lived and slept at the police station overnight in digs shared with female members of the Auxiliary Fire Service.[9] Additional to Eileen's work in the WAPC, she regularly undertook work with the Women's Voluntary Service (WVS) and distributed food parcels to families in Devonport.

In readiness for an air raid, the auxiliary policewomen usually slept in their uniforms or in 'half blues'. The police station itself was struck directly by enemy bombs at least twice, including once while Eileen was on duty. In the immediate aftermath of an air raid the instinct was to flee; however, on this occasion Eileen dutifully instructed her colleagues to remain firmly seated and carry on working. Fortunately the bomb came to rest, unexploded, outside the WAPC office. It was not long before men in uniform arrived and told them to evacuate to Widey Grange, the contingency site for exactly this type of scenario. Knowing there was still work to be done, Eileen collected up as many pieces of paper as she could before she left. The bomb was removed by the military and taken to Dartmoor to be disposed of, where, tragically, it detonated before safe disposal was achieved and killed two British soldiers. Eileen's stoicism in the face of narrowly avoiding death by sheer good fortune typified her outlook on her service in the WAPC. The small matter of an unexploded bomb in the corridor outside her office was not going to prevent her from undertaking her work, vital to the war effort.

Come the end of the Second World War, the WAPC was disbanded and its members offered other positions in the civil service. One option was to take the constable's oath and become a fully sworn police officer, something which Eileen did with gusto after being encouraged by the Chief Constable. Under collar number 314, she became the first new member (WPC Iris Martin was already serving) of the Plymouth City Police Women's Department on 1 April 1946, on a salary of £3 19s per annum.[10] Her pay rose to £4 14s per annum on 6 November 1946, come the end of her probationary period. Soon after she was elevated to a fully sworn officer, she married PC 259 Jim Normington, who had just returned to the force from overseas military service. Typical of policewomen of the era, it was expected of them that they would largely deal with cases concerning women and young children, and this kind of work took up much of Eileen's duty time while serving in uniform on 'B' Division.

A notable arrest of Eileen's was that of Hilda Gustek, also known as Stella Costello, for the abduction of an 18-month-old boy from Plymouth in 1945.[11] Eileen travelled to Cardiff to arrest Gustek in 1948 and conveyed her by train to Plymouth to answer for her crimes. Gustek was also held on charges of desertion from the Auxiliary Territorial Service (ATS), the women's branch of the British Army during the Second World War. A photograph of Gustek, visibly distressed and trying to cover her face, with WPC Normington leading her away by the arm, appeared in an edition of the *Daily Mirror* on 30 September 1948. As a footnote to the story, Gustek was eventually found 'not guilty' of child abduction but was admonished for deserting.

Eileen obtained an attachment to CID on 30 July 1951, a situation made permanent on 31 March 1952.[12] Among Eileen's cases was that of infiltrating illegal gambling establishments in the city, something which on one occasion required her to go undercover at a whist drive with her husband Jim. One can only imagine the interesting, perhaps even fun times the two had working covertly.

Although Eileen never appeared to suffer any professional setbacks by virtue of her gender, she certainly felt it 'bad form' to remain in service as a policewoman when her husband reached the rank of superintendent. Subsequently, Eileen resigned in 1959 and took her police pension, having served with the Plymouth force for twenty years. Enduring interest in the history of policewomen among academics and historians inevitably led to Eileen being contacted innumerable times throughout her retirement, including by the BBC.

In the winter of her years, Eileen gave a talk to an audience of young in-service policewomen in Plymouth as part of the Women in Policing Network's celebration of the centenary of women in policing. A close friendship with retired police officer and author Simon Dell MBE QCB also led to Eileen writing the foreword to Simon's book *The Fair Arm of the Law* in 2016. At the age of 99, Eileen agreed to participate in the University of Plymouth's '50 Years, 50 Voices' oral history project led by Professor Kim Stevenson PhD LLB. This was her final professional interview before she passed away at the grand age of 102 in 2019. Not long before her passing, she was joined at her bedside by the Chief Constable of Devon & Cornwall Police, which now covers the city of Plymouth, Shaun Sawyer QPM.

It was felt by several who knew her that Eileen should be given a send-off befitting her importance to national, local and social history. It was therefore thanks to the gracious permission of Chief Constable Shaun Sawyer that Eileen was conveyed into the chapel of rest by four female pallbearers – Chief Inspector Jane Alford-Mole, Sergeant Miranda Dalton, Police

Constable Louise Edwards, and Police Constable Sally Cliff. The service was led by Lead Police Chaplain Sarah Jeffrey MA and a tribute made by Chief Superintendent Nikki Leaper. The small funeral service, conducted on a pleasant spring afternoon at Efford Crematorium, closed out a remarkable chapter in Plymouth's history and that of the great British policing story in general.

Eileen's retirement flat was within walking distance of the old Greenbank police station building, which has now been converted to student flats with little acknowledgement of its heritage. Even as a centenarian she was incredibly energetic, marching up and down the flights of stairs, troubling those even a third her age to keep pace with her. Her personality was such that when visitors went to leave, she would tell them: 'I always insist on a kiss goodbye.' Before they had a chance to react, Eileen had already planted a 'big one' on their lips. That was Eileen all over: spirited, forthright and very, very cheeky. Eileen did not write any detailed memoirs and was always modest about her achievements and about her place in history. With kind permission from Simon Dell, the following passage written by Eileen is extracted from *The Fair Arm of the Law*:

> It is hard to think that I was born at the same time as the first policewomen appeared on our streets during the years of the Great War. In my own service from 1939 until 1959 in the Plymouth City Police, I became one of the first two sworn female officers in the city force. I saw many changes in the decades in which I served myself. Whatever would it be like if one of those first policewomen in 1915 came ahead one hundred years and saw the work which women in the police service deal with now? So much has altered for the better for us ladies in the force nowadays. Pay, hours, conditions, and the ability to marry without having to give up your job to name but a few significant changes. But I was not alone during those challenging times when Plymouth was being bombed night and after night and we girls held the fort at police headquarters control room, even when an unexploded bomb was dropped through the ceiling![13]

Eileen's modesty of her importance exemplifies so many of her peers across the country. Women who were stepping forward into roles that had previously always been undertaken by men, but doing so with no sense of aggrandisement or the mark they were making on history. Her reflections about the status of women in the police force today, however, demonstrate exactly how important their first steps were.

WINIFRED HOOPER

Winifred Hooper was born near Plymouth in December 1918 and was educated at a girls' boarding school in Bideford, North Devon. Her father owned 3½ acres of woodland in the Whitleigh area (now swallowed up by the city of Plymouth) on which he built a bungalow for the family to live in. During the early years of the war, Winifred's father, who was acquainted with the Chief Constable of Plymouth City Police, enquired with him as to whether there were any jobs available for his daughter. Winifred's friends had already joined the ATS and Women's Auxiliary Air Force (WAAF) and she felt it her duty to do something worthwhile, preferably outdoors in the Traffic Department. Although there were no traffic roles available for women at the time, she was offered a position in the WAPC. Her role, though, was largely concerned with tending to the Chief Constable and filing duties in the registry office at Greenbank police station. Her first day at work was 3 October 1940.

As a result of a negative encounter with the city's only full-time, fully sworn policewoman, Agnes Valentine Mead, Winifred formed the opinion that Mead disliked the WAPC and its members.[14] Although there had been consistent advocation for a Women's Police Department in Plymouth in the interwar years, successive chief constables failed to convince the police Watch Committee to take action, resulting in Mead's singular and somewhat unceremonious appointment in 1937, which was largely due to the influence of Nancy Astor MP. The sudden drive to recruit women into a role for which they had recently been refused no doubt frustrated Mead, as it meant eliminating her unique position within the force.

Like Eileen, Winifred too had a brush with death courtesy of the Luftwaffe. Her intimate account of a close encounter with an enemy bomb during the war is best told in her own words, as transcribed from an audio recording Winifred made in the 1990s:

> It happened just after midnight, a sultry summer's night on June 13th 1943 at Police Headquarters, Greenbank, Plymouth. Every night during the war, three members of the Women's Auxiliary Police Corps slept in to be ready to help 'man' the control room should there be an air raid. This particular night, Yvonne and I were on our own as the third member of our trio was on holiday. We had done our usual spell of office work during the evening having had our supper in the canteen and gone to bed hoping for a quiet night. We had been lucky for quite some time; things had quietened down considerably, so we allowed ourselves the luxury of going to bed in our night attire. That was a big mistake!

We awoke to the wailing of the air raid siren. We tumbled out of bed and threw on a few top garments. We didn't stop to dress properly, thinking as on many occasions past, the 'all clear' would go as we reached the control room or soon after. Little did we think that as we left our so-called little bedroom, that we would not see it again for five days.

As we descended the steps to the control room there was the most frightening, screaming, whistling noise which sounded as if it was aiming for my head, then a loud thud and … nothing more. Thank you, God, for that. Everyone was rooted to the spot, then I remembered Sergeant Kenneth Worley came over to me and offered me his steel helmet to put on. Nobody knew what to do. Then Inspector Denley came down and very calmly announced that we had an unexploded bomb on the court landing just above us. Only those of us who worked with Mr Denley will know and understand how apparently cool and matter-of-factly he dealt with this. Then came the order to evacuate the building. As we left the control room, I think that every telephone that had hitherto remained silent started to ring. It seemed terrible not being able to stay and answer them all. Yvonne and I went to the charge office, which was just inside the main entrance to the building, to await further instructions.

As we got there, we were confronted with two German airmen who had just bailed out over the city and had been brought in by two police officers. They were taken into a nearby office and we were intrigued to see one of them, a blonde, good-looking youth, take out a comb and brush his fair locks! They remained at Greenbank only a short time and later were transferred to Plympton together with other prisoners from Greenbank. The story went around that one of the airmen said that there was no need to worry about the bomb because it was unlikely to go off; the rot having set in in Germany, or words to that effect.

We were then bundled into the prison van and driven by Superintendent Ernie Beale to alternative accommodation at Widey Grange. To date that is the only time I have had a ride in the prison van, and I will never forget it as long as I live. We were thrown from side to side of that van as we sped along. [Shopping street] Mutley Plain looked like an inferno, Timothy White's premises being on fire and flames were reflecting in all the shop windows. As we passed Emmanuel Church, a stick of bombs hit the houses just above Hender's Corner. After what seemed like an interminable drive, we reached Widey Grange to be met by Ben Frowde, a First Police Reserve, who was the caretaker there. There was no electricity in the Grange and somehow nobody knew how to light the Aladdin lamps provided. Having lived in the countryside for many years and used oil lamps, we managed to get some light on the scene. Now to find the telephone switchboard which was in an upstairs room. Neither of us knew too much about working a telephone switchboard, however now was our time to learn. Then Sergeant Charles appeared on the scene. He helped us and insisted on lending me his jacket, as what with being scantily clad and suffering I suppose with a certain amount of shock, and being by now about 3 a.m., I was feeling rather cold.

All I can say is that we sat there for the rest of the night trying to keep contact with Greenbank and waiting, listening, and praying for those brave men who had stayed behind with that unexploded bomb. The morning came and we went home for breakfast, but we had to be back by 10am to begin our job in the office which was soon moved from Greenbank to Widey Grange. At lunchtime a meal was laid on for all staff in the large banqueting hall at Widey Court. I shall always remember walking into that hall seeing the long table laid for lunch and in the centre of the table Ben Frowde had placed a bowl of yellow roses. The sight of those roses must have conveyed to many others as they did to me, a feeling of sanity after the long nightmare. Thank you, Ben, wherever you are, for that kind thought which meant so much at that particular time. Jack Hingston, the acting chief constable, took his place at the head of the table and we all sat around like one big family. We worked at Widey Court for five days and it was pretty chaotic. We were told that the bomb was defused and removed. It was one of the biggest bombs, 1,000kg, to fall on the city. It was said that had it exploded, there would not have been left two stones standing on top of each other. Time passes and memories fade, but I think that when I look back at those days, I will always remember the wonderful friendliness and comradeship which existed between all ranks and … that bowl of yellow roses.[15]

After the war, Winifred remained in the Plymouth City Police force as a civilian dispatch driver, largely concerned in the transport of mail and equipment between the city's police stations, but also rounding up stray dogs. Although she was not a sworn police officer, she wore a smart policewoman's uniform with the number '818' on the shoulder epaulettes, the significance of which is lost to time (there certainly were not that many officers in the force!). She served until 1978 and in that time saw the city of Plymouth rise up from the ruin and rubble left behind by Hitler during those devastating war years in which so many lives were lost. Another great alteration during Winifred's tenure was the abandonment of Greenbank police station in favour of modern facilities at Crownhill on the edge of the city boundary;

Greenbank Police Station War Room, 1940s. Eileen Normington (front)
being handed paper, Winnifred Hooper (left-most telephone box) smiling.

the abolition of Women's Departments and their integration with the male
regulars in 1976; and the amalgamation of Plymouth City Police with the
Cornwall Constabulary and Devon & Exeter Police on 1 June 1967, which
formed the Devon & Cornwall Constabulary as it exists today. She passed
away in 2016 at the age of 98.

Although Eileen's and Winifred's names do not come up often when talking about the history of women in policing in Britain, they were pioneers in
their own right for the simple reason that they did what they set out to do,
and more, in the face of archaic attitudes, in a patriarchal society, under the
cloud of a terrible world war. Eileen exhibited the tenacity and drive to demonstrate that women could make effective police officers, and both women
in their capacity as 'wapsies' and Winifred in her later career, the important and often unsung role played by women in civilian roles within police
forces. They exemplify the work undertaken by the oft-overlooked WAPC
during the war years, which as a body perhaps took the next significant stride
towards integrating women more thoroughly into the police service. If they
could undertake such roles during the war, why, the question follows, could
they not continue to do so afterwards? Eileen was far from alone in transferring her civilian role in the WAPC to that of a full-time constable at the
conclusion of the war. So much so that this transition represents probably
the single largest increase in the numbers of women as a percentage of the

workforce since their initial introduction. Eileen, Winifred and their peers nationally had demonstrated the capabilities and the value of women in the police force, leading to a far increased acceptance of their presence.

At the conclusion of the war, the Home Secretary, Donald Somervell, wrote to all members of the WAPC to express his gratitude at their efforts, albeit in perhaps slightly pejorative language that is demonstrative of the prevailing patriarchal state of society. The women of the WAPC had done their part admirably, but ostensibly only to support and despite the absence of their men. Their efforts are no less diminished by the Home Secretary's mildly tarnished praise, however, in terms that are utterly exemplified by Eileen and Winifred:

> I should like to send a special message of appreciation to those who have served so long and so loyally in a part-time capacity in the Women's Auxiliary Police Corps. Of all the achievements of this country during the war, few have caused such universal admiration as the part played by our women; and to this achievement the Women's Auxiliary Police Corps have contributed their full share. Many of you have husbands, sons or brothers serving in the Armed Forces or have had to bear a heavy burden of family responsibility, and almost all have been engaged for long hours on war work, but whatever your circumstances you have brought to your police duties the same unfailing cheerfulness and courage and the same ready sense of public duty. It is a fine record of which each one of you has reason to be proud.[16]

Their place in history is perhaps best summed up in the words of another pioneer, Joan Lock:

> We shouldn't underestimate what these pioneers achieved. They were very courageous. They were determined to do their duty. These days, it would be impossible to imagine what a police force would be like without women.[17]

SOPHIE ALLOWAY

THE ESTABLISHMENT OF POST-WAR POLICING IN GERMANY

VALERIE REDSHAW

A young WPC Sophie Alloway hands papers to Superintendent Dorothy Peto, officer in charge of Metropolitan Women Police, at New Scotland Yard in the mid-1930s. Sophie Alloway was to reach the same rank and position before her retirement from the police in 1959.

ONE DAY A SCHOOL FRIEND asked Sophie what made her abandon teaching for a career in police work. Her thoughtful and considered response was: 'Someone once jokingly suggested a policewoman's life for me, which I scornfully repudiated. But the idea must have stuck, because I had finished one job and hadn't another and was crossing a London Street one day when a young policeman smiled at me and that decided my future.'[1] That unknown constable's smile was the catalyst for what was to become an outstanding career in London's Metropolitan Police.

Sophie Alloway was born in Auckland, New Zealand on 7 January 1899. The eldest of four daughters, she spent her early life in the small town of Marton, where her father was manager of the Bank of Australasia.

She was educated at a small private school in Marton, at the local high school, and at Nga Tawa, the Wellington Diocesan School. She eventually became a trainee teacher at this school and later completed her teacher training at the Diocesan School in Auckland. For a while she taught at her old school and another in Lower Hutt.

She then gave up teaching and, with a friend, spent four years in Levin developing a poultry and flower farm. Overseas travel being a typical experience for young New Zealanders, the pair went to England in 1930 with the idea of carrying on with small farming there. The first year they spent travelling and exploring farming opportunities. At the time England was in the grip of the Great Depression and the farming idea was soon abandoned. Sophie took a job for a while coaching a girl who was an invalid, and later studied typing and shorthand.

In 1932 she applied to the Recruiting Department of the Metropolitan Police at New Scotland Yard, and in January 1933 she was called to appear before a selection board. After what she has referred to as a 'long and gruelling day', she was informed that she had been successful.

After completing the twelve-week training course at Peel House, in May that year Sophie was posted to 'A' Division in Hyde Park. Her success, of particular interest back in New Zealand where there were no policewomen, was reported in the social notes of the *Timaru Herald*.[2]

For the next two years she continued to study the technical and practical work of a constable to meet the requirements of her probationary period. She had to pass further examinations and qualify in first aid to be confirmed. The policewoman's role at this time was principally concerned with women and children – both as victims of crime and offenders. After her early experiences 'on the beat' at Hyde Park, she then transferred to Paddington.

When the policewomen command at Scotland Yard (Superintendent Dorothy Peto and a sub-divisional inspector) required clerical support, she transferred and became the first woman constable to be given a job there. She quickly demonstrated that she had a flair for administration and what was to follow was the first of a steady series of promotions. In her third year of service, she had begun to study again to pass the civil service examination, a requirement for promotion to the rank of sergeant. In 1938 she reached this rank.

Sophie wrote regular letters to her sisters in New Zealand which were full of her experiences in Britain and her duties in London. When war was declared in 1939, she described the bright sunny Sunday when she went on duty at 8.00 a.m. in peace time and at 4.00 p.m. came off duty in war time:

> It is incredible but true. To see the faces of the people in the street it is difficult to think that much is amiss, and yet there is a strange unreality about it all. You would wonder what the little brown box is that everyone is carrying over their shoulder and why they are all carrying the same thing. You would also wonder why in peaceful England men in khaki are marching and training in streets and open spaces and why the shops are boarded up or protected by sandbags. Also, why there are notices pointing to the nearest trench or air raid shelter or first aid post. You would also think it very strange that there are no lights at night, and that all the windows should be covered with black paint or black curtains.[3]

Sophie goes on to explain that the cardboard box held the gas mask without which no one should leave the house, day or night. The trenches and air-raid shelters were to become places of refuge when warning sirens sounded, the sandbags to help prevent damage, and the soldiers were soon to disappear from the places where they were currently training and living.

In her job she was required to wear a tin helmet, carry a service respirator over one shoulder, and a haversack on the other containing a suit of protective clothing to wear over her uniform if needed. All of which must have become very heavy by the end of the day. The helmet was, however, a godsend when she was patrolling and travelling about in the blackout, on many occasions saving her from bumps on the forehead when she tripped and fell over sandbags or collided with pedestrians, a Belisha beacon or lamppost.

One of the first and most painful duties of the war was the evacuation of children from London to the comparative safety of the more rural parts of Britain. Sophie found this a particularly harrowing task:

> We had children from the poor districts, and most were very good, but it was pitiful to see others. Their cases were so heavy, and they were just blind with misery, so they stumbled and fell. We carried all we could or took their cases for them on the journey from school to the train.

Each policewoman had five or six children to care for, some of whom were refugees recently arrived from Europe and could not speak English. One can only imagine how traumatic this experience could have been for them. Sophie and her team were pleased to learn later that all had arrived safely at their destinations in the Isle of Man (a secret when they left) without a single accident: a feat they were immensely proud of.

In September 1939, Sophie noted that all examinations for promotion had been cancelled. While it was difficult to concentrate on study under war conditions, she was anxious to progress further with her career as she felt cramped in her present position.

It had been announced that recruiting of policewomen was to cease for the near future and this too would affect opportunities for promotion. Within a few days, however, this decision was reversed, and Sophie was delighted to learn that she would be responsible for training the new policewomen recruits.

They were to have a week of intensive training before going out to divisions, followed by a few hours of instruction each week for the following six months. It was expected that she would have a new class about every two months. It would be a challenge to condense into one week the teaching previously given over eleven or twelve weeks, but Sophie thought it would be interesting and felt lucky to have been chosen for the job.

In her letters home, a chief item of news was income tax being increased to 7/6 in the pound. She also mentioned the prohibitive cost of putting up blackout curtains, preparing buckets of earth and water to deal with incendiary bombs if they should land in the house, and that ration cards were to arrive at the end of October. She sent pictures of Hyde Park after excavators had scooped out enormous quantities of earth to fill sandbags.

At the end of 1939, Sophie sat the examination for promotion to the rank of inspector. She notes that it was a reasonably good exam, but the questions were not very much in line with the work done by policewomen. Under war conditions gas masks had to accompany candidates into the exam room, and the first instructions were what should be done if there was an air-raid warning. Her comment on this was that it was 'such a soothing thought for the beginning of a long day of difficult papers'.

In 1940 she was transferred to Southwark while she awaited the result of the promotion examination. In February she learned that she had been successful and her actual promotion would occur 'in due course'. The winter was extremely cold, and Sophie was challenged by a bout of German measles followed by influenza. She was not happy in her new division, where the inspector appeared jealous of her rapid progress in the service. She kept herself busy off duty, working for the welfare centre, which provided warm clothes for the London children evacuated to the country and for the NZ Women's Work Party, which provided comforts for NZ soldiers in Egypt. Her policewomen helped too and made more than seventy socks, cardigans, jerseys and vests for the children.

The war escalated in Europe as Germany invaded other countries and large numbers of refugees arrived from Belgium and Holland by train. Sophie and her staff met them at London's railway stations to help with processing – a task she found heartbreaking: 'for it is terrible to see people arrive almost entirely destitute in a strange country, in many cases unable to speak the language, and having been through so many perils and terrors'.[4]

More enemy aliens were being interned, and Sophie had been making multiple trips to Liverpool with women of varying nationalities. From Liverpool they travelled on to the Isle of Man to an internment camp.

Sophie was also involved with the re-evacuation of many of the London children. The original plan had been to wait until the bomb raids started, but the Nazi invasion in Europe, and Italy entering the war in June, caused a change of plan. Many parents were still reluctant to allow their children to leave London and Sophie thought there would still be too many children in London once bombing began.

The fall of Belgium was followed by the retreat from Dunkirk. On 17 June, France decided to stop fighting and an attack on Britain became seemingly inevitable. Sophie made preparations at home for a raid. When the first alarm sounded at night she would dress, make tea and put it in a flask in case there was no water in the morning. The bath, basins and buckets were filled with water and the stirrup pump ready. Her suitcase was packed. She would then lie down and sleep until the 'all clear' siren sounded. At her bedside was a torch and some cash; her clothes, shoes and suitcase nearby.

Policewomen were asked to volunteer to go to the Isle of Man to look after the female internees. Sophie put her name down but was asked to withdraw. Having second thoughts, she realised that she was anxious not to lose the training of recruits, and did not think it wise to bury herself just at the point when promotion was in the offing. The women who went made an incredibly good impression and there was strong demand for increasing the number of policewomen everywhere to cope with problems arising from the war. Sophie hoped she would continue to get plenty of recruits.

By September 1940, bombing raids became very frequent and sleep was constantly interrupted. Sophie, with no air-raid shelter in the immediate vicinity, was allowed to sleep under the staircase in a vacant flat in her apartment block at night. She would cover herself with a carpet and hope for the best! The barrage put up by the anti-aircraft guns in Hyde Park was deafening but she got used to it and did not mind, as it meant fewer bombs would be dropped. Following a late shift, she would often sleep on a mattress at the police station because of the difficulty of travelling home late at night, especially on her bicycle. She became used to sleeping in her clothes.

As the Battle of Britain raged overhead, people kept a score of the planes downed. One Sunday it was 144. The figures were being kept like a cricket score – people asking, 'Have you heard the latest score?' and the answer would be, 'Last I heard it was fifty for three.'

An enormous amount of damage was done and Sophie found it awful to see houses, hospitals, churches and business places a mass of ruins, along with the terrible loss of civilian life and the long lists of injured people. Each night she wondered if she would see her little flat again, as houses nearby had been destroyed.

One night she was called with colleagues to evacuate people from streets near a spot where a delayed-action bomb had been dropped. The bomb had fallen about an hour before it was found and could explode at any moment. After an hour, the team had got all the people away to shelters or other houses. The last few just having disappeared, there was a roar, a great black column of smoke and showers of falling masonry. The police guarding the street had to run, throw themselves into the gutter and lie flat until things calmed down. All were intact but very dirty and muddy, and mostly pleased to have saved so many people from death or injury.

After weeks of these nightly raids, Sophie remained cheerful. While her house was still standing, a land mine dropped further along the street caused chaos in her bedroom, with ceilings cracked and big chunks missing in it and other rooms.

In November 1940, Sophie went before the selection board for promotion to inspector. She found it fearsome as she was questioned by several chief constables and an assistant commissioner for over twenty minutes. With no current vacancies, she would have to wait quite a while to be promoted.

Bombing seemed to have moved to the industrial Midlands temporarily, but she still had to sleep at the police station after her late shift, because transport was still difficult at night. She continued training policewomen, and describes the visit of the king and queen to Southwark and the wonderful reception they were given. There was an air raid on at the time, but the crowd could not believe royalty was among them and surged around talking freely to them. The mayor and corporation representatives were apparently most upset at being pushed aside.

Sophie's next move was back to the Yard to the Women Police Branch while waiting for promotion. Here she taught part time, supervising others as well as assisting with the office work. She was still organising the escorts of enemy aliens to Liverpool. On one occasion, along with four women constables, they took ten females, and were very proud of the fact that this was done without the assistance of male officers – 'Something of a victory for us.'

Finally, in December 1941, Sophie was promoted to the rank of inspector and posted to Stepney in the East End of London. Here and until the end of the war she continued her devotion to her police career, becoming recognised for her loyalty, courage and organisational ability. The Battle of Britain had been a challenge but the aftermath of destruction, food shortages and social problems provided her with plenty to occupy her and her staff.

When the war ended there was much jubilation in the streets of London, but Sophie did not have long to savour it, for on 30 May she was told she had been seconded to the Foreign Office. She was to be working for the British element of the Control Commission for Germany. In July she flew to Germany with the Public Safety Branch of the Commission, with the rank of Public Safety Officer Two. Her role was to reorganise the German women police in the British Zone of Germany, and in the British Sector of Berlin:

We were airborne at 12.40pm and landed at 3.10pm. It was a particularly good journey. We could see nothing of England because of cloud, though the cloud broke as we approached the coast of France. There were acres and acres of ripening corn. We saw Antwerp quite clearly, also Essen and Dortmund. The destruction was terrible, just devastation for miles and miles. The plane was an ordinary transport with seats along the side, so we had to screw round and get a stiff neck to see out. When we landed, I remembered to stamp heavily on the German soil, but nearly forgot and all but smiled at a little German boy who was sweeping the entrance hall.

An hour and a half's uncomfortable journey in an army lorry with unpadded seats followed before she reached her destination. She noted that the entire journey was through corn fields and vegetable crops and that the people appeared indifferent, although some children and old people waved.

Sophie was accompanied by Inspector Hill, a fellow Metropolitan policewoman, but it appears that her tasks were different and Hill ultimately worked in the Rhine area, and is rarely mentioned by Sophie beyond their early arrival in Germany. Sophie spent most of her time as the only woman among several men. She was the senior female Public Safety Officer in Germany.

The Commission building was surrounded by rusty wire, and she was not sure 'whether we are wired in, or the Germans are wired out'. She describes some of the routine of living in the Commission, detailing how German girls looked after the mess and bedrooms, laundry and shoes. There was a NAAFI (Navy Army Air Force Institute – canteen service) and a free ration of cigarettes, which she traded some of for chocolate and film.[5]

The headquarters was a large building that used to be a bank, with several flats above. Sophie took her turn as security officer for twenty-four hours and had to sleep there all night. She set up a bed in the director's room and insisted that she should be armed.

As part of a team of four, she began surveying a part of Westfalen, visiting public safety officers in the various towns in the administrative district of Westphalia. This brought her into contact with the public as well as the administration. She began to get a truer picture of the damage, and wrote that she got 'some, though not many savage looks from members of the population'. People seemed generally surprised to see a woman in her role.

Most of the travelling was over bad roads with many diversions for 'bridge blown', craters or mines. A sign reading 'mines cleared between these points' was common. The countryside was littered with overturned or wrecked cars, guns, tanks or lorries, crashed aeroplanes and ammunition dumps. The railways were wrecked, and trains and trucks just stayed where they were bombed. The roads were also packed with huge army trucks loaded with German prisoners of war being returned home and displaced persons being moved from one camp to another. In one place, she saw many Russians and Poles waiting to be returned home, but while they remained there they constituted a major problem, as they roamed about at night, marauding at will.

Sophie was horrified by the destruction caused by Allied bombing. One place she visited had borne witness to one raid lasting twenty-eight minutes which had flattened the town. It had been quite substantial with big, well-built houses, churches and business premises, but was reduced to piles of rubble under which were the bodies of thousands of people. No attempt was or could have been made to rescue anybody as the Americans were advancing to capture it after the raid. This was only one of the hundreds of places to suffer the same plight.

By August, Sophie had travelled from Lübeck to Hamburg, where she hoped to remain for some time. She was introduced to Colonel Armitage, the officer in charge of Hamburg, and arranged to meet Colonel Barnes,

Senior Public Safety Officer for the city. The latter was searching for suitable rooms for offices. A temporary one was eventually found in the food office and Sophie was given a 21-year-old German girl as a clerk, a car and a police driver, along with an instant promotion to the rank of Major Alloway.

Her accommodation was in a large room on the third floor of a block of luxury flats, and she chose the best furniture from there and from adjoining flats until it met her requirements. The mess was in the former Gauhaus (Nazi Headquarters), and Sophie took her meals there and was served by former staff of the old America Hamburg Shipping Line. She met regularly with other military staff and attended several social occasions involving talk, then dinner with a band, hock and burgundy between courses, and Curacao with toasts. 'No one knows where it comes from, and no one asks,' she quipped.

She completed her major report and returned to Lübeck to try and persuade the Commission to give her authority to base herself in Hamburg. By September, she was back in Hamburg and finding the work interesting, but things became more difficult when office hours were over. The mess was like a large hotel. The military appeared to resent all the civilians, and while pleasant in conversation, quite definitely did not want to be friendly. There were a great many parties with people staying up to the early hours. She wrote that she 'can't imagine how they managed to do a day's work. The stuff they drink is just poison except for some wine.'

During her down time, she visited the golf links and found that she could join and be provided with clubs. There was a pro and a fine clubhouse on a beautiful course of thirteen holes, but no balls. She was offered a couple of wrecks for practice. (Among her souvenirs of her time in Germany is a golf trophy she won partnering Colonel Armitage, Senior Public Safety Officer for Hamburg, at a Hamburg Golf Club competition.)

In Hamburg, she established herself firmly on the public safety staff and sought a move to a proper office, and subsequently set about finding women recruits for the training school. She invited herself to the police training school at Hiltoup to have discussions about training with the officer in charge. While there, she inspected some police horses that had been in an unbelievably bad condition through neglect, but they had just been turned out to grass and she believed they would soon pull round. Later she drove back through Münster, Osnabrück and Bremen, which were all severely damaged, and noted that it appeared the people just lived in the holes of what was left of their properties, yet looked clean and well dressed.

She found that she increasingly hated the German language but was beginning to pick it up, and ultimately intended to find an instructor and have some coaching in the winter evenings. She set up her permanent office in the old Gestapo building and was pleased that it was large and sunny. Her typist kept the vases fresh with flowers. Applicants for policewomen positions begin to pour in to her, but nearly all were turned down as they had been members of the Nazi Party.

From her new office, Sophie wrote to Police Woman Superintendent Dorothy Peto with a request for a portrait of the royal family to frame and hang in the room. She acquired a new car – a beautiful Mercedes requisitioned from two senior German police officers – and noted that they were not too pleased about that. It did, however, please her driver, of whom she became very fond. The feeling was mutual, and he often went beyond the normal expectations of duty by taking diligent care of her and always ensuring that 'Madam's *blumen* [flower] vase' in the car had fresh flowers. He was also armed where she was not.

Within the year, nine of the policewomen in the city had to be dismissed for their erstwhile Nazi ideas, leaving only thirteen to do all the work and help with the training. Hamburg had had policewomen since 1927, but a fundamental change needed to be made in the German police organisation from punishment to prevention. This seismic attitudinal shift was made both by recruitment and retraining. Most of the time Sophie worked from Hamburg but visited all parts of the British zone, as well as the British Sector of Berlin. She took her job of reorganising the German Women Police very seriously, constantly travelling through the British Sector and back and forth to Berlin, recruiting, training and advising as requests for her assistance came from throughout the country, sometimes, she said, 'feeling like a commercial traveller'.

In December 1945, she was delighted when one of the first thirty women recruits selected out of the 300 mixed gender officers in training topped the class, another was third and another fourth. All the women achieved a high standard.

An article from the *Daily Mail* early in 1946 reported:

Miss Alloway's Girls, German Women Police trainees, called after their British Commander, took part in a raid on Hamburg's Black market today (Thursday). They assisted 300 uniformed police to search a row of apartment houses. British Army rations, cigarettes, clothing and currency, valued at several thousand pounds were seized.[6]

Sophie Alloway (third from right, front row) with some of her German policewomen and officers of the Hamburg Police, 1945. (Courtesy of the Barker Family collection)

One minor problem she encountered initially was persuading the German policewomen to wear uniform. Eventually, this was resolved when she designed an attractive navy blue and silver uniform that was tailor made for each person.

In 1948, Sophie was promoted to the rank of Public Safety Officer One. By this time there were 500 policewomen in the British Zone and 100 in the British Sector of Berlin, and of that total number, 100 were trained to operate in criminal investigations.

Through her deep sympathy and understanding of their problems, Sophie Alloway became well loved and respected by the German women and was received by them in their homes. These friendships endured, and in later years she was able to revisit them. When she returned to Britain at the end of 1948, she was given several parties, farewell presents, formal presentations and kind messages from all sorts of people, German and British. The one that touched her most was on the morning of her departure. Her driver came to take her to the port, and as she came out of her residence, she found a small deputation of Women Police and little children. They presented her with flowers and sprays of fern and the eldest child made a little speech thanking her for what she had done for all the sick and troubled people in Germany, and for the children.

On her return to Britain, Sophie was posted to the Women Police Branch at New Scotland Yard (A4) and took the rank of sub-divisional inspector, later being regraded to chief inspector. Her work here was largely administrative and organisational. In 1953 she was promoted to the rank of superintendent (grade one) and became responsible for Women Police, who at this stage had reached almost 300. When she joined in 1933, the women in the Metropolitan Police had numbered only about ninety.

In 1954, Superintendent Sophie Alloway was awarded the Queen's Police Medal for Distinguished Service – the first woman in the Commonwealth to receive it. Sir John Nott-Bower, Commissioner of the Police of the Metropolis, read the citation, speaking of Sophie's loyalty, courage, organisational ability, both during the Battle of Britain and when chosen for special duty in Germany from 1945 to 1948 to reorganise the German Women's Police Force. Germany was at that time in a state of chaos, and the Nazis had discouraged the employment of women in the public service. He spoke also of her unfailing devotion to duty.

As she went up to receive the medal from Lord Lieutenant, Field Marshal Viscount Alanbrooke KG, GCB, OM, GCVO, DSO, who was conducting the presentation on behalf of Her Majesty the Queen, the press cameramen rushed onto the stage. Her appearance was said to match her outstanding character: 'Tall, upright, immaculate in her navy-blue uniform with silver stars on her shoulder, a peaked cap edged with silver and wearing the Defence and Coronation Medals, she received loud applause.'[7]

Sophie resigned from the Metropolitan Police in 1959 when she reached the age of compulsory retirement, having served for almost twenty-six years. A letter written by her commanding officer said Miss Alloway, throughout her service, had been an excellent police officer, first as a uniformed constable and sergeant, then as an inspector during the war.

The work of women police lay principally among women and juveniles and in the prevention of delinquency and in social and moral welfare. Senior women officers had, therefore, to be fully informed, not only on law and police procedure, but also on all the organisations, both statutory and voluntary, concerned with welfare. She was deeply knowledgeable and genuinely interested in all matters concerning the position and welfare of women, the problems of teenagers and the safety and well-being of children. In addition to the Queen's Police Medal, she was also awarded the Defence Medal, Coronation Medal and the Police Long Service Medal during her career.

She returned to New Zealand in March 1959, settling in the town of Levin. Her youngest sister, Constance, was very pleased to see her, but thought she might find life back in New Zealand a little boring after the excitement of life in London and her experiences in post-war Germany. On the contrary, Sophie was pleased to be home and immediately took up many activities in the community. She joined the National Council of Women and was its national president for two years. It was during her term as president that she initiated the Meals-on-Wheels service, and was in charge of it for almost ten years. She was appointed a Justice of the Peace, and in that capacity also acted as a marriage conciliator. She was a delegate serving on the Horowhenua Road Safety Committee, an official visitor to the Levin Hospital and Training School and was involved with work among young offenders. She was also an avid theatregoer, a member of the Levin Little Theatre, and a very enthusiastic golfer.[8]

She was missed by her colleagues in both London and Germany. Some even made the long journey to New Zealand to visit her, and in later years she was able to revisit her policewomen friends in Germany. She felt that the constructive rehabilitation work she did there was the most important she had achieved. Sophie was a woman who made many contributions to community life in London and in New Zealand. She died in Levin in August 1975, at the age of 76.

PW CHIEF INSPECTOR JESSIE GREEN ALEXANDER

NOTTINGHAM CITY POLICE

ROBERT PHILLIPS AND TOM ANDREWS

Police Woman Inspector Jessie Green Alexander following her promotion in 1951.

THE DAUGHTER OF A MINER, Jessie Green Alexander was born at Woodside by Mauchline in the county of Ayrshire in Scotland on 1 August 1906,[1] long before women would even be considered for the role of constable. Jessie has previously been noted as a voluntary worker with the YMCA before choosing a career in the police. However, on her Nottingham City Police application form dated 7 February 1936, completed in her own immaculate and beautifully old-fashioned cursive handwriting, Miss Alexander provides her former employer as a Mr Montgomery of Dalmore by Mauchline in Scotland. As perhaps a sign of the times, she gives her length of employment as thirteen years, indicating that she took the job at the age of just 14. Her 'trade' is given as 'Hone', but whether this is a spelling error of 'home' (unlikely, given the immaculate and pristine nature of her handwriting, suggestive of the care she took of the application form), or relates to 'honing' of metals (essentially sanding them down for use in engines and similar) is unclear.[2] It is even more ambiguous on her police service card where she is described as a 'Hone Marker'.[3]

The final question at the end of the application form asks potential recruits: 'What are you most proficient in?' Her short reply is somewhat insightful towards either the role of women at the time or alternatively what Jessie anticipated the 'correct' answer to be – 'Shorthand and typing'.[4] Similarly telling is the nature of the pre-printed application form itself. Every single pronoun thereon relates to 'him' or 'his', and also includes details of age and height requirements as well as pay scales for constables. The physical requirements have been amended in fountain pen to relate to women ('twenty – twenty-eight years' to 'twenty-two – thirty-five years'; and taller than 5ft 10in to 5ft 4in) and the pay scales simply crossed out; but then each masculine pronoun has been carefully scored through and amended to its feminine form in the finer cursive handwriting consistent with Jessie's.[5] Whether it was Jessie herself that made these changes it may never be possible to know, but the consistency of handwriting tends towards that conclusion. If that is the case, it is already a measure of the lady who would go on to blaze a trail through the ranks of the Nottingham City Police.

It was perhaps a combination of this meticulousness and the incredible neatness of her handwriting on the application form that attracted the eye of Nottingham's Chief Constable of the time, Captain Athelstan Popkess. He was a man known for being a stickler and perhaps a perfectionist with a rigid sense of discipline,[6] and also not one for necessarily valuing the role of women in policing at this time.[7] Jessie's beautiful cursive script would have no doubt stood her apart from other potential candidates and drawn the eye of the Chief Constable as he was reviewing applications.

Policing was obviously a calling for Jessie, as while applying to Nottingham City she also applied for service to the Glasgow Police in Scotland, being placed on a reserve list. Fortunately, Glasgow's loss would certainly prove to be Nottingham's gain. The tall Scot moved to Nottingham from her native Ayrshire, and only a month after submitting her application form was sworn into service as Police Woman Constable '3' on 9 March 1936 in the Nottingham City Police, joining just three other female officers in the ranks. Her collar number signified her as a replacement for WPC Winifred Hilton, who had resigned from the force on 31 January 1936, triggering the recruitment process for which Jessie was applying.[8] She would go on to become only the second female police officer in the City Police to serve for a total of thirty years.

At the time she joined, Jessie's shifts would have alternated between a week of eight-hour days from 9 a.m. to 6 p.m. with one hour's unpaid lunch break, and an eight-hour split shift of 9 a.m. to 1 p.m. and returning 5 p.m. to 9 p.m. Uniform was provided by the force, excluding footwear, for which the women received an allowance.[9]

Jessie seemingly got on very well with her select band of female compatriots because after only two years with the force she served as a bridesmaid to May Gabbitas, one of her three colleagues. May, who was the daughter of the Leicester City Police Deputy Chief Constable, had been serving with Nottingham for four years, when on 1 October 1938 she married Sergeant Charles Richardson, also of Nottingham City Police.[10] As was the expectation at the time, her marriage meant that May had to resign from the force. This was certainly the first marriage between a policewoman and policeman within Nottingham, and quite possibly one of the first nationally. It was so sensational that it made national news, appearing in the *Daily Mail* alongside a photograph of the happy couple.[11] Marriage was not for Jessie, however, who was to remain married to her career; she would have been unable to serve her full thirty years had she taken vows with a man.

Jessie's City Police service record describes her as 5ft 9½in in height with a fresh complexion, hazel eyes and dark brown hair. Her height was no doubt a key factor in her gaining employment in the Nottingham force, Captain Popkess being particularly renowned for his penchant towards employing tall officers.[12] Initially being posted to the City 'D' Division, she remained in the rank of constable until being promoted to the rank of acting police woman sergeant on 4 July 1945 shortly after the end of the Second World War.

During the war years, PW Constable Alexander received her first commendation on 18 March 1941 from Nottingham magistrates, who were seemingly impressed with her ability in the arrest of a male offender who was charged with stealing silver. Shortly after her promotion to acting PW sergeant, a further commendation was awarded by Nottingham magistrates in December 1945 for 'her astuteness in arresting a reputed [male] thief loitering with intent to commit a felony'. She received yet another commendation on 16 December 1948 for the arrest of a known criminal, 'a man who is of a violent nature', who was subsequently charged for loitering with intent to commit a felony in the city.[13] The suspect was arrested by the unarmed and alone PW Sergeant Alexander, who along with other female officers at the time was equipped only with a police whistle and her wit – handcuffs and truncheon being issued only to their male constables. These commendations show that Jessie was not simply involved in the policing of women and children, as is so often typical of her peers. Instead, these awards show that she was both willing and able to deal with crimes of all nature and give a good account of herself in confrontational situations.

The life of an officer in the Nottingham City Police was somewhat different to that of many other forces at the time, with Chief Constable Popkess placing a keen onus on the physical prowess of his staff. Constables were expected to participate in organised sports and were given time on-duty to undertake this, as well as being expected to participate off-duty. Policewomen were no exception, with one recalling later that she was required to attend the city's Victoria Baths every Sunday morning for swimming and life-saving practice, during which they were paired with a male officer.[14] Jessie would have been required to maintain her physical fitness and be able to 'hold her own' in conflict situations just as her male counterparts would have. Jessie's peers also recall arresting men, and how the detainees would occasionally be heckled for 'being arrested by a woman'.[15]

On 14 February 1946, Acting PW Sergeant Alexander was confirmed in rank which, along with other officer promotions, was mentioned in the *Nottingham Evening Post* on that date.[16] Her promotion also saw her transferred to CID (Policewomen's Department), becoming the first female officer to receive instruction on a Detective Training Course. This milestone course, which cost the force the princely sum of £7, was held at Wakefield between 25 February and 13 April 1946.[17] Having a policewoman attached to CID was not uncommon at the time, with her colleague Ethel Davies having served in that department until 1944.[18] Indeed, their role on the department seems to have been welcomed and encouraged, assisting investigations by undertaking the expected duties of policewomen at the time, 'making enquiries and taking statements in cases where women and children were concerned'.[19] In the force's annual report of 1920, the Chief Constable Lt Col Frank Brook wrote: 'During the year 3 Policewomen have been appointed. They are proving very useful and with added experience the scope of their work and sphere of usefulness will be enlarged.'[20] This was followed up the subsequent year with a statement suggesting that the 'sphere of usefulness' had come to fruition, and 'the 2 Policewomen employed continue to do most useful work, their value depending not so much on patrol duty as enquiry and observation work'.[21] By 1924, Brook reported in a letter to the Committee on Women Police that the expected role of women was 'observation work in connection with detection of crime, betting and licensing offences. Taking statements from women and children in cases of indece[n]cy. Enquiries in connection with women and children. *Patrol duty on special occasions* [emphasis added].'[22]

It therefore does not seem surprising that Jessie was to spend a significant portion of her career in CID, as uniformed patrol by women was reserved solely for 'special occasions'. No doubt the impact of a mere four women additionally patrolling was not felt to be necessary, except as a conversation starter and for the visual impact as a change from normality. It was perhaps Jessie's forthright manner which led to her being put on the official training course, whereas Ethel had not been. It is easy to imagine her asking very blunt direct questions of her senior officers as to why her male counterparts were receiving this additional relevant training and she was not.

Her dedication and hard work continued, and promotion to PW inspector came on 14 March 1951, along with command of the Policewomen's Department, which Jessie formally instigated herself on 7 May that same year.[23] She replaced her predecessor Ethel Davies, who had retired as the force's first PW inspector on 30 September 1949, there seemingly having been no rush to appoint her replacement for some eighteen months.

There can be no doubt that the strict discipline of Captain Popkess had rubbed off on Jessie, as she too is recalled as being a stickler for standards. On one occasion, PW 18 Mary Needham recalled walking into Policewoman Inspector Alexander's office at the City Police Headquarters and failing to salute as was required. Jessie promptly made an appointment for the young policewoman constable to see no less than the Chief Constable himself, whereupon she was promptly informed, 'If you do not alter your ways you can go and exploit your talents elsewhere'.[24]

This was not to be the only example of her being a strict disciplinarian, with Mary further recalling an incident in 1955 when Her Majesty the Queen was due to visit Nottingham. Jessie was in charge of ensuring that her

Nottingham City Policewomen's Department, 1951. Jessie Alexander (front row centre).

subordinates of the Policewomen's Department were turned out impeccably for duty. Poor Mary was reprimanded by her formidable inspector for 'allowing [her] ears to protrude out from under [her] hat too much', and as a result was removed from duty for the royal visit![25] Mary was not alone, either. Describing Jessie as 'firm but fair', PW Joan Siddals recalls that 'being found improperly dressed would result in swift comment from Miss Alexander'. On one occasion, after having her hair styled, Joan found to her absolute horror that her police hat would not fit over the new hairdo, and as a result, 'prayed I didn't have to go to HQ before 5pm so she wouldn't see me!'[26] No doubt she would have been sent back to the hairdressers to have it restyled more appropriately.

During 1952, PW Inspector Alexander received the Queen's Coronation Medal on the accession of Her Majesty Queen Elizabeth II to the throne. During this time, Miss Alexander is recorded as being involved in all aspects of the Policewomen's Department. As well as proving her ability at arresting known violent men, she was well respected by members of the public, who often visited her with their wayward children in order for her to give 'good solid advice or a very stiff talking too if she felt necessary'. In an interview in 1966, 'Miss Alex', as some of her officers called her (but never to her face), said, 'I would try to explain where a girl was making her mistakes and tell her what she should and should not do.'[27] This nurturing tendency extended to looking after the force's police cadets too. Val Gant, who started as a cadet in 1965 and ultimately retired as an inspector herself in 1997, recalls that Jessie treated the female cadets 'very much like her flock'. Although she too remembers that Miss Alexander was 'very careful to ensure that her PW cadets wore minimal make-up, their stockings were straight and uniform immaculate'.[28]

In apparent expectation of primarily dealing with women and children, who seemingly by virtue of their age and gender were more liable to be overcome and faint (although it would be felt that Jessie's own temperament should have suggested otherwise to her), PW Inspector Alexander ordered that her policewomen were also to carry smelling salts in their force-issue handbags.[29]

It was during her time as inspector that Jessie was to oversee a significant expansion within the Policewomen's Department. The growth of the city of Nottingham after the Second World War had been considerable, especially with the building of the Clifton and Broxtowe 'council estates' under the new national social housing policies. As a result of this expansion, the Chief Constable applied to the Home Office for an increase in the authorised strength of the City Police, including numbers of policewomen, which was granted. The Policewomen's Department was permitted to expand nearly threefold, from an establishment of thirteen in 1953 to thirty-six in 1954, comprising one inspector, five sergeants and thirty constables.[30]

The height of Miss Alexander's career came in 1958, when on 9 July she was promoted to Police Woman Chief Inspector, becoming the first female officer to reach this rank in the history of the Nottinghamshire Police (at this time still separate County and City forces). This promotion was announced to the public on 10 July 1958 in the *Nottingham Guardian Journal* newspaper, which announced: 'The Home Office have decided that Nottingham should have a woman Chief Inspector, which will be the top rank for women.'[31] In this same year, she was awarded the Police Long Service and Good Conduct Medal after twenty-two years' unblemished service. During this time, PW Chief Inspector Alexander had seen her department grow from four Home Office authorised female officers in 1936 to an establishment of thirty-five by her promotion to chief inspector. They now also had their own specific department, thanks to her instigation, gaining them far more recognition than they previously had as mere 'attachments' to the CID or being called out to deal with arrested women and children.

There was still not equality with their male counterparts, however. Policewomen were only paid 90 per cent of the wages of policemen, albeit they did not work night shifts; their duties by this time being either days (7 a.m. to 3 p.m.) or evenings (3 p.m. to 11 p.m.). They did, however, operate an on-call rota covering the intervening hours, where they could be called back to duty in the event that an 'incident involving women or children should arise and a female officer needed'.[32] There were also still at this time 'police matrons' who would remain with female prisoners, being collected from their homes by the policewomen simply as and when required.[33] These were often wives of serving police officers or older women who had some connection to the police, but who were not warranted officers and therefore not subject to fixed wages or duties.

For her work with the Nottingham City Police, Policewoman Chief Inspector Jessie Alexander was awarded the British Empire Medal (BEM) on 8 June 1963 on the order of the Queen in Her Majesty's Birthday Honours list. The award was announced in the *London Gazette* on 31 May 1963.[34] The medal itself was presented to a proud Miss Alexander the following month on behalf of Her Majesty at Nottingham City Council House by the Lord Lieutenant of Nottinghamshire, Brigadier Sir Robert Laycock.

It is interesting to note, however, that Jessie's personnel record shows that the incorrect details were added to the file by hand, and actually state that she was awarded the higher award of Most Excellent Order of the British Empire (OBE).[35] No doubt taking their lead from her police personnel file, some publications and private works also refer to the award of an OBE. However, there is no official record of the OBE award in the *London Gazette*, the official publication that meticulously lists all official honours and awards.

Nottinghamshire Police's first female chief inspector retired from the police on 8 March 1966, after a distinguished and nationally honoured career, with a pension of £714 2s 6d per annum. She decided to leave the hustle of the city and returned to her native Scotland and to Ayr, living with her Uncle George in the bungalow she had commissioned for her retirement. The Nottingham Watch Committee compiled a special report on the impending retirement of PW Chief Inspector Alexander for their meeting of 12 January 1966, detailing the highlights of her career; not standard practice for most officers.[36] She was to retire a mere two years prior to the amalgamation of the Nottingham City Police with the surrounding County force; a move at which she would no doubt have felt most aggrieved, in line with many of her peers,[37] given the especially high standing of the Nottingham City force nationally at the time.[38]

A relaxing retirement was not to be for the formidable 'Miss Alex', and it was certainly not to be devoid of hard work. As with the early pioneers such as Margaret Damer Dawson and Katherine Scott, she saw herself as being much more of a social worker. The functions of policewomen at the time in dealing primarily with women and children neatly transposed itself into that role. Perhaps this was a circular result, given the views of those early pioneers into what the role of women in policing should be, and thus it bore to fruition. On finishing her employment, Jessie stated her intention of putting to use her many years of policing and advice to others to help those less fortunate in her native county. The *Evening Post and News* reported an interview on 1 February 1966, quoting Jessie as saying of her retirement: 'There's always work for people who want it. It won't be a lazy life by any means.' Any relaxation time that she did enjoy involved her passion for spending time in her garden, and specifically growing roses.

During her career she had served through and presided over the most significant period of change for women in policing since their first introduction. The during- and post-war expansion of policewomen and associated roles for women in the police saw an increased realisation of both their importance and abilities. It paved the way for an irreversible change in the gender mix of policing, and it was women of unquestionable abilities such as Jessie Alexander who demonstrated their full potential. She undoubtedly had to adapt her ways of working to fit in with the male-dominated workplace, but similarly she made the role her own, introducing the Policewomen's Department with Nottingham, ensuring women received suitable training on the CID, and all the while adopting an almost motherly, if somewhat harsh, persona of her charges – subordinates or 'customers'.

She retired Police Woman Chief Inspector Jessie Green Alexander, British Empire Medal, and died aged 80 in 1986, being laid to rest at Low Coylton cemetery, about 3 miles from where she was born. She was a true police trailblazer, respected by those who served alongside her and her adopted city, to which she devoted her life.

SISLIN FAY ALLEN

BRITAIN'S FIRST BLACK FEMALE POLICE OFFICER

ADAM PICKIN AND TOM ANDREWS

Sislin Fay Allen at her passing out parade. Metropolitan Police publicity photo.

The courage that trailblazers like her showed in joining the police service allowed others to follow a career in policing.[1]

SISLIN FAY ALLEN WAS BORN in St Catherine, Jamaica, on 20 March 1939,[2] the second youngest in a family of ten children. Tragically, her mother died when she was just 13 years old and she was raised by her aunt, who was a judge. After leaving school, Sislin subsequently cared for her ill father until his passing in 1962, developing her abilities in the care field.

Having no parents left to care for, she emigrated to the United Kingdom as part of the Windrush generation, following the British government's recruitment appeals advertising a shortage of nurses. Upon arrival in the UK, she settled in Thornton Heath, Croydon, London. Her initial thoughts on arriving were simply that Britain was 'cold'!

After arriving in the United Kingdom, Allen trained and became a geriatric nurse, successfully applying for a position at Croydon's Queen's Hospital, where she worked for five years. However, since childhood she had aspired to join the police, saying it was a job she always wanted to do, and that if she ever had the opportunity to do it, she would. No doubt her interest in the legal process was heavily influenced by her aunt.

In 1968, at the age of 29, while looking through the *Daily Mail* newspaper on her lunchbreak, she noticed an advert looking for 'both male and female police officers'. Surprised, and thinking 'why not', she cut the advert out and put it in her pocket, telling herself that she would apply as soon as she had the time. As soon as she got home, she finished the application and submitted it without telling her family; she didn't want to tell anyone unless she was successful in her application.

At this time there were no Black female officers in the police at all nationally.[3] Due to this, when she had completed her application form and before posting them back, Sislin added a postscript at the bottom, writing simply 'I am a black woman', as 'I did not want that if I had succeeded and when they saw me, they did not know I was black'.[4]

A few weeks later she received confirmation that she had been successful and invited for interview, shocking her husband and two children when she broke the news.

Mrs Allen attended the famous Metropolitan Police Training School at Peel House, Hendon, where she was the only Black, Asian or Minority Ethnic (BAME) person on her induction. She had joined the police only just less than a year after Norwell Roberts – Britain's first Black male police officer in the modern era, and the first since John Kent's dismissal from Carlisle Police in 1844.[5]

'On the selection day there were so many people there, the hall was filled with the young men. There were ten women, and I was the only Black person [of any gender].' She remembers thinking that she didn't have a chance.[6]

While being interviewed, she was asked why she wanted to leave her nursing profession and become a police officer. She replied it was what she had always wanted to do for a career.

After successfully completing the literacy and numeracy entrance exams and her medical, Mrs Allen was told she had passed the selection process and would be posted to Croydon's Fell Road Police Station, so she could be stationed near her family.[7]

It was not until the conclusion of her passing-out parade that she realised the full scope of her achievement, recalling: 'I nearly broke a leg trying to run away from reporters'. Allen told *Black History Month Magazine* in 2015: 'I realised then that I was a history-maker, but I didn't set out to make history – I just wanted a change of direction.'[8]

Her acceptance at the time shocked many, with one friend having previously told her, 'Oh they wouldn't accept you, they don't accept Black people in the [police] force.'

Some sectors of the public tried to ensure that Sislin's career as the first female BAME police officer was over almost before it had begun. She received a torrent of hate mail in the form of threatening and abusive letters, which occasionally made her want to quit before she even started on the beat, telling *The Guardian* at the time: 'for every nice letter received there had been others full of abuse … I do not know whether I will stick with this job or not … it is not an easy decision to make'.[9] This was compounded by the fact that she also received significant abuse from her own community, who often perceived the police as 'the enemy'.[10] Thankfully, it appears that her superiors soon got wise to this and withheld the hate mail. 'They gave me the good [letters],' she explained, but 'they never, ever gave me the bad ones. They told me about them but they never showed me because they thought it would distress me and maybe they thought I would resign.'[11] Unfortunately, her training had coincided with Conservative MP Enoch Powell's infamous 'Rivers of Blood' speech on 28 April 1968, berating immigration from the Commonwealth, no doubt encouraging and emboldening a significant proportion of the vitriolic correspondence that Sislin received.

Despite the abuse, Sislin started her first day in Croydon, describing it as 'daunting', with members of the public stopping to stare, and some coming up and congratulating her. She patrolled in the new women's police uniform which had just recently been created by top fashion designer and stylist to royalty Norman Hartnell, in 1967.[12]

While certain members of the public were openly hostile towards Mrs Allen, her comrades in blue were not so. 'My colleagues were very accepting

– in Croydon really and truly. I didn't have any problems there. I just did my work.'[13]

After a year or so working at Croydon, Sislin was posted to the Missing Persons Bureau at Scotland Yard, Police Headquarters. After her time there she transferred to Norbury Police Station.

In 1972, Sislin left the Metropolitan Police, handing in her warrant card because of family commitments, and returning to her birth country of Jamaica with her husband and their children. Upon arriving in Jamaica, she was given a congratulatory letter from the country's prime minister.

While she may have left Britain and the Metropolitan Police, she didn't stop policing altogether; instead, she chose to continue her career in the Jamaican Police Force. Working as a police officer in Jamaica wasn't without its own problems, either, with Sislin later saying: 'I discovered doing the job [became] very troublesome again right here …There has at all times been a stigma hooked up to the police – individuals have their very own concepts, however all of that's not warranted.'[14]

The scope of her achievement has been felt ever since, with countless BAME women following in her footsteps, including Marlene Strachan, the first Black female officer to complete thirty years' service.[15] 'There is still a long way to go, but at the end of the day, I was glad I was able to inspire so many people to take up the challenge,' Allen said in 2020, a year before her death. 'They are all doing a good job.'[16] Today still, however, women make up only 30 per cent of the Metropolitan Police strength, and only 15 per cent of those (3.43 per cent of the total police officer workforce) identify as being of BAME heritage.[17] There is clearly still a long way to go to reach parity.

On 4 December 2020, the National Black Police Association bestowed the lifetime achievement award on Mrs Allen, in recognition of her pioneering service in the face of such hostility and adversity. At around this same time, Policing Minister Kit Malthouse MP commented that Allen was owed 'a debt of gratitude for her service' because she was 'an inspiration and paved the way for the many female Black officers who have come after her'.[18] This was a view shared by Commander Dr Alison Heydari, the Metropolitan Police's highest ranking BAME female officer, who stated, 'Sislin's achievements mean a great deal to me actually. She paved the way for black females – and today in the Met and in policing we have so many black females and it all started with Sislin.'[19]

About her own achievements, Mrs Allen instead describes herself as an ordinary mother and optimist. 'The journey for me has been memorable but I think we still have a very long way to go, but at the end of the day, I am glad that I was able to inspire so many people to take up the challenge.'[20] Even in late 2020, following the shocking murder by an American police officer of George Floyd, an unarmed Black man, and the resultant Black Lives Matter movement, Mrs Allen remained proud of both her own service and today's officers, stating: 'there has always been a stigma attached to the police – people have their own ideas but all of that is not warranted. It's a very worthwhile job that I would recommend at any time to anyone.' Although, she does consider more work is required to bridge the gap between the police and the Black youth.[21]

Sislin sadly passed away on 5 July 2021 at her home address in Ocho Rios, Jamaica, aged 83. She is survived by her two daughters, Lorna and Paula.

Allen's legacy cannot be overstated, with her image being displayed on London Underground stations in 2019, on the 100-year anniversary of women joining the Metropolitan Police, as part of a recruitment campaign. She has clearly made significant impressions on those who have followed in her footsteps, as evidenced by the quote from Commander Dr Heydari. As a statement made by the Metropolitan Police upon news of her death reads: 'We are grateful for your service Sislin, you paved the way for so many others.'[22]

DCI JACKIE MALTON

'YOU EITHER FOLLOW THE CROWD OR STAND OUT AND DO THE RIGHT THING'

KATE HALPIN

'WHY DON'T YOU FUCK OFF, you cunt. I'm not working with a woman!' It was not the welcome to the Flying Squad that Detective Sergeant Jackie Malton had expected from Phil, the detective sergeant who had been assigned to work with her when she became the first woman to join the Rotherhithe office in south-east London in 1981. Over the next six months he would go out of his way to undermine her and make her working life as difficult as possible. Jackie could not know it at the time, but her encounter with this officer would ultimately change the course of her life and career beyond the Met.

While it was clear that she was not wanted as a woman by many on 'the Squad', that encounter would ultimately contribute to improving the representation of women in policing and the Criminal Investigation Department (CID) specifically, when Lynda La Plante used Jackie as her police advisor on a drama she was writing in the early 1990s, taking all those negative experiences to develop the character of Detective Chief Inspector (DCI) Jane Tennison and add to her storyline for the first series of *Prime Suspect*. Jane Tennison is frequently cited as one the most popular television detectives both in the UK and abroad, but there would have been no Tennison without the input of Jackie Malton. Jackie is at pains, however, to point out that while everything that happened to Tennison in *Prime Suspect* happened to her, her experiences were over the course of over twenty years rather than two hours!

Given the huge strides made in the representation of women across all ranks and roles in policing, it is easy to forget the position that women in the CID found themselves in during the early 1990s when *Prime Suspect* was first screened. In 2012, Professor Jennifer Brown and Professor Frances Heidensohn provided the context of the environment in the CID nationally at the time: 'At the time the programme was screened there was one woman serving as a DCI (outside of the MPS) compared to 347 men. There were no women serving as detective superintendent or detective chief superintendent.[1]

National workforce data figures breaking down numbers by detective status and rank are not available, but the Metropolitan Police Workforce Data report for April 2023 shows the transformation in the representation of women across all ranks, but especially within the detective ranks. It is notable that at the rank of detective constable the gender split is now nearly 50:50.

Police Officer	Overall Total		
	Total (FTE)	Male (FTE)	Female (FTE)
Commander and above	32.50	26.50	6.00
Chief Superintendent	27.00	20.00	7.00
Detective Chief Superintendent	26.00	17.00	9.00
Superintendent	99.00	78.00	21.00
Detective Superintendent	115.29	79.00	36.29
Chief Inspector	223.96	180.00	43.96
Detective Chief Inspector	210.30	149.80	60.50
Inspector	862.88	686.09	176.79
Detective Inspector	508.19	368.75	139.44
Police Sergeant	3,413.77	2,708.34	705.43
Detective Sergeant	1,576.62	1,105.77	470.85
Police Constable	21,938.67	15,589.27	6,349.40
Detective Constable	5,488.82	2,937.13	2,551.68
Police Officer Total	34,523.01	23,945.66	10,577.35

The change in gender representation cannot be attributed to just one thing, but there is no doubt that the screening of *Prime Suspect* contributed to more women joining both the police and seeking a career in the CID. 'If you can see it, you can be it' is the oft-used quote to inspire people to take on new challenges. In the Metropolitan Police (the Met) in 1992, very few female colleagues would have seen a female DCI – or too many other women supervisors at all, for that matter – in the workplace, but the fact they could see a senior female detective on the television suggested that they at least existed. Vanessa Jardine, the recently appointed Chief Constable of Northumbria

Police, wrote a blog in February 2023 to mark LGBTQ+ History Month, and she was very clear what led to her interest in a police career: 'Growing up, there were three women in my life who really got me to think about a career in policing. I'll never forget their names: Christine Cagney, Mary Beth-Lacey and Jane Tennison (I bet you were thinking I was going to say something much more profound!)'[2]

Jackie's welcome to the Flying Squad was not dissimilar (but definitely more hostile) to the welcome that Lilian Wyles BEM had received sixty years earlier, as the first woman to join the CID in the Metropolitan Women Police Department. Lilian wrote in her memoirs that women were not initially welcomed by the men of the CID:

> Though policewomen had been existence for nearly three years, their duties had been bounded exclusively by the uniform branch. They did not cross the threshold of the CID during that time and were never invited to do so. The officers of that exclusive department barely recognised the existence of women in their midst. When they met them in the passage or on the stairs the CID officer would respond to the policewoman's smile of greeting with the curtest of curt nods. If they thought about them at all, which I much doubt, it was only to express sympathy with their uniformed brothers, who were suffering from this feminine infliction.[3]

Nevertheless, Lilian persisted and joined the CID in 1922, where she would remain for the next twenty-seven years until her retirement. She attributed this feat to her upbringing: 'The years of well-ordered childhood and young girlhood bore fruit when I stood alone among to three to four thousand men who formed the personnel of the Criminal Investigation Department.'[4]

Her early days in the CID certainly did not auger well for a long-term career within the CID:

> I was not wanted in the CID. I was a sop thrown to those who had demanded that woman should be appointed to deal with the child, the girl and the woman in all cases of sexual offences … Here then, was I, a lone woman in a camp of, if not hostile, at least indifferent men attached to Scotland Yard … I had just weathered three years of storm and stress with the uniformed women. Suddenly I had the feeling I could bear no more. The prospect of another struggle was too much for me. I sat down to compose a letter of resignation from the police.[5]

Thankfully fate was to intervene, and Lilian never submitted that letter of resignation. She instead went on to pave the way for the generations of women who followed her into the CID; something that was highlighted when the Metropolitan Police celebrated the centenary of women joining in 2019. She was full of optimism for the future of female detectives at the end of her service:

> The year 1949 saw women firmly entrenched in the Criminal Investigation Department of the Metropolitan Police; from a lone woman officer there is now a permitted strength of forty-eight. The Special Branch also has two women attached to it … In every way the women officers of the CID and Special Branch are trusted and treated in the same manner as the men.[6]

Thirty-three years after Lilian retired so full of optimism, how then did Jackie Malton find herself being given such a hostile reception from a fellow officer to what was, and still is regarded as one of policing's elite teams? And how did this and subsequent encounters change Jackie's life in so many ways?

EARLY YEARS AND JOINING LEICESTER POLICE

Jackie was born in Lincoln in 1951, the year Lilian Wyles published her memoir. She initially grew up in Leicester with her older brother and sister, moving to Grimsby aged 14 as a result of her father's job in the newspaper industry. In her teens, Jackie recognised that she was gay and would not be able to conform to the societal expectations of the 1960s by getting married, having children and being supported by a husband. She recognised that she needed a career that would allow her to support herself. Her favourite subject at school was history – she was always curious to learn why things happened. She had hoped to go to university and pursue a career with the probation service, but it was not to be at that time, given her predicted A-level results. Although her maternal grandfather had served in the Metropolitan Police during the First World War, it was not something that was discussed as a career option.

When her hopes of being a probation officer were dashed because of her predicted A-level grades, she looked to policing and returned to Leicester as a police cadet. The cadet programme acted as a kind of access programme to the police force (as it was called then). She joined the cadets in late 1969, where she undertook the same training alongside the male police cadets, with the only difference being the expectation that the women cadets made the tea! Her tutor was John Peacock, who she describes as a gentle and supportive man who treated the women no differently to the men. It was he who encouraged Jackie to pursue an application for the regular police.

She joined the Leicester and Rutland Women's Police Department as a probationary constable on her 19th birthday in July 1970. It was still some time before the integration of the separate men's and women's police departments, but it was being discussed and on the horizon. Her initial training was undertaken at the regional police training college at Ryton-on-Dunsmore (now home to the College of Policing). The training was also integrated, and it was only when she returned to Leicester at the completion of the three-month residential course that she had her first experience of 'segregation', as the Leicester Women's Police Department was a separate entity from the main police force. The department was overseen by Superintendent Hilda Parkin, who Jackie describes as a fearsome woman who scared her witless! The women officers dealt with offences committed on and by women and children. They also maintained a card index of all those they came into contact with, building up an encyclopaedic knowledge of the local community. Jackie also built up a good rapport with the local prostitutes, started developing her own informants, and made some decent arrests for impactful crimes, leading to an early attachment with the Drug and Vice Squad while still in the early part of her two-year probationary period.

The integration of the two departments was on the horizon as a result of the Equal Pay Act 1970, which would be enacted along with the Sex Discrimination Act in 1975. The Labour government had refused to allow an exemption from the legislation for the police,[7] and a number of the more forward-thinking chief constables around the country acted in advance of the 1975 deadline to integrate the separate male and female departments. Sir Robert Mark, Commissioner of the Met, did this in 1973.[8] Likewise, Alan Goodson, the Chief Constable of Leicester, also took proactive steps to integrate his female department with the men. One of his first initiatives was to train women to be advanced vehicle response drivers alongside the men, in effect bringing integration to the traffic department. Jackie was selected for the training and undertook an intense three-week course to drive the new fleet of Triumph Dolomites. At the conclusion of the course she was partnered with Doreen Newton, and they would patrol together, responding to a whole range of calls, not just those normally assigned to the Women's Department.

Not all of the women working in the separate Women's Police Department were as keen on integration as others. Some felt their specialist skills and knowledge would be lost and others simply did not want to perform the same duties as the men. Police Sergeant Ethel Bush, another key woman in police history when she became the first policewoman to be awarded the George Medal in 1953, was interviewed by the Met's in-house publication to mark her retirement in September 1971 (where her medal and place in history was shockingly never mentioned). She did not hold back on her view on the potential impact of integration: 'I understand that men and women might be integrated. Well that's alright as long as they don't expect us to get up at six o'clock in the morning. If they do the Women Police will decrease in numbers overnight.'[9]

Ethel also expressed her concern about loss of the women's individuality and specialist skills. When full integration did come a few years later, Alan Goodson recognised this by retaining a small number of policewomen in a women-only special enquiry unit that worked alongside the specialist social workers and probation officers.

Having been confirmed as a substantive police constable, Jackie started looking to the future. She took her sergeant's exam in 1973 with only three years' service. At that time the scores were ranked, and she was placed sixth nationally (for both men and women). The top 200 candidates were invited to apply for the national Special Course, the fast-track promotion scheme for promising officers, but it was not to be. However, not long after this disappointment Leicester and Rutland Constabulary advertised for women sergeants in the *Police Review*, and she applied. She knew that Superintendent Parkin found it ridiculous that she was even considering applying and was clearly not keen on the idea. The same could also be said of Chief Constable Goodson, who during the interview process suggested that she was too young and too inexperienced for promotion at that time. She responded that he was one of the youngest chief constables in the country (he was appointed Chief Constable in 1972), and a short time later found herself as Woman Police Sergeant Malton and posted to Syston in north Leicester.

After two years in uniform, she applied to become a detective sergeant within the CID. Not long after taking this post, she found herself as the lone female officer in a fully integrated CID office. She earnt the respect of her male colleagues and thrived through hard work and determination. In 1977, she passed the inspector's promotion examination and made a temporary uniform inspector in another part of Leicester, which she did not enjoy as much as her CID posting.

Her career was clearly flourishing, and she had been able to buy her first house for £8,500 in 1974, which required her father's permission at that time. She kept her private life very distinct from her professional life. She recognised she was gay and attracted to women, but she felt a degree of shame and dared not tell her parents, fearing their reaction. Outside of work she played a lot of sport, including for the force ladies' hockey team. It was sport that would take her to London and the Metropolitan Police, and set her on the path to that fateful first day on the Flying Squad. The Met ladies' hockey team came to Leicester in 1978 and Jackie started a relationship with one of the Met players, both travelling between their respective homes in London and Leicester to see each other. Over time her new circle of London-based friends suggested she transfer to London to make it easier to see her new partner and experience a different style of policing. She sought out the advice of her then chief superintendent, who was honest enough to say that Leicester Police were not entirely sure what to do with her and there was no guarantee of a permanent inspector's post in the near future.

LONDON CALLING!

Jackie's application to transfer to the Metropolitan Police was accepted, and she moved to south-west London to live with her partner in April 1979. The Met were happy to accept her as a uniform sergeant in the first instance, but did not recognise the inspector's qualification she held from Leicester because, as she was to soon find out, things were very different in London. Like many transferees into the Met, she was routinely referred to as a 'carrot cruncher', which was somewhat ironic given that her first Met posting was to the outer London borough of Richmond-upon-Thames, which had enclaves that would have been far more tranquil than some of the parts of Leicester she had policed. Her fellow supervisors would allude to her 'county ways', given that she would not cut corners, always being professional and methodical. She found the Met operating culture quite *laissez faire* in comparison. She felt the police in London were more detached from their communities, and found it alien that at a set time on each shift the whole team would return en masse to the police station for a cup of tea, whereas previously she had cultivated a network of tea spots on Leicester beats to develop relationships and pick up intelligence.

The only other woman of a supervisory rank at her new police division was an inspector called Elizabeth Neville. Elizabeth had been selected for the Home Office Fast Track scheme that Jackie had been unsuccessful at in her interview a few years earlier, but Jackie acknowledged that Elizabeth was clearly destined for the top, given her abilities. (Elizabeth would go on to be the second female chief constable after Pauline Clare when she was appointed Chief Constable of Wiltshire in 1997, awarded the Queen's Police Medal in 1996, and made a Dame Commander in 2003.) Jackie and Elizabeth would occasionally patrol together, as many sergeants and inspectors did, but the senior management intervened to separate them, saying that it was not appropriate for two female supervisors to work together. This seems bizarre now, given that Jackie had been allowed to patrol with Doreen Newton when they were posted to the response cars in Leicester and that female officers would have patrolled in pairs when the police departments were segregated.

Within eighteen months of joining the Met, Jackie transferred back into the CID as a detective sergeant and moved to another south-west London police station. It was from here on in that she would start to gain those different experiences her friends had promised her if she transferred to the Met. In the next few years she would be involved in the investigation of the New Cross Fire, the ensuing Brixton Riots, the disappearance and murder of a young boy on the day of the royal wedding in July 1981, and receive that infamous welcome to the Flying Squad and promotion to West End Central Police Station, where she experienced some of the darkest times of her career, but which would all go into creating one of television's most revered police characters.

No sooner had she settled to life as a detective sergeant in local CID than she was told to go Brockley Police Station in south-east London, where she was to be seconded to the major inquiry team that had been set up to investigate the death of thirteen young Black people after a house party in New Cross on 18 January 1981. Many more partygoers had also received serious physical and psychological injuries. The police team was headed by Commander Graham Stockwell, someone that Jackie describes as her blueprint for leadership.

In 2021, Jackie discussed her role and thoughts about the matter as one of the police participants in *Uprising*, the BBC documentary directed by Sir Steve McQueen and James Rogan that marked the fortieth anniversary of the fire, examining its impact on policing and community relations.[10] The breakdown in the already strained relations between police and the local Black community as a result of the police handling of the New Cross Fire investigation, along with increasing tensions emanating from the increasing use of the 'sus laws' (which in essence allowed the police to stop and search anyone they 'suspected' of intending to commit an offence under Section 4 of the Vagrancy Act 1824), culminating in Operation Swamp – a five-day operation between 6–11 April which saw nearly 1,000 people stopped and searched and 100 arrested, and triggered the Brixton Riots.[11] Jackie was moved from the New Cross Fire team at Brockley to an investigation team based at Kennington Police Station, examining the crimes committed during the riots. All this time she was still on secondment from her south-west London CID team.

While these were obviously major enquiries for the Metropolitan Police, on 31 July 1981 she was recalled to assist in the investigation of Vishal

Mehrotra, an 8-year-old boy who had been reported missing and last been seen near his home in south-west London on the day of the royal wedding. Jackie was tasked by the detective superintendent to be the link between Vishal's family and the police team. In effect, she became the Family Liaison Officer some years before such a role became formally recognised, professionalised and accredited. It is a difficult and sensitive role, recognising that, in some cases, families and loved ones are involved in the disappearance of a victim and so an open and enquiring mind is required, while being sensitive to the situation. Sadly, some of Vishal's remains were found in woodland in Sussex in February 1982, and Jackie had to break the news to his family. Jackie co-wrote her own memoir, *The Real Prime Suspect –From the Beat to the Screen. My Life as a Female Detective*, which was published in August 2022. At that time, she wrote of this investigation:

> What none of us knew then, or when Vishal's remains were subsequently found, was that the person responsible for killing him would get away with it. I knew that Vishal would always be in my heart and in my mind, and that I would never give up hope that someday the perpetrator would be caught.[12]

Since publication of her book, she has been involved in a BBC Sounds podcast series on the case, *Vishal*,[13] made by Colin Campbell, the BBC reporter, which has led to Sussex Police reopening the investigation.[14]

In the early 1980s, Metropolitan Police officers were informed of their postings via the weekly *Police Orders*, and it was via that medium that Jackie learnt she was being posted to the Flying Squad office at Rotherhithe in south-east London. This was a prestigious posting to the team widely known as 'The Sweeney' – Sweeney Todd being the cockney rhyming slang for Flying Squad. The first Flying Squad had been established in 1919 as the 'Mobile Patrol experiment' by Sir Nevil Macready, the Commissioner.[15] That same year, women had first been allowed to join the Met by Sir Nevil after much lobbying. He finally agreed that they could join, and they would be an 'experiment in every sense' as well (there are no prizes for guessing which experiment he tried to discontinue).

The Sweeney had also been the name of the hugely successful ITV drama series that originally aired between 1975–78, starring John Thaw and Dennis Waterman as the fictional Detective Inspector Jack Regan and Detective Sergeant George Carter. Any viewers of the fifty-three episodes of the TV drama may well remember the absence of any female detectives of note. In the same issue of *Police Orders*, Richard, one of her fellow detective sergeants, was posted to Croydon Division. He told Jackie that there had obviously been a mistake, and she was actually going to Croydon and he was joining the Flying Squad. It was soon established that Commander Graham Stockwell was now in charge of the Squad and had personally requested her (the concept of applications for vacancies was some way off).

Given the introduction to her fellow sergeant that opened this chapter, it was clear that even if her colleagues knew the senior officer in charge had recruited her, this was not to provide her with any form of top cover. Such was her commitment to the role that she amicably parted company with her romantic partner, recognising that she would be working long and unsocial hours. It is hard to imagine any of her male colleagues at that time making the same decision with their wives or female partners. The Flying Squad at Rotherhithe made the portrayal of male police officers seen in the BCC drama series *Life on Mars* and *Ashes to Ashes* (which Jackie also advised on) seem quite tame in comparison. Jackie continued to experience hostile bullying from Phil; he nicknamed her 'the Tart'. She endeavoured to fit in with the culture of 'work hard, play hard' for her three years on the squad, even playing five-a-side football with her male colleagues.

The team quickly worked out her sexuality and she subsequently received multiple sex toys, along with the advice that what she needed was to find the right man and more besides, which at the time she laughed off even though she was hurting terribly. Team-building events mainly took place at the pub after any operation and after court cases, whatever the verdict. Six months after joining the team, she asked to see her detective chief inspector, as she could take no more of working with Phil and requested a new working partner. Her DCI agreed and the next two and a half years were some of the most enjoyable of her career, despite some of the compromises she had to make to fit in.

At the beginning of 1984, Jackie was promoted to detective inspector and posted to West End Central Police Station, or the 'Premier Division' (police division, not football league), as her chief superintendent liked to refer to it. As the name suggests, the division covered the West End of London including Mayfair and Soho. She was one of four detective inspectors reporting into DCI Stan Finch, with whom she had worked previously. Jackie arrived only a couple of years after the conclusion of the Operation Countryman investigation into widespread police corruption in the Met and City of London police forces, and much of the focus had been on the West End club and vice scene. Sir Robert Mark, the Met commissioner from 1972–77, said at the time it was his ambition 'to arrest more criminals than we employ'.[16] It was against this backdrop that she had her welcome chat to the division with Ted Stowe, her new chief superintendent. He set out his standards, including that none of his officers were to frequent any nightclubs without express prior permission.

If Jackie had been one of the very few female detectives across the entire Flying Squad, she was an even rarer entity as a female detective inspector. However, she recognised the responsibility she had as both a role model, mentor and confidante to those female officers who felt unable to confide in their male colleagues on some issues.

She had been at West Central for nearly a year when her home phone rang at around 10 p.m. one Sunday evening. It was an anxious-sounding woman, a uniformed sergeant, asking if she would be in the following day as she needed to speak to her. The next day, the acting sergeant came to Jackie's office and relayed her concerns about a nightclub raid she had been on with her new team. A large quantity of drugs had been discarded on the floor and seized by police, but never entered into the police property register. Soon after, she noticed that same team making arrests for possession of drugs and the arrested people claiming that they had been fitted up and the drugs planted on them. Jackie decided the matter needed to be escalated to DCI Finch immediately. Finch made his own discreet enquiries and referred the matter to the Complaints Investigation Bureau (CIB).

CIB acted quickly and arrested three officers, including the team inspector, a sergeant and a constable. This sent shockwaves around the station. The following day she went into the canteen, normally the beating heart of any police station, but on this occasion as she walked in everyone got up and walked out. She was told that there was homophobic graffiti about her scrawled across the walls of the gents' toilets. Latterly, she had pornographic lesbian magazines posted through her letterbox at midnight and the female sergeant had her car smothered with excrement. The message was clear to both officers: not only had they breached the unwritten rule that you do not 'grass' on your colleagues, but they also knew where they lived.

By this time, Ted Stowe had retired and the new chief superintendent (a well-known member of a Masonic lodge) asked to see her and aggressively questioned why she had not spoken to him in the first instance, the intimation being he would have kept it all in-house.

It would be another year before the matter came to trial. The defence teams were considering running a defence that Jackie and the female sergeant were in a relationship and made the allegations as an act of revenge on the inspector. The thought of her sexuality being not only publicised, but in effect weaponised against her, resulted in an acceleration of her drinking.

Ultimately, Jackie was never called to give evidence and two of the three officers were given prison sentences. This did not stop the personal abuse that Jackie received from other colleagues, who asked how she could live with herself being responsible for a father of four going to prison. DCI Stan Finch received no such abuse or ramifications from his colleagues, even though he was the officer who called in the Complaints Investigation Bureau, but Jackie as both a woman and gay became the target. She doesn't think there would have been a problem had she been a heterosexual woman or a man reporting the matter. Jackie was one of the few 'out' female gay officers at that time; her experience led other gay colleagues she knew to say they would definitely *not* be coming out having seen what she had gone through.

In 2021, Jackie appeared in the BBC documentary *Bent Coppers: Crossing the Line of Duty*, some thirty-seven years after the events at West End Central. In it, she described this whole process as being life defining and crushing, she felt incredibly isolated and vilified for doing the right thing. It was the toughest thing she had ever dealt with in her career.[17] She is still clearly haunted by those events at West End Central, and in talking about it on the BBC documentary and in other forums she disclosed the physical and mental impact on her, including panic attacks. Post-traumatic stress disorder (PTSD) was unheard of in the police force in the 1980s and many officers would have turned, as Jackie did, to 'Dr Smirnoff or Dr Gordons' to help. In the early 1990s, when she was asked to help another officer who was reporting wrong-doing against a colleague, this acted as a trigger for a huge panic attack and she ended up being hospitalised, where she was diagnosed with PTSD.

Jackie was to remain at West End Central for three years, when she started to consider another posting to a more specialist investigative unit. In 1987 she found herself unexpectedly posted to the Company Fraud Squad, investigating white collar crime, including many of the frauds associated with the sale of shares from the various government privatisations in the late 1980s. She was initially partnered with a male detective constable who everyone assumed was her boss. After a couple of years, another detective inspector joined the team: none other than Phil, her former Flying Squad nemesis. However, this time Jackie took the initiative and took him outside for a 'chat', where she immediately stood up to him and told him in no uncertain terms (perhaps replaying some of the 'industrial' language that had been part of his first conversation with her on the Flying Squad) that she would not be tolerating any of his previous behaviour towards her, and if he stepped out of line she would have no hesitation in reporting him to the commander. He assured her there would be no issues and there were not.

With six years under her belt as an accomplished detective inspector, Jackie ended the 1980s applying for further promotion, and began the 1990s as a detective chief inspector (DCI) in charge of the Hammersmith and Fulham CID. At that time, she was one of only three female DCIs in the Met. The early 1990s were to be life-changing for her in many ways, but two meetings stand out as having life-changing consequences, and resulted in two master's degrees in different subjects and dual retirement paths.

The first meeting was with Lynda La Plante, the well-known writer and dramatist, who had asked to speak to a senior female detective about a script she was putting together. Jackie's name came up and the character of Tennison was fleshed out. The second meeting was with someone called John at a local Police Consultative meeting, which he was attending on behalf of the local Alcoholics Anonymous (AA) group and making a presentation to showcase the work of AA and how they could work in partnership with the police. He invited Jackie to a meeting, and afterwards John asked her if she had found it useful. She told him she had been hospitalised with the panic attacks linked to the events at West End Central and had come to the realisation that she was sick and tired of being sick and tired, and made a call to John saying, 'I think I might be one of you.' John was to take Jackie to her first AA meeting on 29 December 1992, and she has been sober ever since.

Lynda La Plante had the inspiration for creating the character of Jane Tennison from watching the BBC's *Crimewatch*. She realised she had not seen any senior female detectives making appeals and set out to create her own. Jackie's task was to help bring the character to life. Her experiences over the previous twenty years were distilled into two hours, and she also met Helen Mirren to advise her on how to conduct herself. Lynda wanted to portray Tennison as a gay officer, but Jackie advised her that at that time it would be a step too far. Jackie was concerned at how her colleagues would react to the portrayal of Tennison, the character who has been described as 'a take-no-crap leader battling the overtly misogynist and often corrupt institution that she nevertheless believed in very deeply'.[18]

The support from other police officers was overwhelming. She had nailed it. Brown and Heidensohn's subsequent research confirmed it: 'Qualitative response from officers participating in JB's national survey indicated that the behaviour portrayed in the programme [*Prime Suspect*] did mirror the experiences of woman officers.'[19]

The critical and public reaction was equally overwhelming. *Prime Suspect* has been screened in over seventy-eight countries, seen by over 220 million viewers and won a host of awards. The impact and influence this had cannot be underestimated, given that nearly a third of the population cite 'media fiction' as their main source of information about the police.[20] The lasting impact has been acting as a catalyst in increasing the representation of women in policing, and especially within the CID as considered above.

Jackie continued to make a significant contribution to policing as a DCI, establishing one of the first specialist Community Safety Units set up to investigate domestic abuse. Recognising that many women were reluctant to press formal charges against their assailants, she also set up a project to work with male offenders. She was also an active mentor to the female detectives within her department. Despite having a stellar crime performance on her division, further promotion eluded her as a result of her marks on a numerical aptitude test. In 1997 she was medically retired as a result of a longstanding knee injury.

NEW OPPORTUNITIES

In 1993, a few years before she actually retired, Jackie was interviewed by Angela Lambert for *The Independent* newspaper. The success of *Prime Suspect* had inevitably led to an interest in who was the inspiration for the character. When questioned about her plans for a life beyond the Metropolitan Police, she said, 'I'd like to work with ex-offenders, do more work around issues affecting women and if possible, advise for TV on scripts.'[21]

Jackie was able to put that 1993 plan into practice. Within a few months of retiring, she was asked to become a story consultant to the popular ITV police drama series *The Bill*. She was also to advise on multiple other well-known television dramas. In 2018, she was asked to present a CBS Reality TV series called *The Real Prime Suspect*. She continues to work with production companies on a range of projects and is very much in demand as an inspirational speaker in both the public and private sector. She recently came full circle when invited to speak to the Met's current Flying Squad at a team-building day at the US Embassy.

Throughout her life she had been beset by doubt about her academic abilities. She failed the 'eleven plus' exam, got poor mock A-level grades, and could not pass the numerical aptitude tests that would have seen her promoted to detective superintendent. She perhaps forgets that she came sixth in the country when she sat the police sergeants' exam in Leicester and became one of the youngest ever sergeants in the country. After some gentle persuasion from those she was working with in the drama world, she enrolled on an MA course in Creative Writing, which she swiftly followed up with another MSc degree in Addiction Psychology and Counselling.

For the last seventeen years she has been volunteering in a prison, working with inmates both in group and individual settings. She enjoys the opportunity to help people, and approximately twenty men attend her weekly Alcoholics Anonymous (AA) group at the prison where she works. She remembers that chance meeting with John in 1992; just as AA helped her and was given to her for nothing, she wants to help and give something back.

She has worked with some very dangerous and violent offenders; she has never felt threatened and there is mutual respect between the inmates and the retired Metropolitan Police detective. Many of the inmates have experienced some form of adverse childhood experience,[22] others have very high IQs but very low levels of emotional intelligence. While some would have pleaded not guilty at court to their offences, once inside most accept their offending. She has helped several prepare for release back into the community, and is even the 'next of kin' for one man she supports as he has no one on the outside waiting for him.

When she has some down time she plays for her local walking football team, is the local Neighbourhood Watch co-ordinator in her village, and takes good care of Frank, her Jackapoo dog.

REFLECTIONS

At the time of writing, it is twenty-six years since Jackie retired from the Metropolitan Police. A few years ago, she was asked to consider writing her memoirs, which she agreed to do, but she felt very uncomfortable at the prospect of the being judged by her former colleagues, friends, family and the wider public. This time it would be *her* vulnerabilities and insecurities on show and not those of the fictional DCI Tennison. However, once again those fears were misplaced and the book, co-written with Hélène Mulholland, was published in August 2022. The reaction to the book has provided something of a cathartic release: she finally felt proud of everything she has achieved and found it a moment of huge personal change. Perhaps the only negative was when she was refused membership of a former police officer's Facebook group: it was clear some had still not forgiven her for doing the right thing at West End Central, and there was further reason not to trust her as she was now a journalist (which she is not!), but now she does not fear that rejection and not fitting in. One of the many positives of social media is that many people, former colleagues and complete strangers, have reached out to her and either reminded her of a small act of kindness she did for them while serving, or the inspiration they have got to deal with their own issues having read about her challenges.

As the years have passed it has been all too easy for people to say the portrayal of the Met as experienced by DCI Tennison was from another era, and that both the Met and wider policing have changed and improved for the better. In her article on Tennison in August 2021, Julia Sirmons commented: 'The problems with policing that La Plante illuminates – their poor treatment of Black and Queer communities, and of sex workers as well as the cover-up or enabling of paedophile rings by the highest ranks – all feel sadly relevant today.'[23]

The publication of Jackie's own book coincided with some of the darkest times in the Metropolitan Police's history, with the convictions of two police officers: Wayne Couzens for the kidnap, rape and murder of Sarah Everard in March 2021; and David Carrick for multiple rapes spanning many years. Baroness Casey's *Independent Review into the Standards of Behaviour and Internal Culture of the Metropolitan Police Service* showed that despite the huge strides made in gender representation over the years, there is still a long way to go in changing the internal culture, which she described as institutionally sexist, racist and homophobic.[24] Jackie was invited to write an opinion piece in *The Guardian* once the full Casey review had been published, and again it brought back memories of her experience at West End Central:

> This occurred almost 40 years ago but it seems that on this front, not enough has changed, as an October 2022 interim report into the culture and standards at the Met by Louise Casey recently laid bare. 'Too often', said the report, people who had reported wrongdoing said that they found the system 'stacked against them.' Many officers and staff said that they were made to feel as if they were the problem for speaking up. 'We heard supervisors and managers are actively dissuading their staff from reporting misconduct,' the report continued.[25]

In 2020 she was asked by London Southbank University, where she had studied for her MSc, to give her advice that others could learn from. It was short and sharp but very powerful, and reflected her experience as a trailblazing police officer – one of the country's first openly gay senior female officers: 'So, you either follow the crowd or standout and do the right thing.'[26]

CHIEF CONSTABLE SUE FISH

HIGHLIGHTING MISOGYNY, MENOPAUSE, AND MISCONDUCT

TOM ANDREWS

Sue Fish. Nottinghamshire Police publicity photograph.

IF YOU HAD ASKED HER friends, or even teenage self, whether she expected to become a police officer, let alone a chief constable, the answer probably would have been a hearty laugh at the notion. Describing herself as 'somewhat of a rulebreaker', it took Sue Fish five years and two universities to graduate a three-year degree. During that time, she had no idea what she wanted to do with her life. Graduating from the London School of Economics, several of her friends were heading off to high-paid jobs in the City and were required to entertain clients at strip clubs and lap-dancing bars. Neither of these ideas appealed to the young Sue, who was not interested in the idea of money for money's sake. She was far more drawn to the idea of a career with a sense of purpose where she could make a difference. The university's careers advisor suggested the police or the NHS management scheme, but the prospect of not doing the same thing day in day out and forever testing herself, that her mind linked with a strong sense of fairness as well as right and wrong, attracted Sue to the policing avenue.[1]

Applying to the graduate fast-track 'Special Course' in 1986, she went to a three-day assessment centre involving scenarios and an interview, during which she was asked where she saw herself in five years. 'The correct answer was probably to say leading a team, or chief constable, but I went with honesty. I said that I didn't really know, I would see where it took me. I didn't really know much about the police and felt I would just see how things went,' she reminisces. Perhaps predictably, the resultant feedback explaining her rejection from the programme stated that she 'lacked ambition'. Having made it to the interview stage, though, she was still guaranteed a job with the police. She applied to Nottinghamshire Police in order to be with the man she loved, who lived in the county.

At the time, applicants were subject to a home visit by the local sergeant or inspector, and sure enough, a couple of officers came to visit her, her partner and his 3-year-old son at their house in East Bridgford. This was a very 'weird' experience because Sue recalls that it felt like she was being judged based on her appearance and home. Asking about her domestic arrangements, the officers were informed that she and her partner were not married. This was seemingly scandalous to her guests, who told her that in order to join Nottinghamshire Constabulary she would need to 'regularise her position'. The Chief Constable at the time, Charles McLachlan, was apparently 'a very moral man' who couldn't have female officers 'living in sin'. Sue, confident that her partner would propose, telephoned the force, advising, a little optimistically, that she was now engaged and had fixed a date for her wedding. She was now free to join.

She feels that she was quite fortunate, later discovering that despite the Sex Discrimination Act coming in eleven years earlier, married women applicants were not accepted. Sue understood the rationale to be because married women at the time served an average of just seven years before leaving to become mothers; therefore, they didn't represent a good return on the investment of training.

This wasn't to be the end of the discrimination Sue encountered in her early career by virtue of her gender. At the time, the force only employed 8 per cent, or 165, of its officers as women, whichever was fewer. When she joined her shift at Canning Circus Police Station in May 1987, she was the third woman on the team, where previously they only had two – one for each 'half' of the shift. This presented a conundrum to her sergeant when allocating duties, because he couldn't possibly pair up two women in the 'panda' car and didn't know what to do with her. Sue was also never crewed on the van on weekend nights or offered overtime. After becoming frustrated at this – and, crucially, not afraid to speak her mind – she challenged her inspector, who told her that 'because she was in a dual-income household where she and her husband worked, she didn't need the money. All the men on the shift, their wives stayed at home and didn't earn anything, so they did need it.' She was also to discover that the morals on which Chief Constable McLachlan ostensibly prided himself were seemingly only applicable to the women. Sexual relationships with victims and witnesses were seen as a 'perk of the job' and a significant number of men had numerous ex-wives, as well as mistresses. This was to provide a lasting impression on the young officer, one that she would later have an opportunity to try to do something about.

During her time in the same force, nearly thirty years later as Deputy Chief Constable, Sue oversaw the portfolio of the Professional Standards Department (PSD); the day-to-day running of which she is keen to highlight was done by a colleague, D/Supt Jackie Alexander. It was at this time that the pair fought to highlight the emotional damage that can be done to victims – especially vulnerable ones – who are exploited by police officers for sexual relationships. She believes that sexual exploitation by police officers utterly undermines trust, confidence and legitimacy in policing, as well as referencing the reputational damage to the force through the abuse of trust represented by such an act. The matter became most prominent when the case of PC Simon Jones came to the attention of the PSD. Jones, who was later described by the prosecution barrister as a 'predatory man who pursued the women with unparalleled persistence, vigour and enthusiasm',[2] was proven to have had sex on duty with two vulnerable female victims of crime. He was found guilty of two counts of misconduct in a public office and sentenced to two years in prison. Sentencing Judge Michael Stokes said of Jones: 'to use your position as a police officer in order to engage in reckless sex activities with women who are themselves extremely vulnerable is a very serious matter'.[3]

A serious matter it certainly was, but one that was flying largely under the radar within the police service as a whole nationally. There were suggestions that Jones's attitudes were at the very least common knowledge among his colleagues, both in a former force and after he transferred to Nottinghamshire. Evidence of this had been quite literally writ large on some of Jones's police equipment. He was not, however, reported by any of his peers or supervisors. This, suggests Sue, was an example of the pervasive misogynistic or toxic masculinity attitude, not just in the police but society as a whole. Jones's defence throughout his internal misconduct and criminal proceedings was simply that 'no-one had told [him] it was wrong'.

This may have been the incident that lit the spark in Sue that drove her to action, but she too had been the victim of misogynistic behaviour. At the hands of the very worst gangsters of the criminal underworld, this could to some extent be anticipated. Men with a moral compass which justified the murder of innocents could entirely be expected to demean the position of the female police officer leading the investigation against them, using any means necessary.[4] Sue recalls implementing personal safety plans and varying her routine and commute at the height of investigating the Nottingham 'Bestwood Cartel'.[5] Experiencing criminally misogynistic behaviour on two occasions at the hands of senior police officers should have been far less expected.[6] Yet this was the culture even as recently as the late 2000s, when Sue was sexually assaulted by a fellow chief officer, when she herself was an assistant chief constable (ACC).

It was evident that, while the culture of misogyny could be described by some as 'institutional',[7] it was certainly 'endemic'. Her personal experiences may have ignited the spark, but it was a study undertaken by Nottingham Citizens in 2014 that spurred action.[8] The research spoke to victims of hate crimes, but Sue recalls 'forty percent of women who were victims of hate crime, also said that it was because they were a woman'. She remembers this vividly, realising there was a huge societal issue that no one, men or women, was talking about. Women were leaving jobs, stopping exercising outside and taking the car instead of walking. Why should this be normal and not talked about? Was it because there was no *mechanism* for talking about it?

Deputy Chief Constable Fish had the power to change that. In discussions with the male Chief Constable Chris Eyre and male Police and Crime

Commissioner (PCC) Paddy Tipping, she explained the issue. The question was put back to her that if the force started recording incidents of prejudice against women (rather than the active discrimination covered in gender equality laws), would this not make them guardians of public morals? Sue answered quite plainly that 'if the public can't guard their own morals, then who else will if not the police?'; no doubt with a significant feeling of irony regarding the double-standards of morality demonstrated by the police earlier in her career.

The chief and PCC agreed Sue could implement the initiative, so she committed the force to it a few days later at a women's conference. As plans for the practicalities were still being finalised, the scheme was leaked to the press and a furore erupted. 'Nottinghamshire Police to make wolf-whistling a HATE crime';[9] 'Wolf whistling to become HATE crime as one police force classify the street harassment as misogynistic offence';[10] 'WOLF WHISTLING NOW A HATE CRIME: Police to start recording unwanted sexual advances in same category as racist abuse'[11] ran the tabloid headlines (emphasis in originals). There was a particular irony in this timing, barely a year after *The Sun* had stopped publishing topless pictures for its infamous fifty-year-long 'page 3' feature, following significant public and parliamentary pressure indicative of changing times.[12] Even respectable news outlets who should have known better were joining the ruckus: 'One researcher from [BBC] Radio 4 rang me and said "I understand you've made wolf-whistling illegal?"' recalls Sue. 'I was a little disappointed that the researcher didn't know that a police officer can't simply make up laws.'

In spite of the tabloid uproar, Sue says she was surprised at the ire she experienced from serving and ex-police officers. The most vocal were the retired male police officers, from whom she disappointingly received hate mail, which was itself often very misogynistic in nature. Most surprising, however, were the disparaging and disapproving sentiments from senior female colleagues – what few there even were. Both Cressida Dick (Commissioner of the Metropolitan Police) and Sara Thornton (head of the National Police Chiefs' Council (NPCC)) were vocal in their condemnation, suggesting that Mrs Fish's actions were implying a level of vulnerability on the part of *all* women and that the police should be focussing on real crime. An evaluation of the policy implementation by academics at Nottingham Trent University and the University of Nottingham demonstrated its positive impact.[13] Given the evidence base, the idea of expanding the misogyny hate category nationally was mooted at the NPCC, but the same two chiefs were largely instrumental in preventing it.[14]

'In Nottinghamshire we listened to what women were experiencing,' says Sue. Working in partnership with Citizens UK, women's organisations and academics had shown the nature of the problem, and even if only Nottinghamshire Police were going to try to do something, *anything* about it, then Sue knew that's what she must do. It simply provided women and girls with a knowledge that they could report situations in which they were harassed, intimidated or violated, to a government agency that would listen and potentially do something about it. The value of this this 'evidence-based policing'[15] approach was further demonstrated by the increase in reports every time the force ran an awareness campaign, funded by the PCC's office. This clearly highlighted the need on the part of those victims to tell the police about their experiences, and showed that there was indeed a large, unreported issue occurring.[16]

In 1954, just nine years after the Nazi atrocities of the Holocaust became known, psychologist Gordon Allport coined his five-step 'scale of prejudice'. Starting with 'anti-locution' (hate speech), and descending through 'active avoidance', 'discrimination' and 'physical attack', the ultimate end if hate was left unchecked was 'extermination'.[17] All these stages were evident with misogyny. If anti-locution (speaking derogatively about women, often as 'objects'), discrimination (society's expectations and tolerance) and physical attack (groping) were allowed, then the message was clear: extermination may well be accepted. In the cases of the 'Yorkshire Ripper' and 'Suffolk Strangler', because they targeted 'sex workers', even the police were vaguely tolerant of their activities.[18] Sue knew that if the police could intervene at an early stage and make offenders aware of the effect of their misogyny on victims, then perhaps they could be prevented from descending the scale, in the same way that the government's 'Prevent' anti-radicalisation programme attempts to intervene before extremist ideas escalate into physical attack or extermination.[19] But it was an uphill battle trying to change deeply entrenched societal views, a year before the #MeToo movement raised public consciousness.[20] Especially in a service that had long been particularly misogynistic.

Ever since starting in the police, Sue had faced hurdles because of her gender. Joining in 1987, she was issued with a handbag ('which remained in the plastic wrapping in my locker from the day I was issued it until I retired') and a wooden truncheon half the length of the men's, designed to fit in said handbag. It certainly wasn't designed to do the job for which such personal protective equipment was originally intended. Uniforms too were wholly impractical. Women were issued and expected to wear 'A-line' skirts in the summer months between March to October. These made running very difficult, but also meant that the women on shift were normally the ones sent first over fences to catch fleeing criminals. On one occasion the young PC Fish was in hot pursuit of a suspect who hopped over a spiked fence. This presented a significant obstacle in the skirt, which Sue hitched up to try and scale it, but in spite of this she promptly got stuck. 'My shift never came so quickly or in such numbers to assist me with that conundrum,' she recalls embarrassingly.

Male officers wore blue shirts but women were issued with thin white shirts. Wearing her tunic over the top presented no issues, but regularly a lecherous older inspector would declare uniform to be 'shirt sleeves order' (no tunics); most often when it was cold and raining. He would then make a point of checking in with the female officers on their allocated rendezvous points – but noticeably didn't speak to their faces.

It wasn't all negative experiences during her early career, however. Only a month after completing her two-year probationary period, she passed her sergeants' exams and she was put forward again for the 'Special Course' by her superintendent. On this occasion Sue feels that she was actually a 'beneficiary of the old boys' network'. She was an acting sergeant at the time and one of the team she supervised was also one of the Police Federation representatives for Nottinghamshire. When her interview panel comprised of a Federation 'rep' from a different force area who made no secret of the fact that he'd spoken to Sue's colleague, she became acutely aware of the wide networks across policing. It was clear it could be a double-edged sword, however; it was apparent during the interview that she was positively regarded and benefitted from the network. This encouraged her in her later career to ensure fairness for all, determining that she needed to root out inequality and increase opportunities regardless of connections. She certainly didn't want to be seen as the person that had got where she was through cronyism and felt that others shouldn't benefit simply from who they knew either.

A large part of this drive to support those who worked under her came from her own experience of support when she announced she was pregnant. The ACC at the time, Chris Fox, identified that Sue wasn't going to take the at-the-time stereotypical route of not returning after having her baby. He wrote her a letter encouraging her to remain true to herself and to return to the force if that was her passion; she still has the letter to this day as a reminder of the power of encouragement. Proving ACC Fox's faith in her, Sue successfully passed her inspectors' exam just a few weeks before giving birth. As an inspector, Sue applied for and successfully obtained a secondment to Her Majesty's Inspectorate of Constabulary (HMIC), during which time she was promoted to chief inspector. Once again clearly confirming her abilities, she became the lowest ranked officer ever to lead a force-wide inspection: normally the preserve of superintendents or above. She returned to Nottinghamshire in that rank and was posted to the northernmost part of the county at rural Worksop, a far cry from the city policing she was used to. Sue suspects this was because her father-in-law was chair of the Nottinghamshire bench of magistrates, and as such she was posted 'out of the way' to avoid any negative inference. In this example, the 'networks of policing' quite likely worked against her.

Opportunity was once again grasped when she applied for promotion to superintendent with West Midlands Police in 1997. Her ability clearly shone through, and she was promoted to chief superintendent, in charge of the specialist operations department of firearms, dogs and traffic. Moving to the West Midlands allowed her to gain a qualification as a tactical firearms commander, overseeing perhaps the most high-pressured and responsibility-laden duties in the policing environment. 'I never would have had this opportunity in Notts,' she believes, 'because the force support department was very nepotistic and full of "old boys". Unless you'd gone up through the ranks – and you could only do that if you were male in that department – you wouldn't get an opportunity for courses like that.' There was a very macho culture there at the time, that took Sue some time to overcome on her return to Nottinghamshire as ACC in 2003.

At that time, Nottinghamshire Police was a force in crisis. Labels such as 'Shottingham' were being applied to the city,[21] in response to the epidemic of gun crime that had seen the country's first ever 'routine' armed foot patrols.[22] Chief Constable Steve Green was unprecedently pressured into admitting to a national newspaper that '[Nottinghamshire Police] cannot cope with violent crime'.[23] The idea of returning to her 'home' force, at a time when it was in acute crisis, really appealed to Sue, who relished a challenge. The city and the force's reputation were in freefall, with 'interventions left, right and centre from the HMIC and others'. Sue's wealth of experience as a firearms commander no doubt stood her application to return to 'Shottingham' in very good stead. She vividly remembers her mother warning her about taking the post, though, concerned it would ruin her career or kill her, and 'it nearly did both'.

While the force was under scrutiny for its serious violence and shootings problem, she recalls the Home Office standards unit complaining about the rate of violent crime the force was experiencing, with her suitably curt reply of 'well, people are dying' promptly closing that issue off. The first eighteen months of her time as ACC, she recalls, were chaos. As much as 10 per cent of the force's staff were devoted to murder investigations, with dozens more from other forces coming in to help. As 'ACC Crime' at a time when there was a murder a fortnight, ACC Fish was having to plan two investigations in advance in terms of finding space and equipment for incident rooms, as well as identifying where staff would come from, while also developing a murder prevention strategy. Half the murders were classed as 'Category A – unknown suspects, attracting significant public attention and which require extensive resource allocation'.[24] 'The great and the good of policing were coming to Nottinghamshire and saying they'd not seen anything this bad since the Krays.'

Her position also meant she was in overall charge of Operation Starburst – the force's response to the notorious 'Bestwood Cartel' under Colin Gunn and other associated groups.[25] Gunn was later described by newspapers, following his conviction, as 'Britain's most notorious gangster';[26] and it was ultimately ACC Fish's responsibility to stop him. The media pressure on her during this time was intense, especially following the shooting of 14-year-old schoolgirl Danielle Beccan in October 2004.[27] ACC Fish was the 'face' of the investigation on TV, and says the force received numerous complaints from the public about such a 'young female officer' being in charge of such a serious investigation. By this time she was in her forties and had spent a large part of her career in CID! The sense of purpose the enquiry gave her, however, was second-to-none, seeking justice for this most heinous of crimes being fundamental to what it meant to be a police officer.

Being in charge of such a significant and complex operation didn't come without personal and professional cost. She had to create personal safety plans for her entire family and brief her neighbours about what to do in the event of spotting suspicious activity. It also came at perhaps the ultimate cost, when in an act of cold-blooded revenge for his nephew's death, Colin Gunn had two innocent people murdered.[28] This was ultimately to prove his downfall, being convicted for conspiring to arrange it, but Sue says she will 'always carry the scars of the John and Joan Stirland murders' and whether she could have done anything differently to prevent them. The subsequent inquest (or 'public inquiry masquerading as an inquest') was challenging for Sue, who was required to give evidence on behalf of Nottinghamshire Police. Sue is in no doubt that the conviction of Gunn 'saved the city of Nottingham'. She adds:

This may sound trite, but fundamentally that's what it was about. Companies were moving out to Derby and Leicester or choosing to invest there rather than in Nottingham. Universities were undergoing significant expansion nationally but only in a very limited way for the two Nottingham institutions. Lives were being ruined and there were economic consequences to that.

As a result of the Stirlands' murder, she and other colleagues were investigated by the Independent Police Complaints Commission; only finding out after *several years* that she was not to face any criminal charges on the BBC Radio 4 lunchtime news. No one had thought to tell her first. Her treatment as the subject of this investigation meant that when she was promoted to deputy chief constable and inherited the portfolio in-force for overseeing the PSD, she was determined to improve how they dealt with officers in terms of timeliness and communication. She was also in a position to sign off on the changes around treating sexual misconduct as corruption as outlined above.

Another one of her 'lightbulb moments' happened when a female detective constable and long-time acquaintance of Sue's handed in her resignation only a few years prior to her retirement. 'No-one retired early with only a few years left to work,' thought Sue, 'as that's when you accrue the largest part of your pension.' Determined to find out what had caused this officer to want to leave, Sue conducted her exit interview. It transpired that severe symptoms of the menopause had been exacerbated by a complete lack of sympathy or willingness to make minor adaptations by the officer's sergeant. This had led her to feeling that it wasn't worth continuing to struggle through her shifts, and that she should take early retirement. Appalled that but for the sake of a few simple changes like slight amendments to shift times and the provision of a fan and window seat, the force was losing a career-long detective, Sue offered to sort the issues. The officer declined, having already resolved in her head that she wanted to leave; but if this was the experience of one officer, undergoing a natural process that every woman goes through, was she the only one who felt this way? Sue was in a position to not only find out, but do something about it.

She spoke to the force's Women's Network, who were working on the issue already, in which the retiring officer had had some input. This had been commenced in response to significant demographic changes within the police workforce. When Sue first started in the mid-1980s, the average length of a female officer's service was just seven years, often leaving after having children, no part-time or flexible working, or often leaving on marriage. Now the average length of women's service was fast approaching that of men's — although still some way from being equal.[29] This meant that more and more women were working through their menopause, with roughly 50 per cent suffering from associated symptoms including hot flushes, insomnia, difficulty concentrating or anxiety/depression.[30] More officers and police staff in high-pressure roles with significant amounts of responsibility were also women.[31] Some of the menopausal symptoms could severely impact on their performance at work, through no fault of their own, if just minor adaptations couldn't be made. Solutions seemed so potentially simple, yet weren't in place within Nottinghamshire Police, or indeed many companies nationally. Officers experiencing symptoms 'looked for support but found that there was nothing'.[32]

Sue endorsed the work of the Women's Network, which was largely driven by Detective Constable Keeley Mansell, who had experienced early menopause aged just 42.[33] Mrs Fish, by this time temporary chief constable, ensured that Nottinghamshire Police became the first force in the country to introduce a specific menopause policy and associated guidance for managers on 1 January 2017, written by DC Mansell.[34] DC Mansell went on to win national awards for her pioneering role in both highlighting the issue and developing the policy, which has since been adopted by numerous other forces across the country.[35] Sue highlights the irony of a police force, traditionally a very male-dominated environment, blazing the trail in developing such a crucial supportive document for women. Or perhaps it was exactly *because* it was such a male-dominated environment that such a policy was needed. 'If you want to attract and retain people, you need to demonstrate your values.'

'It was again something that every woman experiences, but no-one talked about,' recalls Sue:

Everyone knows what happens when periods start, it gets taught in schools; but no-one knew what happens when they stop. Even doctors weren't taught about it in training – although that's changing now. They used to just prescribe women anti-depressants! We weren't going mad, it's a natural process that happens to *every* woman.

She is keen to highlight that she was just fortunate enough to be in a position to support the development and implementation of the policy, and that the majority of work was done by Keeley Mansell and the Women's Network. But again, it perhaps took Sue's being there, as a forward-thinking female leader not afraid to consider what might otherwise have been awkward or even taboo subjects, to oversee its introduction. After her retirement, Sue was awarded an honorary doctorate by the University of Nottingham for her work raising the profile of women's issues such as misogyny hate crime and menopause. She stresses she very much sees this as an award for all who contributed to the projects:

> I may have made some of the decisions, but actually the hard work was done by other people. Making decisions is actually quite easy, although you have to take the flak, but you also get all the kudos. I led a whole team of people – a whole county, not just a police force. You never really do anything on your own. I wouldn't have come up with any of the things that appear to have my name attached to them now if it weren't for the work of Jackie Alexander and her team; if it wasn't for Keeley and her colleagues. It's all on the shoulders of other people's work, but someone has to take those decisions. It seems to have been me.

Flak certainly followed the force's new menopause policy, as it had done with the misogyny pilot scheme: 'Nottinghamshire Police [...] to provide "crying rooms" for female officers going through the menopause,' wrote one supposedly feminist author.[36] 'COPS AND SOBBERS' headlined *The Sun*, also taking the 'crying room' angle.[37] 'Police force brings in "patronising and insulting" "have a cry" space for menopausal female officers,' stated the *Daily Mail*.

They even managed to find a woman who worked in a fashion magazine to say that if the 'middle-aged women [in my office] feel a bit overwrought they go home and have a stiff gin and tonic';[38] becoming forgetful or fatigued producing magazine content obviously being highly comparable to the job of a police officer. *The Express* showed the strength of their research with their headline 'Police set aside crying rooms for menopausal WPCs' – a now highly pejorative term that went out of official usage with the Sex Discrimination Act 1975.[39]

It was all water off the proverbial duck's back to the now outgoing chief constable, who had introduced an evidence-based policy to support those who may need it and did not impact on those that didn't.

Sue hadn't always been comfortable or self-aware enough to raise potentially taboo topics without embarrassment or make such bold decisions. She remembers frequently apologising for doing something that a man disagreed with, simply because that was what society expected of women: a tacit subservience. On reflection, she states she was acutely aware that as a senior officer she would do down the rank and play up the subservient woman bit – 'oh I'm so sorry' – but then be really grumpy when she was patronised; only later realising she was actually complicit in the event.

Reflection played a big part of her development later in her career. She will always carry the scars of the murder of John and Joan Stirland, and the 'should have, would have, could haves' about her decisions. But, she is keen to emphasise, there are far more people alive today because of her actions:

> That doesn't negate anyone's premature deaths, but there was a big picture to see as well. If you don't make decisions then you won't make a mistake, but you can't do that. You can learn both from things that go wrong and things that go well. If it goes well though, no-one takes the time to understand why it worked.

'Trust your own judgement,' she espouses, 'and don't try to please everyone else, because you can never please everyone. Make decisions that are right by you.' Sue is happy that all her decisions were made for the right reasons – primarily to help others – but she stresses she always made them according to her own moral compass as it's not possible to fully understand someone else's motives.

Decision-making is also about understanding risks, she warns, and being accountable if they go wrong. She always assimilated advice from specialists such as tactical advisors, but ultimately the buck stopped with her. She cites an example of when the English Defence League (EDL) came to Nottingham to protest and as the chief constable she had the power to potentially ban the event. 'Politically that was all I wanted to do, but I had to uphold their right to protest, as well as the counter-demonstration.' Reflecting again, Sue realises it was incredibly lonely and occasionally scary at the top, but at the time she wasn't aware of it. It was only on looking back that she could comprehend the gravity of some of those decisions. She didn't always necessarily get them right, but she always had courage in them and understands why she made them.

It took Sue some twenty-five years to reach this level of self-awareness. 'If I knew how to help people get there any sooner I'd be very wealthy,' she jokes. But in retirement she does a lot of positive action work with young female and BAME officers. Her advice to them is to know what their core values are; but also to have an acceptance of what they might compromise and what they absolutely won't. 'There are costs associated with standing up for what you believe in though,' she cautions. But she feels almost any opinion can be justified if you gather evidence to support it, just be prepared to accept some costs if you want to put your head above the parapet. She feels like she was in several right places at the right times to have had an extraordinary career, but this does down many of her achievements and the hard work she put in to achieving it.

In retirement, Sue continues to push for more accountability from the police and improvement in women's rights.[40] In light of significant national events that took place after her retirement, most notably the murder of Sarah Everard and the subsequent uproar relating to societal misogyny,[41] Mrs Fish's developments in that arena seem remarkably prescient. Observing the police from outside enables her to comment on it with a sense of detachment and a critical eye which she was unable to wield while still serving. She is disappointed that still only a dozen forces record misogyny-based hate, but no longer being in the police force means she is free to call out issues where she sees them, 'which is quite liberating. I do believe in policing, but there are some things that fundamentally need to change and I can see that more clearly now from the outside.' Sue is adamant that she does not want to put any potential new recruits off joining the police, but wants them all, from any background, to go in with their eyes open and recognise the challenges faced by police officers in the 2020s – which are myriad. She wants the right people to join, though, to drive it forwards. She is hopeful that this is the route that policing is taking, and would encourage anyone with a desire to make an impact to apply. She is still immensely proud of the police service and its 'many, many brilliant officers', done a disservice by others who behave badly.[42]

A MOSTLY UNKNOWABLE HISTORY

LESBIANS IN POLICING

DR CLIFFORD WILLIAMS

Dame Cressida Dick.
(Wikimedia Commons)

FROM 2017 TO 2022, CRESSIDA DICK held the highest position in policing in the United Kingdom: Commissioner of the Police for the Metropolis. She was the first woman to head the largest UK police force. And she was a known lesbian.[1] Dick 'came out' as a lesbian (gay) in April 2017,[2] making her the highest-ranked openly homosexual officer in British police history.[3] Her partner, Helen, was also a police officer.

In the twentieth century it would have been unthinkable for an openly gay or lesbian police officer to reach such a position, but in the early years of twenty-first century attitudes and laws began to change, and homosexual orientation ceased to be a block for officers seeking promotion. Gradually, officers were more likely to feel confident about being 'out' at work.

Lesbians have existed in the police service for as long as women have existed in the police service. Although a matter of some speculation, it seems likely that a good number of women who joined the Women Police Service (WPS) during the First World War were lesbians. But that term was not one that was used then and few women, let alone policewomen, admitted to being in same-sex relationships.

Policing was an attractive occupation to many lesbians. There was, until the mid-twentieth century, a bar in most police forces and in law to married women, alongside an expectation, if not even a requirement, to resign for single policewomen upon getting married. Lesbians could avoid marriage and simultaneously maintain a respectable job by being a police officer.

While lesbian sex has never been illegal (albeit in 1921 there was an attempt in Parliament to make it so), being lesbian has traditionally been taboo and lesbians discriminated against. The police, just like most of society in the twentieth century, treated lesbianism as a disorder, and something that was morally repugnant.[4]

Until recently, lesbians within the police service usually kept quiet about their sexual orientation and relationships. There appears to be little recorded in archives regarding lesbians in policing. However, documents in The National Archives discuss the issue of lesbians in the Women's Auxiliary Air Force (WAAF). A minute sheet dated 2 February 1940 reads:

> Since the commencement of war there has been, from time to time, a certain amount of worry caused by lesbians in the W.A.A.F. Naturally it is a vice which is going to be impossible to keep out of the W.A.A.F. altogether, but obviously every endeavour will be made to lessen it. The great difficulty is to get absolute proof that any person practices this vice.

There is obviously difficulty in discharging such personnel, as frequently a lesbian is extremely efficient in her trade, and as no complete proof can be acquired it is difficult to put the case up to records.

It is no doubt realised that although perversion in men is a criminal offence, this is not so with women. At the same time, it must be understood that where such practices exist with women it is evidently most detrimental to efficiency and discipline and, I understand, to morale and well being.[5]

Such comments can be imagined to have been made, if the topic was discussed, by those responsible for the administration of the police.

COMPANIONS OR LOVERS?

It was not unusual for two women to live together in post-First World War Britain; in fact, the war had made this more likely given the number of men killed. But it is pure speculation as to whether the cases known about of two policewomen living together are cases of two women who shared a bed. Lesbians were able to live together, as two women living together did not attract comment.

Two of the most prominent early policewomen were Margaret Damer Dawson and her deputy Mary Allen. They lived together, presented a very masculine appearance, and never married. Sometimes appearance suggested a woman was lesbian: the stereotype of a manly looking woman with short hair would apply to Mary Allen after she joined the WPS and when she was known to her friends as Robert. Were Dawson and Allen lesbian?

As June Purvis points out, 'the difficulties of researching lesbian life (however defined) in the Women's Social and Political Union (WSPU) are enormous since few lesbians, in a climate hostile to their sexual orientation, left records of their lives where their lesbianism is made explicit'.[6]

Mary Allen had relationships with a number of Suffragettes who were lesbian, including Isobel 'Toto' Goldingham.[7] Through Goldingham, Allen met lesbian author Radclyffe Hall and her companion, Una Troubridge. By this time Allen was living with Helen Bourn Tagart, Damer Dawson having died in 1920.

After the First World War it was not so much the possible association with lesbianism that led the Metropolitan Police and others to shun the Women Police Service, but rather their association with militant Suffragette activity pre-war.[8] At the Bridgeman Committee in 1924, the Commissioner of the Metropolitan Police, Nevil Macready, said: 'The main point was to eliminate any women of extreme views – the vinegary spinster or blighted middle-aged fanatic.'[9]

In Gloucestershire, two policewomen, Marion Sandover and Elizabeth Tonra, lived together and may have been lesbian. They served together in the Women Police Service and then in Gloucestershire Constabulary. Sandover served from 1918 to 1948 and they shared a house together until Tonra died.[10]

WOMEN, POLICE AND MARRIAGE

For most of the twentieth century, policewomen were usually unmarried or widowed. In fact, the Police (Women) Regulations 1931 banned married women.[11] Martin Stallion, in an article in the *Journal of the Police History Society* (2021), points out that some policewomen kept their marriage secret in order to stay in the job.[12]

There was great variety in how and whether police forces employed women during the interwar period.[13] Many police forces had no women police officers until the Second World War, when the Home Office required them to at least create an Auxiliary Police Corps of Women. Even then, many initially refused this, feeling them unnecessary.[14]

In 1946, the ban on employing married women was lifted and the requirement for women to resign upon marriage was officially removed in England and Wales;[15] but the expectation still remained, however, that women would leave the police on getting married.[16] In Scotland and Northern Ireland it was not until 1968 that married women could serve in the police.[17]

HIDDEN HISTORY

In recent years, an area of history sometimes called 'hidden history' has come to the fore. One aspect of this is LGBT (Lesbian, Gay, Bisexual, Trans) history. It is a history that in the past was often covered over or erased, such was the disdain and prejudice for ideas of diverse sexual orientation and gender non-conformity. This prejudice manifested itself in law and policing. Given the stigma and taboo of the topic of lesbianism, there is little evidence in the open written archives of lesbianism in the police service. It is simply never going to be possible to know the extent of lesbianism in twentieth-century policing.

Personnel records that have survived in the archives may give us some insights into issues around lesbians within the service. But, of course, these files, if they have survived, are unlikely to be available for public inspection, given the Data Protection Act.

POLICE LESBIANS IN THE 1960S AND 1970S

Brazier and Rice have written about a couple of personnel files that are held by West Midlands Police which give us a rare archival reference to the issue in the 1960s: 'There is very little mention of same sex relationships within any files in the [West Midlands] museum … The standards of behaviour for police officers have always been high … anything not widely accepted by society at the time has been unacceptable for officers.'[18]

Some personnel files do comment on an officer suspected of being lesbian. One such officer joined in 1965 as a cadet in Walsall Borough Police and then joined the regulars of West Midlands Police in December 1966. The following year, despite good progress, she submitted a file to resign. Her chief superintendent said she had become friendly with a woman officer from West Bromwich and he believed they wished to live together, hence the resignation. She changed her mind about resigning and was soon continuing to work well as an officer. 'In January 1968 it was reported that the WPC [Woman Police Constable] from West Bromwich had been staying in this officer's room in the policewomen's hostel and they had been found on two occasions embracing each other and kissing.'[19] The WPC had been told off for regularly engaging in conversations with the other female officer.

In June 1968, the officer again applied to resign, which she did, and then applied for a role in the Territorial and Army Reserve. A reference request from the army to West Midlands Police was returned confirming her police service dates, but did not recommend her for a role. In November 1970, she applied for a traffic warden job in Warwickshire and Coventry Constabulary. Her reference for that job read as follows: 'Whilst in my force, this officer developed an emotional attachment to another policewoman, and as a result the latter part of her service was not entirely satisfactory … I would hesitate to employ her.'[20]

On 9 February 1970, an article appeared in the *Express and Star* entitled 'Women in love without men'.[21] In the article, 'Susan' talks about losing her job as a police officer when her superintendent found out she was a lesbian. The article appears on the file of the officer and also in the file for the West Bromwich woman officer. She also left the police, earlier than Susan, and also applied for the Territorial and Army Reserve without success.

On the West Midlands Police Museum website there is the story of Jean Summers, who joined Birmingham City Police as a cadet in 1967 and then the regulars in 1968:

From a very early age, Jean intuitively knew she was 'different' but had no-one with whom she could confide in about her sexuality: she was gay. Jean was painfully shy and locked within herself. Whilst Jean enjoyed working with her male colleagues, she wasn't interested in relationships with men. She was absolutely terrified of her fellow officers finding out

about it, as being gay in the police service was not spoken about openly at
that time.

Following amalgamation of the Birmingham Police into West Midlands
Police in 1974, in line with force policy, many serving Birmingham City
police officers were moved to work outside the city boundary.

Summers relates her experience of being lesbian in the police service:

> I didn't want to leave [Birmingham]. I joined Birmingham City Ambulance
> Service – at the end of my first shift, I found a note on my clocking-in card
> … one of the other women ambulance drivers was asking me out on a
> date. A number of dates later, she took me to a gay club in Wolverhampton
> where to my absolute amazement, I found several of my former police col-
> leagues. If only someone had talked to me…[22]

1990S AND GAY OFFICERS START TO 'COME OUT'

Before the 1990s, the number of openly gay or lesbian police officers in
Britain could probably be counted on the fingers of two hands. It was only
in the 1990s that a few more brave souls began to put their heads above the
parapet and become open about their sexual orientation. One officer did go
public, after he and his partner (another police officer) had been outed by
their force. Hampshire police constables Lee Hunt and Richard Adair were
'discovered' by their ACPO (Association of Chief Police Officers) team to
be a gay couple living together in 1983. Immediately, they were called to
headquarters in Winchester and posted to work at separate locations in the
two vice squads in the constabulary. They were put on monthly reports and
ordered to live apart! Despite these efforts to rid the force of them, Hunt and
Adair stuck it out, and in 1991 Hunt gave his story to the *Police Review*.[23]

For gay or bisexual police officers, the workplace continued to be a hostile
environment in the 1990s and very few admitted their sexual orientation.
Why would they? The likely consequences were hostility, harassment and
humiliation at work.

Jackie Malton, who served in Leicestershire and then the Metropolitan
Police, became the real-life woman detective figure that Lynda La Plante based
her Detective Chief Inspector Jane Tennison character on in *Prime Suspect*.[24]
Jackie was an out gay woman in the Criminal Investigation Department
(CID) and witnessed directly plenty of behaviour which demonstrated less
than complete acceptance of lesbianism in the CID. Jackie related: 'I had
enough sex toys to open up my own sex shop. Graffiti on the walls "is the

D/I a dyke" in the gents loo at West End Central and pornographic lesbian magazines through the letter box in my own home twice!'[25]

Despite all the hostility, quite a lot of progress was being made in some of the larger police forces. The Metropolitan Police attended the 'Gay Lifestyles' exhibition in London in 1993 and 1994. They had a stall promoting crime prevention and recruitment to the police service. In 1994, Detective Inspector Margaret Palmer was on the stall. Margaret, who joined the police in 1974, reflected on how things were different when she joined. At last (in 1994) she could be open about being a lesbian and she was proud of it.[26]

Alison Halford, in her foreword to Marc Burke's study of lesbian, gay and bisexual police officers, *Coming Out of the Blue* (1993), states:

> Any mention of homosexuality or gayness in police circles usually produces a standard reaction of derision and contempt for those who are or are suspected of being 'that way inclined'. Being gay or lesbian is not acceptable in the eyes of the majority of our law enforcers and the further up the police sub-culture you go, the more scathing and brutal the condemnation becomes.[27]

Halford herself perceived personal prejudice which led to her challenging decisions made not to promote her beyond the high office she reached in Merseyside. This she documented in her autobiography, *No Way Up the Greasy Pole*.[28] In 1992, her industrial tribunal for sex discrimination was reported in the press. The *Pink Paper* stated that the Chairman of the Merseyside Police Authority had said she was unfit to be a senior police officer 'because she was a lesbian and it was bad for discipline'.[29] Halford was backed by the Equal Opportunities Commission in her case against the Chief Constable of Merseyside.[30] Whether Halford was a lesbian or not was not the issue at stake. The issue at the tribunal was whether she had suffered sex discrimination in the nine failed promotion attempts she made between 1987 and 1990. Halford stated in her 1993 book that there was no evidence she was a lesbian other than she had been seen attending a football match at Tranmere Rovers with a woman.[31] And she did not 'come out' as a lesbian in her book.

Marc Burke's 1993 book was a landmark study which captures the stories, almost all anonymously recorded, of officers who had to deal with abuse, discrimination and ridicule within the police service, to add to all the negative things thrown at them by some members of the public. Most of the collated stories are from gay and bisexual men, but a few lesbian and bisexual women also speak up. For example, a West Yorkshire policewoman with five years' service:

I don't normally tell anyone about my true sexual orientation because I am frightened of the consequences. I wouldn't get my CID board for a start ... I don't have a boyfriend but I often invent one and I also have a friend who comes to all my dos, and I go to his – he's gay – and it works quite well.[32]

For some, being open and honest about their lesbianism eventually led to acceptance. A Metropolitan woman officer with seven years' experience states that she was thrown off the crime squad when she was outed after taking part in a Gay Pride march. She was returned to the shift she had been on and declared openly to them that she was a lesbian. Many of them admired her for being open about that. A week later, the chief superintendent who had thrown her off the crime squad told her he thought she had learned her lesson and could go back onto the crime squad.[33]

There are many accounts in the book which describe the hostility gay and lesbian officers faced. But there are also many contributions from women who found companionship and respect in the police. Because they did not get married and leave like so many women, and because they were invariably willing to get 'stuck in', they fitted into the service.[34] There were informal networks of lesbians, and in one force the hockey team was predominantly lesbian. An invitation to join in the hockey in West Midlands Police was said to be an invite to join a lesbian clan.[35]

Whereas gay men were perceived as a threat to the male 'macho' police culture and to the heterosexual officers therein, the lesbian officers presented no threat to those men. But being open about being lesbian or being identified openly as lesbian could lead to problems. One female City of London officer described how she was identified as lesbian, and her associations questioned, after she reported an incident off duty when she was at the London Lesbian and Gay Centre. Being associated with such a place led to an internal inquiry: 'after all the Gay centre was where "certain marches" are arranged and depart from'.[36]

LESBIAN POLICE OFFICERS BECOME MORE VISIBLE

BBC television featured a bisexual woman police officer in the drama *Between the Lines*, broadcast 1992–94. Siobhan Redmond played Maureen Connell, who during the three series had a boyfriend and later a girlfriend. While some police officers are shown in the drama making disapproving comments, her bisexuality is generally accepted.[37]

Charlotte Taylor was the only lesbian out of seven lesbian and gay police officers who featured in the 200th issue of *Gay Times* in May 1995. At that time she was a constable at Holloway Road, London. The following month, and following a lot of media interest outside the gay press, Taylor commented in *Diva*: 'I don't regret being in the photo, but it hasn't been easy. Lesbian and gay officers shouldn't have to be headline news. But the only way to overcome the problem is to increase awareness.'[38]

In 1997, the lesbian lifestyle magazine *Diva* carried an article asking if the police service was a suitable job for a lesbian.[39] The author of the article, Kate Slater, found that none of the friends she knew who were lesbian and in the police were willing to speak openly about their work. Only one was willing to give an interview, and that was anonymously as 'Lucy'. 'Lucy' talks about the regular offensive comments about gays and lesbians and how most lesbian and gay officers lead double lives. Sam Greatrex, who worked as a community contact officer for Hampshire Constabulary, is also quoted in the article. Sam acted as a contact point between gay people and the police on the Isle of Wight before transferring to the New Forest. She states: 'I wanted to give gay people a face behind the uniform. I'd go out and address the gay community about issues that affected them such as legislative measures, and make myself available at all times to discuss anything they needed to.'[40] The article concludes: 'Sam Greatrex provides a positive antidote to the more gloomy discoveries I made. Perhaps it is only a matter of time before the whole of an essentially conservative institution realises the huge contribution that lesbian and gay police officers can make to the rest of our society.'[41]

The majority of gay and lesbian police officers up until the turn of the century would keep a low profile. Why 'come out' when such a move would be likely to result in ridicule, prejudice and often pressure to leave? Many officers simply quit the service, some because the strain of leading a double life was untenable. Many who stayed did not seek promotion, instead preferring to remain away from the spotlight of leadership and the danger of being exposed as gay or lesbian. Others faced discrimination in the process of trying to get promoted. How much discrimination they faced is impossible to judge.

LESBIAN AND GAY POLICE SUPPORT

In London, where many gay men flocked, it was in the Metropolitan Police that gay police men first started organising themselves collectively. What started as an advert for a barbecue grew into a gay police association. The Lesbian and Gay Police Association (LAGPA) was born out of a social in 1990. Gradually, gay and lesbian police officers in other forces started to join the Gay Police Association and other social events were set up. Generally, officers on shifts found that as long as the gay officer was a good cop, the rest of the shift and the sergeant caused no problems and accepted them. By 1995, LAGPA had 200 members.[42] This was, of course, a small fraction of the lesbian and gay police officers in UK police forces at the time, but was probably quite representative of those who were 'out'.

At the same time, watchdogs had been set up to monitor police activity and behaviour, particularly in relation to the policing of Black men. Policing of gay men was also closely monitored. The Greater London Council gave practical support to organisations such as GALOP (a police watchdog monitoring policing of gay and lesbian people), set up in 1982.

Efforts were made by the police to improve relations between the police and the gay and lesbian public. The London Lesbian and Gay Police Initiative (LLGPI), for example, was set up by 1993.[43]

The police attitude to homosexuality generally softened in the late 1990s, and the focus in vice squads started shifting from homosexual offences (such as soliciting and importuning) to a new form of offence: computer-related child pornography.

Some senior officers demonstrated support for lesbian and gay police officers, while the Police Federation lagged behind and was resistant to embracing this aspect of diversity within the police. Sally Bourner 'came out' as gay when she was a sergeant in West Midlands Police in 1995.[44] She was helped and supported by two senior women officers: Anne Summers (West Midlands Police's Deputy Chief Constable) and Cressida Dick.[45] Anne Summers was the ACPO (Association of Chief Police Officers) spokeswoman on gay and lesbian issues when, in 1997, ACPO endorsed a policing charter drawn up by the National Advisory Group – Policing Lesbian and Gay Communities. The charter included calls for: training on lesbian and gay issues for officers at all levels; the creation of an environment where officers can 'come out' without fear of prejudice; recruitment campaigns in the gay press; and appointment of officers to liaise with the lesbian and gay communities.[46] Some forces did already have such lesbian/gay liaison officers.[47]

In 1998, former Chief Inspector Lyn Smith won a sex discrimination case against North Yorkshire Police. Smith said she was passed over for promotion after she left her husband and rumours circulated that she was a lesbian. The rumours and stress nearly caused her to commit suicide. The tribunal in Leeds found in her favour.[48]

In 1999, two West Midlands women officers had an unofficial wedding blessing. PC Sarah Thomas, who became Thomas-West (serving in Wolverhampton), and Acting Inspector Janet West (covering Smethwick), wed in an unofficial ceremony. They are thought to be the first gay officers to 'wed' in Britain. A West Midlands Police spokesman said at the time: 'We welcome officers from all aspects of society, regardless of sexuality, gender or race.'[49]

Partnership policing grew rapidly in the late 1990s and early 2000s.[50] A whole new integrated multi-agency and preventative approach to crime and disorder was matched with the police becoming increasingly aware and sensitive to the needs of what were then called 'minority groups'. By 2000, the police had embraced diversity training, initially concentrating on 'ethnic minorities' and then, as the subsequent century progressed, this came to include people identifying as gay and lesbian. Later still, understanding trans-sexual people was added to the diversity agenda for police.[51] The Macpherson Report left the police service with no alternative.[52]

ACPO embraced this new approach. Hate crime *against* gay men now became a priority above offences committed in and around toilets *by* gay men. Some police forces started recruitment adverts in the gay press, much to the horror of some Police Federation branches.[53] These adverts were primarily aimed at gay men. It is suspected there may have been a feeling that there was no shortage of lesbians in the police service, even if most were not openly 'out'.

INTO THE TWENTY-FIRST CENTURY

In 2016, Sara Glen was appointed Deputy Chief Constable in Hampshire.[54] Fifteen years earlier, she had testified in court about the attempt by her lesbian police officer lover to strangle her while they shared the same bed in which she nearly lost her life. At the time she was reluctant to report the incident for fear of being 'outed'. The police officer who was charged was sent to prison.[55] Being outed as lesbian in 2001 did not appear to be detrimental to Glen's career. It probably would have been ten years earlier.

In 2001, the Lesbian and Gay Police Association (LAGPA) published 'Understanding Lesbian and Gay Police Employees. A reference document for police managers and support workers' (author: Vic Codling). The document explains issues such as 'coming out' and not to assume everyone in the service is straight. The document states that many lesbians now prefer to be described as 'gay', and Point 8 is:

Lesbians often experience more than one prejudice. There is often a (quite dangerous) presumption that it appears easier for lesbians in the police service than for gay men. This is not always the case. In a male dominated police service, lesbians can be more at risk than other women because of sexism and anti-lesbian activity.

At the time, sexual orientation was not catered for within the employment tribunal process. This was rectified a couple of years later.

Julie Fry and Kelly Whiting, both serving in Hampshire Constabulary, came out in 1999 and joined LAGPA.[56] The first gay social event organised for Hampshire Constabulary was held at a Pizza Express in Winchester in 1999. In 2003, these two pioneering lesbian police women, together with a gay police-man, established a support group in Hampshire Constabulary known as the Hampshire Lesbian, Gay, Bisexual and Transgender Resource Group. The Hampshire group was fully endorsed by the Chief Constable and his team. Kelly Whiting chaired the group, and then later Julie Fry assumed the respon-sibility.[57] Such staff support groups were springing up all round Britain.

Until the Equality Act 2010 listed sexual orientation as a protected charac-teristic, there was no specific law prohibiting discrimination against lesbians, although a European Union directive implemented on 1 December 2003 outlawed discrimination on the grounds of sexual orientation. By 2003, all police forces in UK had included a reference to sexual orientation in their equal opportunities statements.

By 2010, when the Equality Act came into being, there was no need for any lesbian, gay or bisexual officer not to feel confident that their sexual orientation and identity would be accepted. Forces had established support groups for LGBT officers and staff, and allowed them to march in uniform at Pride events.[58] This would have seemed like an idea of fantasy even just twenty years earlier.

A survey of 836 lesbian, gay and bisexual (LGB) police officers by Jones and Williams in 2013 found significant improvements for LGB police offi-cers since the work by Marc Burke twenty years previously. Nearly half the respondents in their survey were women, and the survey found that lesbian and bisexual women were less likely to report having experienced discrimination than their male colleagues. Overall, just 20 per cent of the 836 officers reported experiencing homophobic discrimination within the police organisation, and this percentage was lower for the women. The authors recognised that changes within the police organisation had enabled these significant improvements. National work had set a marker for all forty-three forces. Jones and Williams talk of a 'new contemporary organisational culture within which the concept of difference and the benefits it affords to the organisation is embraced, encouraged and protected'.

Furthermore, they state:

Police frameworks have been introduced nationally that promote and support this mission of equality and diversity across the ranks, so that minority
officers feel comfortable to utilise and embed their subjective and inter-
subjective identity characteristics into the role without fear or experience
professional recourse or institutional bias.[59]

Being lesbian was no longer an issue, albeit being a gay man might still be
difficult. But any officer demonstrating discrimination was now likely to
face disciplinary action and the boot was certainly on a different foot from
that in twentieth-century policing.

Suzette Davenport made headlines in June 2014 when she came out
at a Gay Pride event in Gloucestershire, making her the first openly gay
chief constable.[60]

In 2022, data was published on what proportion of lesbian, gay and bisexual identifying officers were serving in the police. This data, broken down by
each police force, did not, however, give the figures by sex, and so we do not
know what proportion of women police officers were identifying as lesbian.[61]
The policing landscape is one that is very different today to that experienced
last century.

Unfortunately, progress in diversity has been matched by deterioration
in efficiency and service, brought about by cuts in service which started in
2008. Detection rates and prosecution rates have fallen dramatically; so low
that many people have little confidence in the police now.[62] It is no longer an
issue whether an officer is male or female and what their sexual orientation is,
but the general status of being a police officer is now much lower than when
being a known or 'out' lesbian could be a problem.

BIBLIOGRAPHY

Allen, Mary S. (1925) *The Pioneer Policewoman*, London: Chatto and Windus

Boyd, Nina (2013) *From Suffragette to Fascist: the many lives of Mary Sophia Allen*, Stroud: The History Press

Brazier, Corinne & Rice, Steve (2017) *A Fair Cop: 1917–2017 celebrating 100 years of policewomen in the West Midlands*, Birmingham: West Midlands Police

Burke, Marc E. (1993) *Coming Out of the Blue*, London: Cassell

Jackson, Sophie (2014) *Women on Duty: A history of the first female police force*, Stroud: Fonthill Media

Jones, Matthew & Williams, Matthew L. (2013) 'Twenty years on: lesbian, gay and bisexual police officers' experience of workplace discrimination in England and Wales', *Policing and Society*, **25**(2), pp.188–211

Lock, Joan (2014) *The British Policewoman: her story*, London: Robert Hale

WOMEN CHIEF POLICE OFFICERS OF THE UNITED KINGDOM, 1995-2023

ANTHONY RAE MA

THE FIRST: PAULINE ANN CLARE CBE, QPM, DL, SSSTJ, BA (HONS), CHIEF CONSTABLE OF THE LANCASHIRE CONSTABULARY 1995–2002

Pauline Clare shortly before retirement.
Publicity photo, Lancashire Constabulary.

ON 14 JUNE 1995, LANCASHIRE Police Authority appointed Pauline Clare the first female chief constable in the UK. Following a press conference, Mrs Clare expressed her own thoughts in the *Lancashire Constabulary Journal*:

> I made it quite clear to everybody at the conference that the Chief Constable's job was mine on merit. It had nothing to do with my being a woman but everything to do with being the best candidate with 28 years of relevant policing skills and qualifications. I emphasised how proud I am to be a woman and how extremely proud I am of my achievements. I realise just how significant it is to be the first woman Chief Constable and I am very conscious of making history, but I will not let any of this stand in the way of the job. [1]

The Police Authority said her gender was irrelevant in her appointment ahead of four senior male officers on the shortlist. They offered her a four-year contract; she asked for seven, and she got it. Chief Constable James Sharples, with whom Pauline worked as Assistant Chief Constable of Merseyside in 1992, said, 'This is not a token gesture, Mrs Clare is a woman of considerable skills and talent who has justifiably reached the top of her profession. She has got where she has purely on merit.'[2]

Pauline had joined Lancashire Constabulary as a police cadet in 1964. 'As a 17-year-old I was acutely aware that the Constabulary was segregated; policewomen belonged to their own department and had their own conditions of service in what was regarded very much as a man's world.'[3]

In 1966, Pauline was appointed as a constable to the Policewomen's Department at Seaforth Division (the home of fictional TV series *Z Cars*) and then worked as a juvenile liaison officer in Kirkby. She had no thoughts of a job for life: 'You were expected to work for a few years, then get married and have a family. I didn't expect to spend the next thirty years in the service.'[4] But with an establishment of only 125 policewomen, just 3 per cent of the force's strength, there was little competition for the few promotions, and in 1970 Pauline was promoted to sergeant in Kirkby.[5] In 1973, 'by the time I was twenty-six, I was an inspector and very firmly on the promotion ladder,' covering the whole of Sefton Division.[6] In 1974 she attended the inspector's course at Bramshill Police College but on returning to Southport, after boundary changes, was now part of the new Merseyside Police. Initially, Pauline supervised women across the division and then, after the Sex Discrimination Act, as a shift inspector in Southport.

In 1983, Pauline was given the choice of a three-year full-time university place on a Bramshill scholarship or promotion to chief inspector. 'I decided to take the promotion, and think about getting a degree through the Open

University in my own time.'[7] She set aside fourteen hours a week for seven years to study and achieved it.[8] The second half of her service, her achievements, honours and awards speaks for itself:

- 1983 Chief Inspector at Liverpool City Centre
- 1987 Superintendent, Community Affairs
- 1988 Sub-Divisional Commander, Southport
- 1991 Chief Superintendent, Commander of Sefton Division
- 1991 Open University BA (Honours) degree in psychology
- 1992 Assistant Chief Constable (Crime) Merseyside Police
- 1993 Lancashire Woman of the Year
- 1994 Assistant Chief Constable (Operations) Merseyside Police
- 1994 Deputy Chief Constable, Cheshire Constabulary
- 1994 University of Central Lancashire Honorary Fellowship
- 1995 Chief Constable Lancashire Constabulary
- 1995 North West Woman of Achievement
- 1995 Appointed as Serving Sister, Order of St John
- 1996 Queen's Police Medal for Distinguished Service
- 1997 Honorary Colonel of the Lancashire Army Cadet Force
- 1998 Commissioned Deputy Lieutenant Lancashire County
- 1999 Open University Honorary Doctor of the University
- 1999 Hosted Police History Society Conference at Constabulary HQ
- 2002 Appointed as Commander, Order of the British Empire

Eighty years after Edith Smith became the first sworn woman constable in Grantham, Pauline Clare became the first woman chief constable. Taking up her appointment on 31 July 1995, she served seven years in that post until 24 July 2002. By 2023, fifty-seven women had been appointed to chief officer ranks. Four others served seven years or more: Justine Curran (seven); Dame Elizabeth Neville (seven); Dame Sara Thornton (nine); and Dame Cressida Dick (ten). Since 1995, appointments have been made by thirty-six (65 per cent) of the fifty-eight UK forces. At the end of 2023, there were nineteen women chief officers serving in sixteen (31 per cent) of fifty-one forces (reduced by the 2013 amalgamation of Scottish forces).

In total, seventy-one appointments had been made (seven women were appointed twice, two three times and one four times) including substantive appointments of forty chief constables; one City of London Police commissioner; one Metropolitan Police commissioner; one deputy commissioner and eight assistant commissioners: an equivalent rank to chief constable.

In addition, there were sixteen temporary and four acting appointments to chief constable or equivalent ranks.

Their names, honours and awards are listed in the following tables.

Women Appointed to the Substantive Rank of Chief Constable or Commissioner of the City of London or Metropolitan Police

From–To	Name and Gazetted Honours	Police Force
1995–2002	Pauline Ann Clare CBE QPM	Lancashire
1997–2004	Dame Elizabeth Louise Neville DBE QPM	Wiltshire
1999–2004	Jane Stichbury CBE QPM	Dorset
2002–06	Maria Assumpta Wallis QPM	Devon/Cornwall
2002–07	Della Mary Cannings QPM	North Yorkshire
2004–09	Barbara Wilding CBE QPM	South Wales
2005–10	Gillian Parker QPM	Bedfordshire
2005–10	Julie Anne Spence OBE QPM	Cambridgeshire
2006–15	Dame Sara Joanne Thornton DBE CBE QPM	Thames Valley
2008–12	Julia Hodson QPM	Nottinghamshire
2008–12	Norma Graham QPM	Fife
2010–13	Justine Curran★★ QPM	Tayside
2010–15	Susan Karen Sim QPM	Northumbria
2011–13	Carmel Maria P. Napier QPM	Gwent
2012–15	Lynne Gillian Owens★★ CBE QPM	Surrey
2013–16	Jacqueline Cheer★★ QPM	Cleveland
2013–15	Colette Francesca Paul QPM	Bedfordshire
2013–17	Suzette Louise Davenport QPM	Gloucestershire
2013–17	Justine Curran★★★ QPM	Humberside
2013–18	Deborah Simpson★★ QPM	Dorset
2014–19	Dionne Marie Collins CBE QPM	West Yorkshire
2015–17	Hilary Jane Sawyers★★ QPM	Staffordshire
2016–22	Olivia Clare Pinkney QPM	Hampshire

2017–22	Dame Cressida Rose Dick★★★ DBE CBE QPM Commissioner	Metropolitan
2018–23	Michelle Prudencear Skeer OBE QPM	Cumbria
2018–	Lisa Jayne Winward★★ QPM	North Yorkshire
2019–23	Joanna Farrell	Durham
2019–	Pamela Charlotte Kelly QPM	Gwent
2020–	Jo Shiner	Sussex
2020–	Rachel Julie Swann QPM	Derbyshire
2021–	Lucy Clare D'Orsi QPM	British Transport
2021–	Serena Margaret Kennedy KPM	Merseyside
2021–	Lauren Poultney	South Yorkshire
2021–	Debbie Tedds	Warwickshire
2021–	Sarah Jane Crew QPM	Avon & Somerset
2021–23	Pippa Mills★	West Mercia
2022–	Angela McLaren Commissioner	City of London
2022–	Rachel Kearton	Suffolk
2022–	Amanda Jane Blakeman KPM	North Wales
2023–	Vanessa Jardine	Northumbria
2023–	Joanna Farrell★★	Scotland
2023–	Rachel Bacon	Durham

Women Appointed to the Substantive Metropolitan Police Rank of Assistant or Deputy Commissioner, Being an Equivalent Rank to Chief Constable

From–To	Name and Gazetted Honours	Metropolitan
2009–14	Cressida Rose Dick★ CBE QPM	Assistant Commissioner
2010–12	Lynne Gillian Owens★ QPM	Assistant Commissioner
2014–16	Helen King QPM	Assistant Commissioner

2015–18	Patricia Ferguson Gallan QPM	Assistant Commissioner
2017–22	Helen Elizabeth Ball QPM★	Assistant Commissioner
2020–	Louisa Helen Rolfe OBE	Assistant Commissioner
2022–	Barbara Ann Gray LVO QPM	Assistant Commissioner
2023–	Pippa Mills★★	Assistant Commissioner
2023–	Dame Lynne Gillian Owens★★★★ DCB CBE QPM	Deputy Commissioner

Women Appointed to Temporary or Acting Chief Constable or the Equivalent Metropolitan Assistant or Deputy Commissioner

From–To	Name and Gazetted Honours	Police Force
2005–06	Carole Anne Howlett QPM	Norfolk
2009	Judith Kyle Gillespie CBE OBE (Acting)	Northern Ireland
2009	Rose Mary Fitzpatrick CBE QPM Assistant Commissioner	Metropolitan
2009–10	Justine Curran★ QPM	Tayside
2011–12	Cressida Rose Dick★★ CBE QPM (Acting) Deputy Commissioner	Metropolitan
2011–13	Carmel Maria Philomena Napier QPM	Gwent
2011–13	Jacqueline Cheer★ QPM	Cleveland
2012–13	Deborah Simpson★ QPM	Dorset
2012–13	Jackie Roberts QPM	Dyfed-Powys
2014–15	Hilary Jane Sawyers★ QPM	Staffordshire
2016–17	Susannah Kate Fish OBE QPM	Nottinghamshire
2017	Fiona Helen Taylor QPM Assistant Commissioner	Metropolitan

2017–19	Janette Elise McCormick QPM	Cheshire
2018	Lisa Jayne Winward★ QPM	North Yorkshire
2021	Emma Elizabeth Barnett KPM	Staffordshire
2021	Claire Parmenter	Dyfed-Powys
2021–22	Amanda Pearson Assistant Commissioner	Metropolitan
2021–22	Helen McMillan (Acting)	Cleveland
2022	Helen Elizabeth Ball★★ QPM (Acting) Deputy Commissioner	Metropolitan
2022–2023	Dame Lynne Gillian Owens★★★ DCB CBE QPM Deputy Commissioner	Metropolitan

Notes: Temporary and Acting appointments are normally limited to months or weeks
*First   **Second   ***Third   ****Fourth Appointment
Honours and Awards are from The Gazette – Official Public Record
DCB – Dame Commander of the Order of the Bath
DBE – Dame Commander of the Order of the British Empire
CBE – Commander of the Order of the British Empire
OBE – Officer of the Order of the British Empire
KPM/QPM – King's/Queen's Police Medal

SOURCES
Stallion, M. & Wall D. (2012), *The British Police: Forces and Chief Officers 1829–2012*, Bramshill, Hook: The Police History Society

Websites
UK police forces: via www.police.uk/
Honours and Awards: The Gazette: Official Public Record, www.thegazette.co.uk/
Who's Who 2022, Oxford University Press: www.ukwhoswho.com/
News: Police Oracle: www.policeoracle.com/
News: Police Professional: www.policeprofessional.com/

All accessed November 2023

ROLL OF HONOUR

IN REMEMBRANCE OF WOMEN POLICE OFFICERS OF THE UNITED KINGDOM WHO HAVE LOST THEIR LIVES IN THE LINE OF DUTY

ANTHONY RAE MA

INTRODUCTION

The story of the sacrifice of women in policing starts with the outbreak of the Second World War and the need for more women to replace men going off to war. In 1939, national regular police strengths of some 74,000 included just 263 women police officers.[1] In 1942, there were also over forty police-women in national railway company police forces; and in 1943, the Royal Ulster Constabulary (RUC) recruited its first seven women police officers. By 1945, there were 463 regular policewomen, including the RUC. In addition, 121 former policewomen joined the First Police Reserve and the wartime Women's Auxiliary Police Corps (WAPC) provided 652 attested officers for street duties and 3,000 unattested for policing roles.

Three women police employees were killed during the war. The first, albeit not an attested officer, is named on the City of London Police war memorial as Nurse Evelyn Rolfe. Aged 65, with thirty years' service in the force, she was fatally injured in 1940 when the unique police hospital at Bishopsgate Police Station was bombed during an enemy air raid. Railway policewoman Lilian Gale, recruited in 1943, became the first attested policewoman to be fatally injured on duty, when run over by a railway engine in January 1944. Metropolitan WPC Bertha Gleghorn, recruited in 1940, was killed when an enemy flying bomb fell on her police station in 1944.

In 1945, Barbara Denis De Vitré, a policewoman since 1928, became the first woman appointed to HMIC to assist with all issues relating to policewomen. In 1946, numbers rose to 760 nationally and Police Women

Departments began to be established in all forces, although run separately, with different pay and conditions to men. In 1948, Miss Denis De Vitré was appointed an Assistant Inspector of Constabulary, and in 1951 she was made an OBE. In 1960, she died age 54 after ill health, by which time there were 2,545 women police in Great Britain, fifty-six in the RUC and 120 in the British Transport Police.

By 1965, fifty years after the first woman was attested into the office of constable, only five had died, just two in the twenty years since the war, both in accidents. But things were about to change; with equality in work would come equality of sacrifice, as women officers began to be employed on more operational duties. In June 1965, Policewoman Myra Waller was killed when her MG traffic patrol car crashed while attending an emergency call. Worse was to come.

Between 1960 and 1975, policewomen numbers in Great Britain more than doubled to some 6,500. Following the Sex Discrimination Act 1975, Police Women Departments were dissolved and integrated into male ranks with equal pay and conditions, and policewomen became women police. In 1995, they were simply police officers, and Pauline Clare became the first female chief constable in the UK; in England and Wales alone, there were 17,650 female police officers.[2] The fifty years following 1965 saw the true cost of equality, as a staggering sixty-two women paid the ultimate price.

Of the sixty-eight officers on 'The Roll', fifty-two lost their lives on operational duty, of which nineteen were killed by criminal acts: eight in bomb explosions (two in war, six by terrorists); six shot (three by terrorists); two stabbed; three struck by vehicles. Twenty-eight were killed by accident or misadventure: twenty-two in road accidents (sixteen in police vehicles); three drowned (two training, one in a rescue); one in a helicopter crash; one in a rail accident; one in a fall. Five died of natural causes. A further sixteen died in road accidents travelling to or from work which constitutes part of a tour of duty. Forty-eight were from forces in England, thirteen from Northern Ireland and seven from Scotland.

Rank designations varied over the years, but by 1940 most forces used the generic 'policewoman' description as a rank, formally 'Police Woman' or 'PW', rather than 'Police Constable' or 'PC' then used by male officers. The Metropolitan Police was an exception, using 'WPC' from the start and 'PC' from 1993; the Royal Ulster Constabulary dispensed with 'Police' for all, and used 'Woman Constable' or 'W/Con.' After the 1975 Act, the PW rank changed to WPC, and by the end of the century the single rank of PC was in general use for all. This Roll shows the officers' formal ranks used at the time.

Within these pages are the names of heroines but mostly the names of ordinary women – mothers, wives, partners, daughters, sisters, girlfriends and colleagues. What makes them extraordinary is not how they died but how they lived – doing an often dangerous and thankless job, forgotten until needed, protecting communities for which, in the course of their duties, they lost their lives. Sadly, as long as police officers are prepared to take risks in the protection of their communities, it is inevitable that the Roll of Honour will never be complete but remains a tribute to all these women.

LEST WE FORGET

Evelyn Rolfe SRN
Police Nurse, City of London Police
Died 9 September 1940, aged 65

Evelyn was a resident nurse at the City Police Hospital on the top floor of Bishopsgate Police Station. During a late-night enemy air raid on 8 September, a high-explosive bomb hit the building and she sustained multiple injuries, dying in the early hours at St Bartholomew's Hospital. Evelyn was unmarried with no immediate surviving family; she had worked as a nurse for some forty years, at least thirty of which were dedicated to caring for sick and injured police officers.

Lilian Daisy Gale
Police Woman
Great Western Railway (GWR) Police
Died 6 January 1944, aged 26

Lilian was patrolling Plymouth GWR docks on 5 January when she was accidentally run over by a railway engine, which severed both legs. She died as a result of these injuries the following day in hospital. Lilian joined the police in April 1943 after service as a clerk in an RAF munitions unit. She was survived by her husband, an army officer serving overseas.

Bertha Massey Gleghorn
Woman Police Constable
Metropolitan Police
Died 19 June 1944, aged 33

Bertha was resuming her beat after a morning refreshment break at Tottenham Court Road Police Station, when a German V-1 flying bomb exploded in the rear yard, burying her in rubble. She was pulled out alive but died from her injuries the same day at Middlesex Hospital. Bertha, appointed in January 1940, received a Commissioner's Commendation in 1942. She was single and was survived by her mother and stepfather.

Catherine Phyllis Godfrey
Police Woman
Leicestershire Constabulary
Died 3 May 1947, aged 31

Catherine was recalled to duty late at night on 23 April to deal with a violent female prisoner at Hinckley. While cycling to the police station in a severe gale, her head struck the branch of a fallen tree and she sustained a fractured skull and spine, dying ten days later. Catherine was appointed on 13 May 1946 after serving with the Auxiliary Territorial Service. She was single and left behind her parents, six brothers and three sisters.

Mary Jean Baldwin
Police Woman Sergeant
Birmingham City Police
Died 26 June 1959, aged 34

Mary was in Selly Oak Hospital on 8 June, after interviewing a patient, when she fell on the stairs, breaking her ankle. While convalescing at home she collapsed and died when a blood clot from her injury caused a pulmonary embolism; an inquest returned a verdict of accidental death. Mary was appointed in 1949, joined CID in 1953, and was promoted to sergeant in 1955. A single woman, she left her parents, brother and sister.

Myra Waller
Police Woman
Lancashire Constabulary
Died 20 June 1965, aged 24

Myra answered an emergency call to the scene of a road accident on the late evening of 19 June, when her MG traffic patrol car collided head-on with a car near Lancaster and she received multiple injuries, from which she died in hospital. Appointed in March 1961, she joined Lancaster Traffic Branch in January 1964. She was single and her parents' only child.

June Randell
Police Woman
Hull City Police
Died 10 March 1966, aged 21

June was riding her moped to report for duty at Crowle Street Police Station, Hull, at 8 a.m., when an articulated lorry turned left across her path without indicating. It knocked her to the ground and she was killed when the trailer ran over her. June had joined the force on 7 December 1964; a single woman, she was survived by her parents and sister.

Carol Anne Waddington
Police Woman
Rochdale Borough Police
Died 21 December 1968, aged 19

Carol was a passenger in a car returning to Rochdale from Bruche Police Training Centre with two colleagues, when the car accidentally collided with a stationary lorry at Prestwich and she died instantly from a fractured skull. Carol was a Queen's Guide and police cadet when appointed constable on 4 October 1968; she was survived by her parents, sister and her fiancé, a serving constable at Rochdale.

Ann Lakey
Police Woman
Teesside Constabulary
Died 19 October 1970, aged 24

Ann was observer in a police patrol car which crashed at Grangetown when responding to an emergency burglar alarm call, and died as a result of her injuries. Ann had worked in the magistrates' court as a typist, and as a special constable, before joining the force, working from Southbank Police Station. Ann was single, her mother died when she was 3 and she was survived by her father, stepmother and sibling.

Barbara Lynne Wilkinson
Police Woman
Lancashire Constabulary
Died 13 November 1971, aged 20

Barbara was returning from participating with the Constabulary Policewomen's First Aid Team in a competition in Northwich when her car was in collision with two other vehicles at Tarleton and she received fatal head injuries. Appointed in July 1970, she had been stationed at Preston and since May 1971 at Kirkby. Barbara was single and survived by her mother.

Karpal Kaur Sandhu
Woman Police Constable
Metropolitan Police
Died 5 November 1973, aged 30

Karpal returned home from duty late at night on 4 November and was attacked outside her house by her estranged husband, who disagreed with her occupation. She called out, identifying herself as a WPC and her husband, fearing arrest, stabbed her in the neck. She died the next morning in hospital. Karpal was the first female Asian officer nationally when appointed in 1971. She was survived by her two young children.

Lesley Anne Beet
Police Cadet
Essex & Southend on Sea Joint Constabulary
Died 13 March 1974, aged 18

Leslie was with a supervised party of police cadets canoeing on the River Chelmer, near police headquarters, Chelmsford, when her canoe capsized and, despite attempts to save her, she was drowned. She had joined the cadets from school, at her second attempt, on 3 September 1973. Leslie was survived by her parents who were both special constables. Fellow cadets planted a flowering tree in her memory.

Mildred Ann Harrison
Woman Reserve Constable (Part Time)
Royal Ulster Constabulary GC
Died 16 March 1975, aged 26

Mildred was on foot patrol with a colleague in Bangor, Co. Down, passing licensed premises when a canister bomb, placed by terrorists on the windowsill, exploded, killing her almost immediately. Mildred was a housewife and had been a part-time reservist for just two months; she was survived by her husband and two daughters aged 6 and 3 years.

Margaret Cherry Campbell
Woman Reserve Constable (Part Time)
Royal Ulster Constabulary GC
Died 21 November 1975, aged 24

Margaret was assisting other officers at the scene of a road accident in Londonderry, during the early hours of 1 November, when a speeding car collided with a police Land Rover injuring eight people, including Margaret, who sustained a fractured skull from which she died three weeks later in Altnagelvin Hospital. Margaret was a single woman.

Linda Emmeline Baggley

Woman Reserve Constable (Part Time)
Royal Ulster Constabulary GC
Died 2 June 1976, aged 19

Linda was on foot patrol duty with a colleague in Londonderry late at night on 23 May when they were both shot in a terrorist attack; she received gunshot wounds in the face and head, from which she died ten days later in Belfast Victoria Hospital. A single woman, Linda joined the RUC Reserve in July 1975, eighteen months after her father was shot dead on RUC Reserve duty. She left behind her mother, sister and brother.

Shirley Moses

Woman Police Constable
Northumbria Police
Died 29 August 1976, aged 21

Shirley was on patrol with a male colleague in Sunderland at 1.40 a.m. when the police car she was driving spun off the road, made greasy by rain after a summer drought. The car crashed into railings, one of which pierced the windscreen and struck her in the forehead, severing an artery and fracturing her skull. She died soon after. Shirley was single.

Norma Spence

Civilian Search Unit Officer
Royal Ulster Constabulary GC
Died 3 March 1978, aged 25

Norma was working with a soldier at an army checkpoint in Belfast, when four terrorists shot dead the soldier; as Norma tried to run away, she was also shot three times and killed. Norma joined the unit in January 1975. She was survived by her parents, brother and her fiancé, a soldier.

Elizabeth Burton
Woman Police Sergeant
Lillian Sullivan
Woman Police Constable
West Yorkshire
Metropolitan Police
Died 15 May 1978,
aged 40 and 41

Elizabeth and Lillian died with three male colleagues travelling to the Police Federation Conference at Blackpool when their coach crashed near Wakefield. Elizabeth, 40 and single, was appointed in 1958 and was a juvenile liaison officer. Lilian, 41 and married, joined in 1969 and worked in the Prosecutions Department.

Isabella Janet Greenshields Harris
Woman Police Constable
Dumfries and Galloway Constabulary
Died 7 November 1978, aged 27

Isabella was driving a traffic patrol car, with a constable, a police cadet and Department of Transport traffic examiner, on the A74. On passing an articulated lorry it jack-knifed, throwing their police car into the opposite carriageway, landing upside down on a lorry and killing all four officers. Isabella joined the force in 1975 and the Traffic Department in June 1978. She was single and left behind her parents and siblings.

Sharon Bury
Police Cadet
Avon and Somerset Constabulary
Died 8 February 1980, aged 16

Sharon was on adventure training at Foreland Point, Devon, when a large wave swept her off rocks, and despite rescue attempts she was lost at sea, her body being recovered six days later. An inquest found she drowned after sustaining a broken neck, rendering her helpless. Sharon had joined the cadets in September 1979. She left behind her parents and sister.

Joanne Margaret Best
Woman Constable
Royal Ulster Constabulary GC
Died 28 October 1980, aged 21

Joanne was with four officers on mobile patrol in Belfast about 1.25 a.m., following an earlier pursuit, when they were seen driving at high speed using the blue light and siren. The Land Rover drove through a red light and was in collision with an articulated lorry and wrecked; the five constables died at the scene or shortly afterwards. Joanne had eight months' service and left behind her parents, three sisters and two brothers.

Deborah Nicholson
Woman Police Constable
Greater Manchester Police
Died 6 November 1980, aged 24

Deborah was on a mobile beat in Wigan on an early shift and visited a local factory, where she suddenly became unwell and collapsed while speaking with the security officer who tried to revive her. On arrival at hospital, she was found to have died from a viral infection of the heart. Debbie was stationed at Pemberton and was survived by her parents and sisters.

Martha Doreen Elizabeth Harkness
Woman Constable
Royal Ulster Constabulary GC
Died 25 July 1981, aged 22

Doreen was with a team operating a vehicle checkpoint on the Magherafelt-Moneymore Road, County Londonderry, at 12.55 a.m. when she was struck by one of two vehicles, which failed to stop at the checkpoint. She died from her injuries a short time later. Doreen joined the RUC in September 1977 and served in Belfast before transferring to Magherafelt in January 1981. She was single and left behind her parents, brothers and sisters.

Elaine Evans
Inspector
Merseyside Police
Died 5 October 1981, aged 33

Elaine was travelling to report for duty on 3 October 1981 when her car was in collision with another vehicle at Fazakerley and she received fatal injuries. She died in hospital at Liverpool two days later. Elaine was survived by her husband and their 1-year-old daughter.

Mabel Elizabeth Cheyne
Woman Reserve Constable (Part Time)
Royal Ulster Constabulary GC
Died 23 April 1982, aged 29

Elizabeth was with two colleagues on patrol, responding to an emergency call of an assault at a pub in Armagh City at 8.40 p.m. when their police car lost control on a bend, colliding with a stone bridge wall. All three officers died at the scene. Elizabeth was appointed in October 1977 and was stationed at Armagh. She left behind her husband and son aged 5.

Mandy Dawn Rayner
Woman Police Constable
Hertfordshire Constabulary
Died 13 October 1982, aged 18

Mandy was observer in a stationary police car near Royston about 11.35 p.m., when a drunk driver, pursued by police, deliberately rammed their car, killing Mandy and seriously injuring the police driver. The offender was sentenced to five years' imprisonment for manslaughter. Mandy, a former cadet, had just four months' service and five weeks' operational duty when she died. She was survived by her parents and younger sister.

Angela Bradley
Woman Police Constable
Lancashire Constabulary
Died 5 January 1983, aged 23

Angela and three colleagues responded to a man drowning in a very rough sea at Blackpool, making two attempts to rescue the man using ropes and a lifebelt. All were then engulfed and swept away by huge waves battering the sea wall. Angela drowned with PCs Gordon Connolly, Colin Morrison and the man; PC Pat Abram was rescued unconscious. Angela was appointed in October 1977. She was survived by her parents and sister.

Jane Philippa Arbuthnot
Woman Police Constable
Metropolitan Police
Died 17 December 1983, aged 22

Jane was among police officers investigating a suspected terrorist car bomb and evacuating around the Harrods store in Knightsbridge when, about 1.20 p.m., the device exploded causing six fatalities and many injuries. Jane and Sergeant Noel Lane died instantly of multiple injuries, and Inspector Stephen Dodd died on the 24th. Jane joined in March 1981, serving at Chelsea. She left her parents, two brothers and sister.

Joanne Mary Cochran
Woman Police Constable
Thames Valley Police
Died 29 March 1984, aged 20

Joanne was observer in a patrol car following a vehicle on the A40 at Oxford near the end of a night shift, when her driver swerved to avoid a polythene sack blown across the road and their car hit the kerb, overturned, and she was fatally injured. Joanne had nine months' service, living in single quarters at Cowley Police Station. She was survived by her mother and a sibling.

Yvonne Joyce Fletcher
Woman Police Constable
Metropolitan Police
Died 17 April 1984, aged 25

Yvonne was with colleagues facing about seventy demonstrators outside the Libyan Embassy in St James's Square, London, about 10.20 a.m., when two submachine guns were fired from the building towards the crowd, wounding eleven and killing Yvonne, who was shot through the back and died in hospital. The suspects left the country under diplomatic immunity. Yvonne, with seven years' service, left behind her parents, sisters and fiancé.

Ivy Winifred Kelly
Woman Detective Constable
Rosemary Elizabeth McGookin
Woman Constable
Royal Ulster Constabulary
GC
Died 28 February 1985, aged 29 and 27

Ivy and Rosemary were having their evening meal in the portacabin canteen of the Newry RUC Station at 6.30 p.m. when the station complex was hit by several bombs during a heavy mortar attack by terrorists. The canteen was destroyed by a direct hit, the explosion killing them both, along with seven other officers. This was the largest number of RUC officers killed by terrorists in a single incident. A further twelve police and twenty-five civilians were injured. Ivy had ten years' service and was attached to the drug squad at Lurgan. Rosemary joined in March 1978 and was stationed in Newry. She was married to an RUC officer, and both resided in Portadown.

Tracy Ellen Doak
Woman Constable
Royal Ulster Constabulary GC
Died 20 May 1985, aged 21

Tracy, together with three colleagues, was in an armoured police car, one of two patrols waiting near the former customs post at Killeen, Newry, to take over the escort of a security van carrying a cross-border shipment of money estimated at IR£2 million. At 9.53 a.m., a 1,000lb bomb placed in a trailer near the road was detonated by terrorists across the border, destroying their police car and killing all four officers. Tracy had three years' service and was stationed at Newry. She was single and lived in Coleraine and was survived by her parents.

Deborah Leat
Woman Police Constable
Avon and Somerset Constabulary
Died 27 November 1986, aged 20

Deborah was driving a police patrol car with a PC in Bristol about 3.10 a.m. when a suspect car failed to stop for them and sped through red traffic lights. As she pursued it at high speed around a corner, she lost control of the police car, which crashed into a tree, killing her. Deborah, a former police cadet, joined the constabulary in July 1984, being stationed at Staple Hill Police Station. She was single and was survived by her parents.

Jacqueline Ann Brown
Woman Police Constable
Hertfordshire Constabulary
Died 6 June 1989, aged 23

Jacqueline was driving a police patrol car with a sergeant escorting a prisoner at 1.15 a.m., when she lost control on a sharp bend at Harpenden, struck the kerb, and overturned, sustaining severe head injuries from which she later died in hospital. Jacqueline had two years' service, stationed at Hatfield. She left her husband, a police sergeant, and her parents.

Jo-Ann Jennings
Woman Police Constable
Essex Police
Died 12 November 1989, aged 23

Jo-Ann was in a police patrol car driven by a colleague about 2.55 a.m., responding to police assistance calls to an illegal 'acid house' party near Brentwood, when their car left the road and collided with a tree, causing serious injuries to the driver and multiple injuries to Jo-Ann, who died the same day in Orsett Hospital. She was a special constable before joining the force in February 1987 and left behind her parents and sister.

Colleen Linda McMurray
Woman Constable
Royal Ulster Constabulary GC
Died 28 March 1992, aged 34

Colleen was observer in the first of two police patrol vehicles on Merchants Quay, Newry, at 11.35 p.m. when terrorists remotely fired a horizontal mortar hidden in a nearby car. The bomb struck their vehicle side on. The driver lost his legs and Colleen was seriously injured and died in hospital the next day. She had fifteen years' service. Stationed at Newry, she left behind her police officer husband, parents and three sisters.

METROPOLITAN POLICE

Sharon Rena Kay Sawyer
Police Constable
Metropolitan Police
Died 1 March 1993, aged 32

Sharon was travelling on her motorcycle to a Territorial Support Group public order shield training day, when she was involved in a road traffic collision and sustained fatal injuries. Sharon was a member of '5 Area TSG', based at Barnes; she had five years' service and previously served in Brixton. She was survived by her parents, brother and two daughters.

Gina Corin Rutherford
Woman Police Constable
South Yorkshire Police
Died 7 February 1994, aged 25

Gina was on mobile patrol as a passenger about 5 a.m. when the police car skidded off an icy road, plunging upside down into the River Dearne. Gina was trapped inside the car, and despite attempts by the driver and a fireman, she drowned before she could be freed. Gina, a former soldier, had eighteen months service at Bolton-upon-Dearne. She was single and living with a police friend; she left behind her parents and two brothers.

Gail Doreen Pirnie
Police Constable
Metropolitan Police
Died 26 October 1994, aged 42

Gail was undergoing a baton training course at the Peel Centre, Hendon, when at 2.10 p.m., having just completed a training exercise, she collapsed and died from heart failure. Gail served twenty years with the force and was stationed at Hendon. A single woman, from Pitlochry, Perthshire, she was survived by her mother, sister and brother.

Sandra Jane Edwards
Woman Police Constable
South Yorkshire Police
Died 10 May 1995, aged 28

Sandra was driving a traffic patrol car in a high-speed pursuit of a suspected stolen car at Cudworth, near Barnsley, about 2.15 a.m. on 8 May, when the police car left the road on a sharp bend and collided with a stone wall. She sustained serious head injuries of which she died two days later. Sandra had ten years' service, and had recently joined the traffic branch. She was awaiting a divorce to remarry, and left behind her parents.

STRATHCLYDE
POLICE

Melanie Igoe
Woman Police Constable
Strathclyde Police
Died 30 May 1995, aged 28

Melanie was undergoing instruction on a standard motorcycle training course for traffic officers in the afternoon, when she lost control of her 125cc police motorcycle on a bend near Largs, collided with an oncoming car and was killed. Melanie joined the force in February 1988, serving at Shettleston before transfer to the traffic branch in 1993. She left behind her police sergeant husband of ten months and her parents.

Philippa Jane Parish
Woman Police Constable
Hampshire Constabulary
Died 13 March 1996, aged 29

Philippa was the observer in a police area car at Winchester responding to an alarm call at 4.30 a.m. when the driver lost control while avoiding an object in the road, colliding with a brick wall, and she was killed. 'Pippa' joined the force in September 1987 and was stationed at North Walls, Winchester. She was survived by her husband, a serving officer, and her parents.

Vanessa Rosemary Carroll
Inspector
West Midlands Police
Died 28 April 1996, aged 35

Vanessa was a month into a six-month posting with the British Police Contingent in Bosnia, helping set up a unified police force in Mostar. At 7.15 p.m., driving with a sergeant at Metkovic near the Croatia border, she swerved to avoid an oncoming car, was thrown from her vehicle and killed. Vanessa had sixteen years' service and left behind her mother and sister.

Nina Alexandra MacKay
Police Constable
Metropolitan Police
Died 24 October 1997, aged 25

Nina was with a Territorial Support Group unit at about 8.35 p.m. when she forced entry to a flat at Stratford to arrest a violent wanted suspect. She was immediately attacked and stabbed in the chest by the man and died in hospital. Nina had five years' service, stationed at Charing Cross and on '3 Area' TSG since November 1996. She left behind her mother, her father, a retired Metropolitan officer, and her brother, a serving officer.

STRATHCLYDE
POLICE

Jacqueline Ann Haswell
Police Constable
Strathclyde Police
Died 7 August 2000, aged 30

Jackie was driving from her home in Stewarton to report for duty at Paisley in the early morning, when she lost control of her car and crashed into a tree, sustaining multiple injuries and a fractured skull from which she died in hospital. Jackie was appointed in January 2000, after working as a force support officer at Kilmarnock. She was a single woman.

Alison Armitage
Police Constable
Greater Manchester Police
Died 5 March 2001, aged 29

Alison was with colleagues on plainclothes observations of a stolen car in Oldham at 4.40 p.m. when a suspect got into the car; to stop him driving away, she went to the rear of the car, which reversed, knocking her down, then ran over her twice, causing multiple injuries from which she later died. Alison had five years' service and was attached to the Operational Support Unit. She was single, and was survived by her parents and two sisters.

Sarah Jane Minskip
Police Constable
Avon and Somerset Constabulary
Died 4 February 2004, aged 26

Sarah was travelling home from an extended tour of night duty after dealing with a prisoner at Taunton, about 7.00 a.m., when her motorcycle was in collision with a van, which turned across her path at Ashill. She sustained head injuries from which she died at the scene. Sarah had eight months' service and was stationed at Taunton. She was survived by her fiancé, with whom she lived at Chard, and her mother and brother.

Catherine Margaret Sutcliffe
Police Constable
Lancashire Constabulary
Died 20 August 2004, aged 34

Cate was on routine patrol duties on Sunday, 8 August, and during a non-confrontational incident at Waddington she collapsed from a brain aneurism. She underwent surgery for cerebral bleeding at Royal Preston Hospital but subsequently lapsed into a coma and died. Cate had twelve years' service, and left behind her partner, parents and brother.

Cheryl Rosemarie Lloyd
Police Constable
Suffolk Constabulary
Died 18 June 2005, aged 42

Cheryl was driving a police patrol car with a colleague at about 8.00 p.m., responding to an urgent call for police assistance, when she lost control of the car on a bend, crashed into a stationary lorry and died instantly from head injuries. A former special constable, Cheryl, with five years' service, was an advanced driver on the urban response vehicle at Ipswich. She was survived by her mother, two sisters and her partner.

Siobhan Mary Majella McCann
Constable
Police Service of Northern Ireland
Died 10 July 2005, aged 41

Siobhan was driving in a convoy of armoured Land Rovers to a public order operation, when she lost control of the vehicle, which crashed at Desertmartin, Co. Londonderry, and she was fatally injured. Siobhan had two years' service, stationed at Londonderry. She was survived by her son, her parents, three sisters, two brothers and her fiancé, a serving officer.

Sharon Beshenivsky
Police Constable
West Yorkshire Police
Died 18 November 2005, aged 38

Sharon responded with a colleague to an alarm at a travel agency in Bradford, when they were confronted by three armed robbers leaving the premises. Shots were fired and she was hit in the chest and killed, and her colleague was injured. Sharon, a former community support officer, had nine months' service. She left her husband, their two sons and daughter, a stepdaughter and stepson, the children aged 4–14 years.

Karen Balfour
Police Constable
Lothian and Borders Police
Died 5 January 2006, aged 37

Karen was driving from her Houndslow home to report for duty at Duns Police Station at 8.25 a.m., when her car was in collision with a van near Greenlaw and she was fatally injured. Karen had fourteen years' service and was based on a community policing team working with youth groups. She was survived by her husband, parents, brother and three sisters.

Deborah Adele Harman-Burton
Police Constable
West Midlands Police
Died 24 March 2006, aged 28

Debbie was travelling home from night duty at Coventry with her partner, a serving officer, driving their car when it was involved in a three-vehicle collision near Kenilworth. She was killed and her partner injured. Debbie, a former police call handler, was appointed in August 2003. She was survived by her partner, her parents and two sisters.

Stacey Victoria Pyke
Police Constable
Lincolnshire Police
Died 15 January 2007, aged 20

Stacey was driving to her home in Yaxley, Cambridgeshire, at 7.15 a.m. after finishing her first night duty at Spalding, when her vehicle was in a head-on collision with a car near Market Deeping and she died at the scene. Stacey had less than six months' service, having been appointed in August 2006, and was stationed at Spalding Police Station. She was survived by her parents, her younger sister and her boyfriend.

Kirsty Leanne Allan
Police Constable
Fife Constabulary
Died 2 March 2007, aged 24

Kirsty was travelling from her home at Dunfermline at 7.50 a.m. to report for duty at Oakley, when she lost control of her car on an icy road and it overturned, causing injuries from which she died soon after. Kirsty was appointed in February 2005 and had just completed her probation; she was stationed at West Fife Villages police station at Oakley. She was survived by her parents, husband and son aged 3 years.

Katie Louise Mitchell
Police Constable
Kent Police
Died 3 October 2007, aged 39

Katie was travelling to report for day duty at Tonbridge when she lost control of her motorcycle and was struck by a car at Goudhurst, killing her instantly. Katie, a graduate of Leeds University, had ten years' service stationed at Tonbridge. She was a volunteer with the Wildlife Heritage Foundation. Katie left behind her parents and was their only child.

Dee Marie Weatherley
Detective Constable
Thames Valley Police
Died 13 December 2008, aged 31

Dee was travelling to report for duty at Aylesbury, in the early morning, when her car was struck by a vehicle which crossed the carriageway from the opposite direction at Hoggeston, and she was fatally injured. Dee was appointed in November 2003 and joined the CID in 2006. She left her partner, a serving officer, with whom she had been expecting a baby, her parents, stepfather and her sister.

Diane Christine Donald
Detective Constable
Strathclyde Police
Died 21 January 2009, aged 40

Diane was driving from her home in Erskine to report for duty at Govan Police Office in the early morning, when her car left the M8 motorway in icy road conditions and struck a tree and she was killed. Diane, a former prison officer, was appointed in 2001 and joined CID in 2007, stationed in Glasgow. She was single and was survived by her father and brother.

Laura Ruth Williams
Police Constable
Metropolitan Police
Died 19 February 2009, aged 41

Laura collapsed unconscious at Greenwich Park Police Station. She was taken to hospital but died the next day of a brain haemorrhage. Laura joined Royal Parks Constabulary in 1998; she was diagnosed with leukaemia in 2001, returning to work after treatment. Following amalgamation with the Metropolitan Police, she worked response and as a 'safer parks' officer. She left her partner and two sons aged 5 and 2.

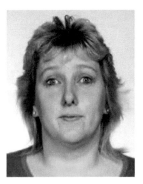

Karen Lynn Paterson
Police Constable
Cambridgeshire Constabulary
Died 6 January 2012, aged 44

Karen was returning home from night duty at Peterborough in the early morning when her car was in collision with another vehicle at Langtoft, Lincolnshire. Karen joined Surrey Police in 1987, transferring to Cambridgeshire in 1997; she was based at Thorpe Wood in Peterborough and also worked out of Bridge Street Police Station as a schools' liaison officer. She left her husband and their two sons and her parents.

Fiona Susan Bone
Police Constable
Nicola Hughes
Police Constable
Greater Manchester Police
Died 18 September 2012, aged 32 and 23

Fiona and Nicola were on Tameside Division van patrol together about 10.50 a.m. when they attended a routine call reporting an attempted house burglary at Mottram. As they walked to the door, a wanted double murderer came out, immediately shooting both officers repeatedly with a pistol, and despite their body armour both fell, suffering multiple gunshot wounds from over thirty shots. The man then exploded a hand grenade and drove to a police station to surrender. Fiona died at the scene and Nicola was dead on arrival at hospital. Their killer received four whole-life prison terms. Both officers worked from Hyde Police Station. Fiona had five years' service. She left behind her parents and sister, and her partner and her daughter, with whom she lived. Nicola had three years' service. She left her father, her mother and younger brother with whom she lived.

Adele Yvette Cashman
Detective Constable
Metropolitan Police
Died 5 November 2012, aged 30

Adele responded with crime squad officers to assist patrols chasing thieves in Belsize Park, Camden; while pursuing a suspect on foot she collapsed and soon afterwards died in hospital of heart failure. Adele had six years' service in both Wandsworth and, since 2010, on CID at Kentish Town Police Station. She was survived by her parents, three brothers and a sister.

Philippa Reynolds
Constable
Police Service of Northern Ireland
Died 9 February 2013, aged 27

Philippa was on routine patrol in Londonderry about 3.30 a.m. when the unmarked police car in which she was a passenger was struck by a stolen vehicle; Philippa was killed instantly and two other officers in the police car were injured. Philippa, a former teacher, had two years' service and was a member of the response section stationed at Strand Road Police Station, Derry. She was survived by her parents and two older sisters.

Kirsty Mary Nelis
Police Constable
Police Scotland
Died 29 November 2013, aged 36

Kirsty, PC Anthony Collins and the pilot were killed when their Air Support Unit helicopter crashed through the roof of a public house in Glasgow at 10.22 p.m., fatally injuring seven others. A sheriff's inquiry found the crash was due to pilot failures. Kirsty had thirteen years' service and was a helicopter observer on Operations Support Division. She left her husband, a serving officer, two stepchildren, parents and brother.

Sharon Garrett
Detective Constable
Cambridgeshire Constabulary
Died 6 June 2014, aged 48

Sharon was driving home from day duty when she was killed in a five-vehicle collision on the A141 at Wyton. A lorry driver received six years in prison for causing death by dangerous driving. Sharon joined the force in 1991, serving in several roles, most recently with the Economic Crime Unit. She was survived by her husband, a serving officer, and two children.

LEST WE FORGET

HISTORY OF THE POLICE ROLL OF HONOUR

The author, retired Lancashire Constabulary Sergeant Tony Rae, established the National Police Officers Roll of Honour research project in 1995 and founded the Police Roll of Honour Trust charity in 2000, following twenty years' research into police line-of-duty deaths.

Joining the force in 1974, he was posted to Blackpool where, in 1971, Superintendent Gerald Richardson GC was murdered and two constables wounded foiling an armed robbery. Transferring in 1980 to the Metropolitan Police, he began researching police murders after finding Belton Cobb's *Murdered on Duty* in the Met library. In his thirty months there, ten police officers were murdered on duty in Great Britain, including two in the Met, plus thirty-five serving and four retired RUC officers murdered by terrorists in Northern Ireland.

On 4 January 1983, Tony rejoined the Lancashire Constabulary; on the 5th, WPC Angela Bradley and PCs Gordon Connolly and Colin Morrison drowned attempting a sea rescue at Blackpool. Angela and Gordon were friends as well as colleagues, with whom he had served on the same shift for three years before joining the Met. They received no national bravery awards but their sacrifice was inspirational; finding no historic records of such deaths existed, he determined to put on record and remember all who had lost their lives in the line of duty.

In 1985, he joined the Police History Society and *Police Review* published his Roll of Honour of 204 police officers unlawfully killed since 1829. By 1995, he had found over 3,000 deaths on duty, 1,000 in the previous thirty years alone. His National Police Officers Roll of Honour Research Project was established and gained the personal support of Lancashire's Chief Constable Pauline Clare, resulting in support from the Association of Chief Police Officers and UK police forces.

In 1999, his List of Remembrance of Met deaths on duty since 1829 was published in *The Official Encyclopedia of Scotland Yard*. In December 2000, Tony was seconded by the Met to research and write their new *Book of Remembrance*, which was dedicated at Hendon by HM the Queen in October 2001. At the request and criteria of Michael Winner, an exclusive Roll was produced to pay special tribute to some 1,600 police heroes and heroines who had been killed as a result of criminal acts, effecting arrests, acts of gallantry or other hazardous duty, for display at the National Police Memorial, unveiled by HM the Queen in 2005. These Rolls were in addition to the Trust's Roll of Honour published by the Police Federation for the National Police Memorial Day from 2004 to 2009.

During 2010–11, the Trust's UK Police Memorial Project group delivered the first proposals approved by the National Memorial Arboretum (NMA), which were handed over to the police service, ultimately resulting in the NMA UK Police Memorial in 2021. In 2012, Tony left the Trust, which he had chaired for most of its twelve years, pursuing academic research study to ensure the Roll's integrity and gaining a master's degree in history at Lancaster University in 2016.

The charity was left in the safe hands of the vice chair, former Met Chief Superintendent Sidney MacKay, whose daughter Nina had been murdered on duty in 1997. In 2018, under Sid's leadership as chairman, the Trust was Incorporated by Royal Charter granted by HM the Queen. In 2019 the Trust became a Memorial Partner to the Police Arboretum Memorial Trust for the UK Police Memorial. In 2020, Sid was awarded the British Empire Medal for services to Police Remembrance, before handing over the chair to the National Police Chaplain Revd Canon David Wilbraham MBE. In April 2023 the Trust merged with the National Police Memorial Day charity to create the new Police Remembrance Trust.

BIBLIOGRAPHY

MARTIN STALLION AND TOM ANDREWS

Much of the large and growing literature on both police history and the women's movement in Britain will include at least some reference to the role of women in the service. To keep it within reasonable bounds, this brief list only includes items which are exclusively about women police. The place of publication is London, unless otherwise stated.

General

Amidon, Lynne Amy (1986) 'Ladies in Blue: Feminism and Policing in Britain in the Late Nineteenth and Early Twentieth Centuries' (PhD Thesis) New York: New York State University, available online at: www.proquest.com/openview/e541586 03ce66add369426663ab4ad25/1?pq-origsite=gscholar&cbl=18750&diss=y [accessed July 2022]

Bland, Lucy (1985) 'In the Name of Protection: The Policing of Women in the First World War' in Brophy, Julia & Smart, Carol (eds) *Women-In-Law: Explorations in Law, Family, and Sexuality*, Routledge, pp.23–49

Brown, Jennifer (1998) 'Aspects of Discriminatory Treatment of Women Police Officers Serving in Forces in England and Wales', *The British Journal of Criminology* **38**(2), pp.265–82

Carrier, John (1983) 'The acceptance and statutory recognition of women as police officers in England and Wales with special reference to the Metropolitan Police, 1914–1931' (PhD thesis) London School of Economics and Political Science, available online at: ethos.bl.uk/OrderDetails.do?uin=uk.bl.ethos.273854

Carrier, John (1988) *The Campaign for the Employment of Women as Police Officers*, Aldershot: Avebury

Coffey, Sarah, Brown, Jennifer and Savage, Stephen (1992) 'Policewomen's Career Aspirations: Some Reflections on the Role and Capabilities of Women in Policing in Britain', *Police Studies: International Review of Police Development*, **15**, pp.13–19

Committee on the Employment of Women on Police Duties (1920) *Report*, His Majesty's Stationery Office (HMSO), Cmd 877
    Minutes of evidence. HMSO, 1921, Cmd 1133
Departmental Committee on the Employment of Policewomen (1924) *Report*, HMSO, Cmd 2224
Douglas, R.M. (1999) *Feminist Freikorps: the British Voluntary Women Police, 1914–1940*, Praeger
Emsley, Clive (2009) *The Great British Bobby: A History of British Policing from the 18th Century to the Present*, Quercus. Note: Chapter 7 specifically: 'War, Women and Wages: Policing the Home Front 1914–1918', pp.178–88
Heidensohn, Frances (1992) *Women in control?: The Role of Women in Law Enforcement*, Oxford: Oxford University Press. Note: Considers American and British perspectives.
Heidensohn, Frances (1993) '"We can handle it out here". Women officers in Britain and the USA and the Policing of Public Order', *Policing and Society: An International Journal of Research and Policy*, 4(4), pp.293–303
Jackson, Louise A. (2006) *Women Police: Gender, Welfare and Surveillance in the Twentieth Century*, Manchester: Manchester University Press
Jackson, Sophie (2014) *Women on Duty: a History of the First Female Police Force*, Stroud: Fonthill
Jones, Sandra (1986) *Policewomen and Equality: Formal Policy v Informal Practice?* Basingstoke: Macmillan
Levine, Philippa (1994) '"Walking the streets in a way no decent woman should": women police in World War 1', *Journal of Modern History*, **66**, pp.34–78
Lock, Joan (2014) *The British Policewoman: Her Story* [New ed.], Robert Hale
Lucas, Norman (1986) *WPC 'Courage'*, Weidenfeld and Nicolson
Lucas, Norman (1988) *Heroines in Blue*, Weidenfeld and Nicolson
Natarajan, Mangai (ed.) (2005) *Women Police*, Routledge. Note: Takes a global perspective but has chapters considering British policing.
Owings, Chloe (1925) *Women Police: a Study of the Development and Status of the Women Police Movement*, New York: Frederick H. Hitchcock. Reprint: (1969) Montclair, NY: Patterson Smith
Rae, Anthony (2002) 'Police heroines: a record of sacrifices women officers have made', *Police Review*, **110**(5693), pp. 24–25
Rae, Anthony (2002) 'Roll of Honour women officers who have been killed while on duty', *Police Review*, **110**(5694), pp. 26–27
Rose, Sonya (2010) 'Girls and GIs: Race, Sex and Diplomacy in Second World War Britain', *The International History Review*, **19**(1), pp.146–60
Scheerhout, John (2013) *Lured to their Deaths – Caging a Killer: Inside Story of the Police Murders that Shocked a Nation*, Liverpool: Trinity Mirror Media
Smith, Clare (2019) 'Elegance with Authority: Norman Hartnell's Designs for the Uniform of Metropolitan Police Women', *Journal of British Police History*, **4**, available online at: british-police-history.uk/cgi-bin/journal.cgi?a=a2142d42a288d075&m=2 927a23e0026c37f#2 [accessed July 2022]
Tancred, Edith (1951) *Women Police, from the Records of the National Council of Women of Great Britain 1914–1950*, National Council of Women

Westmarland, Louise (2001) *Gender and Policing*, Cullompton: Willan

Williams, Clifford (2018) 'From Imprisonment to Patrol: The Role of Some Suffragettes in the Development of Women Policing', *Journal of the Police History Society*, **32**, pp.53–56

Woodeson, Alison (2006) 'The first women police: a force for equality or infringement?', *Women's History Review*, **2**(2), pp.217–32

Women Police in Specific Forces

Avon and Somerset
Williams, Clifford (2016) 'Women Policing the Area of Avon and Somerset Constabulary, 1916–1945', *Journal of the Police History Society*, **31**, pp.50–55

Carlisle
Brader, Chris (1998) 'Copperettes and flighty girls: women and policing in Carlisle and the borders during World War 1', *North East History*, **32**, pp.1–26

Devon and Cornwall
Dell, Simon (2016) *The Fair Arm of the Law: (the Story of the Westcountry's Policewomen)*, Tavistock: Policing Heritage

Fife
(1995) *Policewomen in Fife Constabulary: 50th Anniversary 1945–1995*, Dunfermline: Kingdom

Gloucestershire
Williams, Clifford (2019) 'The First Policewomen of Cheltenham: in Wartime and Peacetime, 1918-1945', *Cheltenham Local History Society Journal,* **35**, pp.53–62

Hampshire
Williams, Clifford (2016) *A History of Women Policing Hampshire and the Isle of Wight 1915–2016*, Netley: Hampshire Constabulary History Society

Hove
Oakensen, Derek (1991) 'A solution looking for a problem?: Women Police in the Borough of Hove 1919–1947', *PICA magazine*, 1/91, pp.13–17

Metropolitan
Jackson, Louise A. (2003) 'Care or Control?: The Metropolitan Women Police and child welfare 1919–1969', *Historical Journal*, **46**, pp.623–48

Rees, Jennifer and Strange, Robert J. (2019) *Voices from the Blue: the Real Lives of Policewomen*, Robinson. Note: A collection of reminiscences by female Met officers, from 1918 onwards.

Nottinghamshire
Phillips, Robert (2022) 'The Early Years of Women Police in the County of Nottinghamshire', *Journal of the Police History Society*, **36**, pp.105–09

Royal Ulster
Brewer, John (1991) 'Hercules, Hippolyte and the Amazons – or Policewomen in the RUC', *British Journal of Sociology*, **42**(2), pp.231–47
Cameron, Margaret (1993) *The Women in Green: a History of the Royal Ulster Constabulary's Policewomen: Golden Jubilee 1943–1993*, Belfast: RUC Historical Society

Sussex
Oakensen, Derek (2015) 'Antipathy to Ambivalence: Politics and Women Police in Sussex, 1915–45', *Sussex Archaeological Collections*, **153**, pp.171–89

West Midlands
Brazier, Corinne and Rice, Steve (2017) *A Fair Cop: 1917–2017: Celebrating 100 Years of Policewomen in the West Midlands*, Birmingham: West Midlands Police Museum

Biographies and Memoirs

The forces, dates of services and ranks are those covered by the work, not necessarily the officer's final position. Where an officer served continuously in two forces, one of which later became part of the other (e.g., Glasgow and Strathclyde), only the later force name is listed.

Alexander, Jessie 1936–66 Nottingham City, Ch. Insp.:
Phillips, Robert (2021) '"It won't be a lazy life by any means": PW Chief Inspector Jessie Alexander', *Journal of the Police History Society*, **35**, pp.11–13

Allen, Mary Sophia 1914–25 Women's Auxiliary Service, Commandant:
Allen, Mary S. (1925) *The Pioneer Policewoman*, Chatto and Windus
Allen, Mary S. and Heynemann, Julie Helen (1934) *Woman at the Crossroads*, Unicorn Press. Note: A history of the women's movement, based on her own experiences: pp.68–91 cover the women police.
1914–36 Women's Auxiliary Service, Commandant:
Allen, Mary S. (1936) *Lady in Blue*, Stanley Paul
Boyd, Nina (2013) *From Suffragette to Fascist: the Many Lives of Mary Sophia Allen*, Stroud: The History Press

Barnett, Helen 1985–96 Metropolitan, PC:
Barnett, Helen and Armitage, Helen (1999) *Urban Warrior: My Deadly Life with the Police Armed Response Unit*, John Blake

Beaumont, Carol 1976–93 South Yorkshire, PC:
Beaumont, Howard (2009) *Carol's Story*, Guildford: Grosvenor House

Birkett Mason, Daisy 1941–71 Metropolitan, Det. Ch. Insp.:
Rogerson, Bill, '"Aunt Daisy": Memories of Daisy Birkett Mason MBE, the First
  Female DCI in the Met Police', *Journal of the Police History Society*, **35**, pp.19–21

Bloggs, E.E. (pseudonym) 200? Un-named provincial force, PC:
Bloggs, E.E. (2007) *Diary of an On-Call Girl*, Wolvey: Monday Books

Bristow, Carol 1964–94 Metropolitan, Det. Insp.:
Bristow, C. (1998) *Central 822*, Bantam

Brooke, Danni 2013 Metropolitan, DC:
Brooke, D. (2023) *The Girl for the Job: True Stories from My Life as an Undercover Cop*,
  Macmillan

Cameron, Ash 198?–200? Metropolitan, Det. Sgt:
Cameron, A. (2013) *Confessions of an Undercover Cop*, Friday Project

Clement-Green, Chris 1984–2000 Thames Valley, PS:
Clement-Green, C. (2017) *Into the Valley*, Mirror Books

Condor, Stella 1951–56 Metropolitan, PC:
Condor, S. (1960) *Woman on the Beat: the True Story of a Policewoman*, Hale

Crockford, Gwendoline 1951–62 Berkshire, Sgt:
D'Alessandro, Ruth (2022) *Calling WPC Crockford: the Story of a 1950s Policewoman*,
  Welbeck

Cunningham, Jean Moffat 1954–81 Lothian and Borders, Supt:
Barnsley, George (2021) 'Supt Jean Moffat Cunningham QPM', *Journal of the Police
  History Society*, **35**, pp.82–83

Davis, Jacquieline 1977–8? Metropolitan, PC:
Davis, J. (1998) *The Circuit*, Penguin

Denis de Vitré, Barbara Mary 1928–60 Sheffield, Leicester, Kent, HM Inspectorate,
Asst HMI:
Stanley, Clifford R. (1972) *The Purpose of a Lifetime: a Profile of Barbara Mary Denis de Vitré
  OBE, Britain's First Woman Assistant Inspector of Constabulary*, Chichester: Barry Rose

Fletcher, Yvonne 1977–84 Metropolitan, PC:
Johnson, Matt and Murray, John (2023) *No Ordinary Day: Espionage, Betrayal, Terrorism
  and Corruption – the Truth Behind the Murder of WPC Yvonne Fletcher*, Ad Lib Publishers

Gleghorn, Bertha 1940–44 Metropolitan, PC:
Foster, Keith (2019) 'Not Forgotten: WPC Bertha Massey Gleghorn: The First
   Female Metropolitan Police Constable Killed in the Line of Duty', *Journal of the
   Police History Society*, **33**, pp.11–12

Halford, Alison 1962–92 Metropolitan, Merseyside, ACC:
Halford, Alison and Barnes, Trevor (1993) *No Way Up the Greasy Pole*, Constable

Hilton, Jennifer, Baroness 1956–67 Metropolitan, Insp.:
Hilton, J. (1967) *The Gentle Arm of the Law: Life as a Policewoman*, Reading: Educational
   Explorers
1956–90 Metropolitan, Commander:
Hilton, J. (2020) *Copper Lady: Life in the Met and Lords*, Stroud: Amberley

Howard, Gladys 1947–76 Hampshire, Insp.:
Howard, G. (2018) *Never a Dull Moment: Memoirs of a Portsmouth Woman*, Blue Lamp Books
Williams, Clifford (2018) 'Gladys Irene Howard (1916–2017): A Portsmouth Police
   Pioneer', *Journal of the Police History Society*, **32**, pp.26–28

Hughes, Nicola 2009–12 Greater Manchester, PC:
Hughes, Bryn (2016) *An Extraordinary Sacrifice: the Story of PC Nicola Hughes,
   16.10.1988–18.9.2012*, Cirencester: Mereo

King, Christine 1982–96 Cambridgeshire, DC:
King, C. (2008) *No One was Listening*, Athena

King, Gladys Lillian 1915(?)–19 London, Women's Police Service:
Scollan, Maureen (2014) 'Gladys Lilian King and the Work of the Women Police in
   London's Strand 1918–19: a Memoir', *Women's History Review*, **23**(2), pp.256–71

Kemp, Olive 1945–76 Thames Valley, PC:
Edwards, Lisa (2016) 'WPC 1 Olive Kemp: the First WPC of the Buckinghamshire
   Constabulary', *Journal of the Police History Society*, **30**, pp.15–17

Lock, Joan 1954–60 Metropolitan, PC:
Lock, J. (1968) *Lady Policeman*, Michael Joseph

Low, Pauline C. 1960–90 Avon and Somerset, Ch. Supt:
Low, P. (2008) *Policing by Cartoon: My Memories of a Police Career 1960–1990*, Somerton:
   Forge-Avalon

MacKay, Julie 1988–2020 Avon and Somerset, Gloucestershire, Det. Supt:
MacKay, J. (2022) *To Hunt a Killer: How I Brought Melanie Road's Murderer to Justice*,
   Harper Element

Malton, Jackie 1970–97 Leicestershire, Metropolitan, Det. Ch. Insp.:
Malton, J. (2022) *The Real Prime Suspect: From the Beat to the Screen. My Life as a Female Detective*, Endeavour

Matthews, Sophie A. (pseudonym?) 2003–14 Metropolitan, DC:
Matthews, S. (2014) *The Thinner Blue Line: the Life of a Female Metropolitan Police Officer*, Bloomington, IN: AuthorHouse

McDonald, Jess 2017–23 Metropolitan, DC:
McDonald, J. (2023) *No Comment: What I Wish I'd Known About Becoming a Detective*, Raven Books

Perkins, Vanessa 1975–91 Metropolitan, PS:
Perkins, Vanessa and Owen, Maureen (1991) *Sorry, Vessa*, Chapmans

Peto, Dorothy Olivia Georgiana 1930–46 Metropolitan, Supt:
Peto, D. (1992) *The Memoirs of Miss Dorothy Olivia Georgiana Peto OBE*, Organising Committee for European Conference on Equal Opportunities in Police

Phillips, Carole 1969–2000 Hertfordshire, Bedfordshire, Supt:
Phillips, C. (2015) *Blue Line, Pink Thread: Memoirs of Police Officer Carole Phillips*, Austin Macauley

Pottinger, Linda 1980–98 Hertfordshire, PC:
Pottinger, L. (2007) *Somewhere Over the Rainbow: an Autobiography of the Life, Love and Loss of a 'Northchurch' Girl*, Milton Keynes: AuthorHouse

Ramsay, Anne 1992–2006 Strathclyde, DC:
Ramsay, Anne and Taylor, Diane (2008) *Girl in Blue: How One Woman Survived Fourteen Years in the Police Force*, Macmillan

Raval, Purnima 1980–2015 Metropolitan, PC:
Raval, Purnima and Virdi, Gurpal (2021) 'Celebrating Diversity in the Met: Purnima Raval and Karpal Kaur Sandhu', *Journal of the Police History Society*, **35**, pp.29–34

Rhodes, Pamela (real name Patricia Crayton) 1951–53 North Riding, PC:
Rhodes, Pamela and Wheeler, Jo (2013) *Bobby on the Beat*, Penguin

Sandhu, Karpal Kaur 1971–73 Metropolitan, PC:
Raval, Purnima and Virdi, Gurpal (2021) 'Celebrating Diversity in the Met: Purnima Raval and Karpal Kaur Sandhu', *Journal of the Police History Society*, **35**, pp.29–34

Sandhu, Parm 1989–2019 Metropolitan, Ch. Supt:
Sandhu, P. (2021) *Black and Blue: One Woman's Story of Policing and Prejudice*, Atlantic Books

Scott, Katherine 1915–18 Hawick Burgh Police area, Women Patrols Leader:
Barbour, G.F. (1929) *Katherine Scott: A Memoir*, Edinburgh: Blackwood

Scott, Maureen Ingram 1963–93 Strathclyde, DC:
Scott, M. (2003) *A Fair Cop*, Glasgow: Clydeside Press

Smith, Edith 1915–17 Lincolnshire, Constable:
Lock, Joan (2006) 'Edith Smith: Grantham's Other "First"', *Journal of the Police History Society*, **21**, pp.5–6

Vinten, Alice 2004–14 Metropolitan, PC:
Vinten, A. (2018) *Girl on the Line: Life and Death in the Metropolitan Police,* Two Roads

Watson, Dorothy Gladys 1919–52 Hove Borough, Essex, PS:
Stallion, Martin (2021) '"Not so Elementary my Dear Watson": The Deeds and Deceptions of a Colchester Policewoman', *Journal of the Police History Society*, **35**, pp.56–59

Willoughby-Easter, Lois 1967–73 Metropolitan, PC:
Willoughby-Easter, L. (2019) *A Girl in Blue*, Blue Lamp Books

Wyles, Lilian 1919–49 Metropolitan, Det. Insp.:
Wyles, L. (1952) *A Woman at Scotland Yard: Reflections on the Struggles and Achievements of Thirty Years in the Metropolitan Police*, Faber

ENDNOTES

Introduction

1   As of 31 March 2021 this still only stood at 32.4% of the workforce, however. Available online at: www.gov.uk/government/statistics/police-workforce-england-and-wales-31-march-2021/police-workforce-england-and-wales-31-march-2021#headline-workforce-figures [accessed February 2022].

2   *The Telegraph*, 1 July 2021.

3   British Association for Women in Policing, available online at: www.bawp.org/women-policing-history/ [accessed June 2022].

4   Virdi, Gurpal and Raval, Purnima (2021) 'Celebrating Diversity in the Met: Karpal Kaur Sandhu and Purnima Raval', *Journal of the Police History Society*, **35**, pp.29–34.

5   Plaque at Lincoln Castle.

6   Dew, Paul (2021) 'First WPC, 1451', *Newsletter of the Police History Society*, Vol. 106, p.41.

7   Bennett, Martyn (ed.) (1995) *A Nottinghamshire Village in War and Peace: the Accounts of the Constables of Upton, 1640–1666*, Nottinghamshire: The Thoroton Society.

8   Cox, J.C. (1890) *Three Centuries of Derbyshire Annals Vol.1*, London: Bemrose and Sons, p.112.

9   'Another Warning to Strangers', *The Liverpool Standard*, 28 July 1835, p.2.

10 Emsley, Clive, *The Great British Bobby: A History of British Policing from the 18th Century to the Present*, London: Quercus.

11 Blackstone, G.V. (1957) *A History of the British Fire Service*, London: Routledge; cited in Everitt, Geoffrey G. (1971) 'The Development of Law and Order in Nottingham', MA Thesis, University of Sussex, Nottinghamshire Archives Office M/24550.

12 Jones, Sandra (1986) *Policewomen and Equality*, London: Macmillan, p.3; Woodeson, Alison (1993) 'The first women police: a force for equality or infringement?', *The Women's History Review*, **2**(2), pp.217–32.

13 Report of the Committee on the Employment of Women on Police Duties (1920), CMD 877, The National Archives 3AMS/B/12/04.

14 Astor, Viscountess (28 March 1922) *Hansard*, Vol. 152, cc.1259–81.

15 Nottingham City Police Annual Reports 1920 and 1921, Nottinghamshire Archives Office, CA/PO/.

16 Report of the Committee on the Employment of Women on Police Duties (1920), CMD 877, The National Archives 3AMS/B/12/04; cited by Astor, Viscountess (28 March 1922) *Hansard*, Vol. 152, cc.1259–81.

17 *Home Office Circular 820*, 183/3 (22 August 1939), The National Archives.

18 Andrews, Tom (2020) *The Greatest Policeman? A Biography of Capt. Athelstan Popkess Chief Constable of Nottingham City Police 1930–1959*, London: Blue Lamp Books.

19 Phillips, Robert and Andrews, Tom (2015) *100 Years of Women in Policing*, Nottinghamshire: Nottinghamshire Police, pp.9–11.

20 *Appendix to Home Office Circular 820*, 183/3 (22 August 1939), The National Archives.

21 Phillips, Robert and Andrews, Tom (2015) *100 Years of Women in Policing*, Nottinghamshire: Nottinghamshire Police.

22 *Leamington Spa Courier*, 29 November 1946.

23 Clinkinbeard, Samantha, Solomon, Starr & Rief, Rachael (2021) 'Why Did You Become a Police Officer? Entry-Related Motives and Concerns of Women and Men in Policing', *Journal of Criminal Justice and Behavior*, **48**(6), pp.715–33.

Chapter 1

1   Awcock, Hannah (2019) *Mary Damer Dawson*. Available online at: turbulentlondon.com/2019/10/24/turbulent-london-mary-damer-dawson-1873-1920/ [accessed July 2021].

2   Cree, Vivienne (2016) '"Khaki Fever" During the First World War: A Historical Case Study of Social Works' Approach towards Young Women, Sex and Moral Danger', *British Journal of Social Work*, **46** (7), pp.1839–54.

3   *The Times*, 17 November 1914.

4   Jackson, L. (2006) *Women Police: Gender, Welfare and Surveillance in the Twentieth Century*, Manchester: Manchester University Press.

5   Critchley, T.A. (1978) *A History of Police in England and Wales*, Constable & Co., pp.184–85.

6   Allen, Mary S. (1925) *The Pioneer Policewoman*, London: Chatto and Windus; and (1936) *Lady in Blue*, London: Stanley Paul & Co.

7   Allen, *The Pioneer Policewoman*, p.8.

8   Boyd, Nina (2014) *Animal Rights and Public Wrongs*, England: CreateSpace, pp.48, 73.

9   *Ibid.*, p.49.

10 Allen, *The Pioneer Policewoman*, p.12.

11 *Baird Report* (1920), Evidence 905.

12 *The Vote*, 21 and 28 August 1914.

13 Boyd, *Animal Rights and Public Wrongs*, pp.50–52.

14 Lock, Joan (2014) *The British Policewoman*, London: Robert Hale, p.21.

15 Allen, *The Pioneer Policewoman*, p.12.

16 Allen, *Lady in Blue*, p.27.

17 Allen, *The Pioneer Policewoman*, p.18.

18 Baker, Michael (1985) *Our Three Selves: The Life of Radclyffe Hall*, England: Hamish Hamilton.

19 Purvis, June (1995) 'Deeds not Words: The Daily Lives of Militant Suffragettes in Edwardian Britain', *Women's Studies International Forum*, **18**(2), pp.91–101.

20 Allen, *The Pioneer Policewoman*, p.41.
21 *The People*, 29 November 1915.
22 Quoted in Lock, *The British Policewoman*, p.91.
23 Lock, *The British Policewoman*, p.136.
24 Allen, *Lady in Blue*, p.32.
25 Allen, *The Pioneer Policewoman*, p.33.
26 *Ibid.*, p.37.
27 *Ibid.*, p.38.
28 Lock, *The British Policewoman*, p.29.
29 *The Times*, 15 March 1916.
30 Allen, *The Pioneer Policewoman*, p.167.
31 *Baird Report* (1920), Evidence 964.
32 Allen, *The Pioneer Policewoman*, pp.71, 273.
33 *Ibid.*, p.62.
34 *Baird Report* (1920), Evidence 1008.
35 Allen, *The Pioneer Policewoman*, pp.101–02.
36 Personal communication from Peter White, Hythe resident.
37 Lock, *The British Policewoman*, p.85.
38 *Ibid.*, p.91.
39 *Ibid.*, p.90.
40 *The Times*, 22 December 1919.
41 *Baird Report* (1920), Evidence 967.
42 *Ibid.*, Evidence 1063–64.
43 Dunning's report to the Home Office, 1917, quoted in Lock, *The British Policewoman*, p.75.
44 Quoted in Lock, *The British Policewoman*, p.110.
45 Macready, Nevil (1924) *Annals of an Active Life*, London: Hutchinson & Co., p.399.
46 Quoted in Lock, *The British Policewoman*, p.117.
47 *Baird Report* (1920), Evidence 1010–13.
48 Allen, *The Pioneer Policewoman*, pp.167–70.
49 Lock, *The British Policewoman*, pp.125–26.
50 Allen, *The Pioneer Policewoman*, pp.167–70.
51 Wyles, Lilian (1951) *A Woman at Scotland Yard*, London: Faber and Faber, pp.99–101.
52 Allen, *The Pioneer Policewoman*, p.8.
53 Wyles, *A Woman at Scotland Yard*, p.99.
54 The author would also like to thank Rod Elwood for searching his personal library for references to Margaret Damer Dawson, including the memoirs of Mary Allen.

Chapter 2
1 Boyce, A.J. and Lavery, E., (1999) *The Lady in Green: Biography of Miss Mary Hare, 1865–1945*, British Deaf History Society Publications.
2 Mayhall, L.E.N., (2003) *The Militant Suffrage Movement: Citizenship and Resistance in Britain, 1860–1930*, Oxford: Oxford University Press, p.134.

3   Crawford, E. (2000) *The Women's Suffrage Movement, A Reference Guide 1866–1928*, Routledge, p.274. *Brighton Gazette*, 26 September, 3 October, 11 November 1908. The *Gazette* reported these meetings in that unmistakeably mildly patronising style that, coincidentally, was to characterise much of the reporting of meetings of the WPV in Brighton.

4   *The Vote*, 24 April 1914.

5   The local branch of the National Union of Women's Suffrage Societies advertised its meetings at the Suffrage Club at 7 Havelock Road regularly, and to distance itself from Suffragettes called itself 'Hastings, St Leonards and East Sussex Suffrage Society (NON MILITANT)' (*sic*) in any advertisements in the local press. Elizabeth Crawford (*Women's Suffrage*, p.197) identifies the St Leonards arsonist as a member of the more militant Women's Social and Political Union, Kitty Marion. Mary Hare was obviously aware of this attack in St Leonards as she referred to it in some of her WFL speeches. *Hastings and St Leonards Observer*, 10 May 1913, 24 May 1913, 31 May 1913, 1 November 1913, 8 November 1913. In East Sussex Record Office (hereafter ESRO), SPA 5/6/4, (which is part of a file entitled 'Militant Suffragettes' formerly kept by Hastings Borough Police) there is a circular letter from Bristol City Police warning about suspected Suffragettes buying large numbers of wicker baskets that were thought to be being used to disguise bombs, and a lengthy supplement to the *Police Gazette* of 16 July 1914 about known or suspected suffragist supporters. The *Police Gazette* frequently contained photographs and descriptions of convicted Suffragettes, those whose identities were sought, those subject to recall to prison, and men thought to be actively helping their cause.

6   *East Grinstead Observer*, 19 July 1913, 26 July 1913.

7   Some indication of progress made in some courts can be found in a report from West London Police Court, where two members of the WPV were about to leave the court while it 'heard certain cases at which women are not supposed to be present' when the magistrate invited them to remain if they wanted to; so they did (*London Daily News*, 6 February 1915).

8   The offender was sentenced to five years' imprisonment. *The Vote*, 13 March, 30 August, 16 October and 18 December 1914; *Kent and Sussex Courier*, 13 March 1914; *Votes For Women*, 14 March 1914; *West Sussex Gazette*, 19 March 1914. On the WFL's campaign to redress the imbalance see Radford, J., 'Women and Policing: Contradictions Old and New', in Hanmer, J., Radford, J., & Stanko, E., (1989) *Women, Policing and Male Violence: International Perspectives*, London: Routledge, pp.13–45.

9   On the Plymouth Watch Committee's proposals, see Mayhall, *Militant Suffrage*, p.128. The WFL's concerns were not misplaced. In June 1918 the controversial Defence of the Realm Regulation 40D was introduced. Designed to reduce the spread of venereal disease in the military, it was in many respects also a reincarnation of the old Contagious Diseases Acts. It too was withdrawn after vigorous protests.

10 *Special Constables Act*, 1914 (4&5 Geo.V, chap.61). *Common Cause*, 2 October 1914. Letter to Sir Edward Ward, dated 13 August, reproduced in *The Vote*, 21 August 1914. In this same issue, Nina Boyle 'Head of Political and Militant Department'

of the WFL announced the launch of the WPV (on 12 August). Although the Undersecretary of State was in one sense correct when he suggested that the employment of women as *full-time constables* would need new legislation, their employment as special constables would not. There was already legislative provision to pay special constables a daily rate and (as anyone at the Home Office should have known) the 1914 Act was about to become law.

11   *The Vote*, 28 August, 13 November 1914, 12 February 1915; *Brighton Graphic*, 4 April 1915. Boyle's comment is cited in: Bland, L., in Brophy, J. and Smart, C., (eds), (1985) *Women-In-Law, Explorations in Law, Family and Sexuality*, London: Routledge, p.34. Philippa Levine argues that eventually 'Boyle's WPV faded into obscurity, ignored by the authorities because of its continued commitment to a feminist perspective'; Levine, P., '"Walking the Streets in a Way No Decent Woman Should": Women Police in World War 1', *Journal of Modern History*, March 1988, Issue 1, pp.34–78.

12   There is little evidence that, for instance, the three nominated senior officers of the WPV after this meeting (Nina Boyle, 'Chief', Edith Watson, 'Head of Investigations', and Eva Christy, 'Mounted Section') spent extra time in Brighton or were much concerned with local arrangements. *The Vote*, 9 April 1915, Woodeson, 'First Women Police'. *Brighton Graphic*, 4 April 1915. *Brighton Gazette*, 10 March 1915.

13   *Sussex Daily News*, 19 March 1915 and 22 March 1915.

14   *Brighton Herald*, 20 March 1915; *Brighton Gazette*, 10 March 1915, 20 March 1915, 24 March 1915, 27 March 1915. ESRO, DB/B/12/30, Brighton Watch Committee minutes, August 1914 to January 1916 (hereafter Btn. WC Mins).

15   *Daily Mirror*, 25 March 1915; *The Times*, 27 March 1915.

16   *Brighton Herald*, 27 March 1915; *Sussex Daily News*, 26 October 1915. The press in Hastings, having reported the arrival of the WPV in Brighton in a supportive way, then took an opposite view once Gentle's views became known; *Hastings and St Leonards Observer*, 27 March 1915, 17 April 1915. Apart from pictures of their training the Brighton WPV seem also to have circulated other group photographs (see for example, *The Graphic (London)*, 17 April 1915).

17   For instance, when the Women Patrols were formed in Chichester in early March 1915, the local newspaper took particular care to reassure its readers that it was entirely unconnected with the WPV (*Chichester Observer*, 10 March 1915).

18   Locally, Alice, Countess of Chichester was president of the Brighton and Hove Women Patrol Committee and the Brighton's mayoress was chairman. Chief Constable Gentle and the mayors of Brighton and Hove sat on the committee (interestingly, the Chief Constable of Hove didn't). When a separate committee was established in Hove in 1917, the mayoress of Hove became Chief Patrol and committee meetings were held at her house.

19   *Brighton Herald*, 27 March 1915; *Brighton Graphic*, 3 and 10 April 1915; *Eastbourne Gazette*, 7 April 1915. The *Brighton and Hove and South Sussex Graphic* started publication only in December 1914. It is difficult to know if Gentle's objection to the WPV wearing uniforms was a dislike of uniforms per se, or if it reflected the possibly embarrassing fact that the only uniforms that the Brighton Special Constabulary had at that time were caps and armbands.

20 *Brighton Graphic*, 10 April 1915; *Weekly Dispatch*, 30 May 1915. The *Dispatch* article seems to represent the official line of both organisations. The WPV were said then to be sixty strong and, in London at least, spent a lot of time in courts, something that was regularly reported in *The Vote*. But in Croydon, for instance, members of the WPV were rebuked by magistrates after it was found that someone who had been referred by the court to the probation officer for reports had also been seen and interviewed by members of the WPV before they even got to the court-nominated official (*West Sussex Gazette*, 26 August 1915).

21 *Brighton Graphic*, 15 October 1915; *Common Cause*, 15 October 1915; *Birmingham Daily Post*, 18 October 1915; *The Vote*, 22 October 1915; *Sussex Daily News*, 26 October 1915; *Brighton Guardian*, 27 October 1915; ESRO, SPA/3/1/13, *Chief Constable's Report Book 3*, Mar 1910–Feb 1924. This was apparently the third time that year that Nina Boyle had been arrested for not complying with regulations issued under the Aliens Restriction Act of that year. She had earlier successfully sued the Bristol Police for unlawful imprisonment. Although often assumed to be South African, Boyle was born in Bexley, Kent in 1865. (Eustace, C.L. (1993) 'Daring to Be Free: The Evolution of Women's Political Identities in the Women's Freedom League, 1907–1930', University of York, Unpublished D.Phil thesis, chaps. 3 and 5.).

22 *Brighton Herald*, 27 November 1915; *The Vote*, 4 February 1916; *Eastbourne Gazette*, 22 March 1916; *Eastbourne Chronicle*, 25 March 1916; *Church League For Women's Suffrage*, 1 April 1916. There was supposed to have been another WFL meeting at Hove Town Hall on 6 November addressed by Nina Boyle and Mary Hare, but for whatever reason it never took place (*The Vote*, 30 October 1915).

23 Coincidentally, the first three women to be employed by Sussex police forces were part-time matrons at Hove, Hastings and Brighton, in 1907, 1908 and 1909 respectively. Oakensen, D., (2015) 'Antipathy to Ambivalence: Politics and Women Police in Sussex, 1915–45', *Sussex Archaeological Collections*, **153**, Issue 1, pp. 171–89. The appointment at Hastings followed a circular letter from the Home Office that suggested that forces who did not employ a matron to supervise female prisoners would not be likely to be certified as 'efficient' (*Hastings Observer*, 16 May 1908).

24 Mary Hare was also president of the Brighton branch of the WSNAC. Even the report on the November meeting in Brighton in the League's own newspaper, *The Vote*, took several weeks to appear and was rather muted when it did so (24 December 1915).

25 There seem to have been two branches of the post-February 1915 WPV, the largest being in London and apparently still operating in February 1916. Though it is difficult to be precise, membership of the Brighton branch may never have exceeded more than a dozen at any one time. It was perhaps no coincidence that the WSNAC was also 'placed in abeyance' in June 1916. *Report of the Women's Freedom League, October 1915 to April 1919*. Available online at: digital.library.lse.ac.uk/objects/lse:sux766qak/read/single#page/102/mode/1up [accessed July 2021].

26 Certainly, Mary Hare seems to have had little to do with policing in any form after she moved to Burgess Hill, although she remained (certainly until after 1928) a member of the WFL. She was elected as a Labour Party member of the Burgess

Hill Urban District Council in 1919 and remained a councillor for over a decade. *Mid Sussex Times*, 1 April 1919. Ironically, in April 1923, as part of a WFL lobby against plans to reduce the pay of women teachers at the annual conference of the National Union of Teachers, Mary Hare chaired a public meeting in Brighton and shared the platform with Commandant Mary Allen of the renamed Women's Auxiliary Service (who spoke on the work of women police); *The Vote*, 23 March, 13 April 1923.

27 *Bexhill Observer*, 12 May, 16 & 23 June, 14 July, 4 August, 17 November 1917, 9 February, 23 March 1918; *West Sussex Gazette*, 10 May 1917. ESRO, DR/B/1/29, Bexhill Borough Council minutes (Nov 1916–Oct 1917). The dissenting voice on Bexhill Corporation was Councillor George Coppard. He was a retired sergeant from the East Sussex Constabulary. Some of the time of the Women Police was taken up in distributing charitable donations to the 'necessitous poor' in the town, and reported accordingly in the local press.

28 *Sussex Express*, 14 December 1917; *Eastbourne Chronicle*, 3 November 1917; *Bexhill Observer*, 9 February, 23 March 1918; *Brighton Herald*, 9 February 1918. Coincidentally (or perhaps not), at the same meeting that the report from Bexhill was considered, the vicar of Rye parish church wrote to the ESSJC asking for permission to employ a policewoman in Rye, paid for by local subscription. The committee rejected the proposal.

29 For instance, it was noted that during 1918, of twenty-one women admitted to St Monica's Rescue Home in St Leonards (run by the Rural Deanery of Hastings and Rye) as a result of police action in Hastings, Bexhill, Rye and surrounding areas, four were referred by Bexhill Women Police (*Bexhill Observer*, 1 February 1919).

30 *Bexhill Observer*, 22 June, 7 December 1918, 28 June, 19 July, 15 November 1919, 24 April 1920. Oakensen (2015) 'Antipathy to Ambivalence'.

31 ESRO, DB/B12/30, Brighton Watch Committee minutes; DO/A/17/7, DO/A/17/8, Hove Watch Committee minutes; *The Vote*, 10 November 1916; Walbrook, H.M. (1920) *Hove and the Great War, A Record and Review*, Hove: Cliftonville Press, p.135. The 'Duties of Policewomen' for the Hove Borough force, dated October 1921, would not be unfamiliar to either the former WPV or the Women Patrols in that town; ESRO, SPA/ACC6572/2. The Police Act 1919 effectively increased the power of watch committees and chief constables so that, in Brighton for instance, while the full council supported the appointment of women officers the Watch Committee didn't, so Chief Constable Griffin got his way.

32 *The Vote*, 9 April 1915.

Chapter 3

1 Barbour, G.F. (1929) *Katherine Scott: A Memoir*, Edinburgh: Blackwood, p.33.

2 *Ibid.*, p.6. Scott's mother was the granddaughter of the former Prime Minister Lord Aberdeen. Katherine appears to have shortened her name by 1914.

3 *Ibid.*, p.5.

4 *Ibid.*, p.7.

5 *Hawick Express*, 1 October 1915.

6 *Southern Reporter*, 18 June 1925.

7 Cathels, David (1887) *Ourselves and Our Times*, Hawick: Kennedy.

8   *Hawick Express*, 20 February 1903.
9   Bogle, Kenneth R. (2004) *Scotland's Common Ridings*, Gloucestershire: Tempus, p.110.
10 *Ibid.*, p.120.
11 Parties of men from burghs across Scotland once patrolled their boundaries on horseback as a matter of course. The purpose was to check that no neighbouring landowner or other person had encroached on the town's lands. The first record of Hawick Common Riding is 1640, although the event is probably much older.
12 Smout, T.C. (1986) *A Century of the Scottish People 1830–1950*, Edinburgh: Fontana, p.136.
13 *Hawick News*, 16 June 1883.
14 Scottish Borders Council Museum and Gallery Service (1999) *Stobs Camp*, Hawick: Scott and Paterson, p.2.
15 *Berwickshire News*, 2 July 1907.
16 *Hawick Express*, 29 January 1915, p.3.
17 *Ibid*.
18 Munro, Kevin (2014) *Scotland's First World War*, Edinburgh: Historic Scotland, p.88.
19 *Hawick Express*, 5 February 1915, p.3.
20 *Hawick Express*, 8 January 1915.
21 *Hawick Express*, 18 August 1915.
22 *Hawick Express*, 19 February 1915, p.3.
23 Charman, Terry (2014) *The First World War on the Home Front*, London: Andre Deutsch, p.107.
24 Rowland, Peter (1975) *Lloyd George*, London: Barrie and Jenkins, p.301.
25 Pugh, Martin (1988) *Lloyd George*, Harlow: Longman, p.89.
26 Levine, Philippa (Mar. 1994) '"Walking the Streets in a Way No Decent Woman Should": Women Police in World War 1', *The Journal of Modern History*, **66** (1), p.43.
27 *Berwickshire News*, 23 March 1915.
28 Jackson, Louise A. et al. (2020) *Police and Community in Twentieth-Century Scotland*, Edinburgh: Edinburgh University Press, p.177.
29 *Report of the Women Patrol for Scotland*, Imperial War Museum, (hereafter IWM) EMP. 42. 3/2, p.1.
30 Levine, 'Walking the Streets in a Way No Decent Woman Should', p.42.
31 NUWW, *How Women Can Help*, IWM, EMP. 42. 5/51, p.1.
32 Levine, 'Walking the Streets in a Way No Decent Woman Should', p.46.
33 NUWW, *How Women Can Help*, IWM, EMP. 42. 5/51, pp.1–2.
34 *Ibid.*, pp.2–3. I have tried to find information on the work of the WP in Peebles without success. Hawick and the region of Stobs Camp was certainly a far busier centre for the army.
35 Barbour, *Katherine Scott*, p.25.
36 Robertson, Derek (2018) *Hawick and District and the Great War 1914–1918*, Hawick: Richardson, p.304.
37 Barbour, *Katherine Scott*, p.27.
38 *Southern Reporter*, 1 June 1916.

39   NUWW, Women Patrols Committee for Scotland, IWM, EMP. 42/55, p.3.

40   NUWW, Report of the Women Patrol's Committee, IWM, EMP.42. 5/22, p.3.

41   *Southern Reporter*, 20 May 1915.

42   *Hawick Express*, 9 July 1915.

43   *The Scotsman*, 23 September 1915.

44   *The Scotsman*, 9 August 1915.

45   *Hawick Express*, 26 March 1915.

46   *Hawick Express*, 18 June 1915.

47   *Police Review and Parade Gossip*, 18 June 1915, p.297.

48   NUWW, The Women Patrol Committee, IWM, EMP. 42.5/21, p.3.

49   *Evening Telegraph and Post*, 8 December 1915.

50   *Hawick News*, 23 April 1915.

51   Barbour, *Katherine Scott*, p.29.

52   *Kelso Chronicle*, 22 February 1918.

53   *Southern Reporter*, 14 January 1915; *Hawick Express*, 19 October 1917 and
     13 September 1918.

54   Barbour, *Katherine Scott*, p.31.

55   *Southern Reporter*, 24 June 1915.

56   NUWW, The Women Patrols for Scotland, IWM, EMP. 42. 3/2, p.6.

57   *Southern Reporter*, 2 February 1928.

58   *The Scotsman*, 26 September 1918.

59   *Police Review and Parade Gossip*, 7 April 1916, p.159.

60   *Hawick Express*, 10 May 1918.

61   *The Scotsman*, 18 July 1918.

62   *Hawick Town Council Minute Book No. 14*, Scottish Borders Archive (hereafter
     SBA), BH/2/14, p.619.

63   *Ibid.*, p.653.

64   *Hawick Express*, 24 October 1919.

65   Jackson et al., *Police and Community in Twentieth-Century Scotland*, p.180.

66   Replies to a list of questions forwarded by the Home Office by the Secretary on
     the Employment of Women on Police Duties, SBA, D/90/83/34, f. 2.

67   Jackson et al., *Police and Community in Twentieth-Century Scotland*, p.188.

68   Roxburgh County Police. Women's Auxiliary Police Corps, SBA, D/90/98/1–14.

69   Barbour, *Katherine Scott*, p.28.

70   *Hawick Express*, 10 December 1952. Berwick, Roxburgh and Selkirk Police was
     formed in 1948.

71   *Jedburgh Gazette*, 26 March 1954.

72   *The Scotsman*, 31 October 2020.

73   Barbour, *Katherine Scott*, p.108.

74   *Ibid.*, p.113.

75   *Ibid.*, p.128.

76   *Ibid.*, p.130.

77   *The Scotsman*, 31 January 1928.

Chapter 4

1   Metropolitan Police Historical Museum Advisory Board (1970) *The Memoirs of Miss Dorothy Olivia Georgiana Peto O.B.E.*, unpublished, p.4.

2   *Baird Report* (1920) evidence.

3   Brazier, Corinne & Rice, Steve (2017) *A Fair Cop: Celebrating 100 Years of Policewomen in the West Midlands*, Birmingham: Self-published, p.7.

4   *Ibid.*

5   Geddes, Eric (1921) 'Second Interim Report of the Geddes Committee (Committee on National Expenditure)', The National Archives CAB 27/166.

6   Wyles, Lilian (1952) *A Woman at Scotland Yard: Reflections on the Struggles and Achievements of Thirty Years in the Metropolitan Police*, London: Faber & Faber, pp.111–12.

7   Lock, Joan (5 December 1986) 'Scarcely Out of Uniform', *The Police Review*.

8   *Ibid.*

9   Becke, Shirley (1974) *The Job: The Newspaper of the Metropolitan Police*.

10 Lock, Joan (1979) *The British Policewoman: Her Story*, London: Robert Hale, p.181.

11 Supplement to the *London Gazette*, 8 June 1944, p.2650.

12 Fido, Martin & Skinner, Keith (1999) *The Official Encyclopedia of Scotland Yard*, London: Virgin Books, pp.196–97.

Chapter 5

1   Edward Smith is the curatorial assistant at the Metropolitan Police Heritage Centre (MPHC) and all information is derived from their extensive collection unless otherwise stated. The editor is grateful for the assistance of the MPHC in compiling this chapter.

2   Wyles, Lilian (1952), *A Woman at Scotland Yard: Reflections on the Struggles and Achievements of Thirty Years in the Metropolitan Police*, London: Faber and Faber, pp.23–26.

3   The National Archives, RG15.

4   WP (Women Police) series, D00001–D00008, MPHC collections.

5   Wyles, Lilian, *A Woman at Scotland Yard*, pp.98–126.

6   Lock, Joan (1979) *The British Policewoman: Her Story*, London: Robert Hale, p.145.

7   Peto, Dorothy (1993) *The Memoirs of Miss Dorothy Olivia Georgiana Peto OBE*, London: Organising Committee for the European Conference on Equal Opportunities in the Police, pp.25–41.

8   Doughan, David (2004) 'Dawson, Margaret Mary Damer (1873–1920)', *Oxford Dictionary of National Biography*.

9   Lock, Joan, *The British Policewoman*, p.91.

10 Allen, Mary Sophia (1925), *The Pioneer Policewoman*, London: Chatto and Windus, pp.129–31, 179–83.

11 Lock, Joan, *The British Policewoman*, pp.130–32.

12 Wyles, Lilian, *A Woman at Scotland Yard*, pp.99–102.

13 Allen, Mary Sophia (1925) *The Pioneer Policewoman*, pp.176–79.

14 Smith, Edward (2020) 'Stanley [née Croll Dalgairns], Sofia Annie (1873–1953)', *Oxford Dictionary of National Biography*.

15 Smith, Edward (2020) 'Metropolitan Dockyard Police', *The Journal of British Police History, Issue VII*, available online at: british-police-history.uk/cgi-bin/journal. cgi?a=a2142d42a288d075&m=ec48d91aec125332#4 [accessed June 2022].
16 Lock, Joan, *The British Policewoman*, p.89.
17 The National Archives, MEPO 7/80.
18 'Wilful Glasgow Wife – Refuses to Rejoin Her Husband', *Sunday Post*, 26 June 1921, p.3; 'Glasgow Merchant Deserted by Wife', *Aberdeen Press and Journal*, 27 June 1921, p.6.
19 Wyles, Lilian, *A Woman at Scotland Yard*, p.25.
20 *Ibid.*, p.24.
21 WP (Women Police) series, D00002, MPHC collections.
22 WP (Women Police) series, D00001, MPHC collections.
23 WP (Women Police) series, D00004, MPHC collections.
24 WP (Women Police) series, D00008, MPHC collections.
25 WP (Women Police) series, D00007, MPHC collections.
26 WP (Women Police) series, D00006, MPHC collections.
27 *Hansard*, Vol. 155, 29 June 1922, available online at: hansard.parliament.uk/ Commons/1922-06-29/debates/7a245527-f177-4366-9061-6f7dffb09b47/ HomeOffice? [accessed June 2022].
28 WP (Women Police) series, D00005, MPHC collections.
29 Wyles, Lilian, *A Woman at Scotland Yard*, pp.108–10.
30 Lock, Joan, *The British Policewoman*, pp.135–46.

Chapter 6

1 'Social Welfare Work at Stafford', *Staffordshire Advertiser*, 2 November 1918.
2 Letter from Chief Constable to Stafford Town Council, 3 June 1919, Staffordshire Archive Service (SAS) ref D/1323/T/12/2.
3 *Staffordshire Sentinel*, 14 November 1919 and *Staffordshire Advertiser*, 6 December 1919.
4 'Stoke on Trent Council', *Staffordshire Sentinel*, 23 July 1920.
5 *Ibid.*
6 'Women police', *Staffordshire Sentinel*, 13 May 1921.
7 'Women police for the potteries', *Staffordshire Sentinel*, 16 June 1921.
8 'No more women officers at present', *Staffordshire Sentinel*, 10 February.
9 'Women police patrols', *Staffordshire Sentinel*, 16 February 1924.
10 'Policewomen in the Potteries', *Staffordshire Sentinel*, 1 June 1931.
11 Letters to both from Watch Committee (SAS) 5/12/27, ref D/1323/T/12/2.
12 Home Office Circular 820,183/3, 22 August 1939, The National Archives.
13 Staffordshire Police minutes dated 7 October 1939, SJC minutes Jan 1938–Mar 1941, (SAS) CC/C/1/12.
14 Home Office circular to police forces No. 801.044/68, 8 August 1940, Stoke-on-Trent City Archives (STCA) ref C/PC/14/2/41.
15 Copy of report from Chief Constable to Watch Committee, 5 September 1940, (STCA) ref C/PC/14/2/41.
16 W.A.P.C. Syllabus of Course of Instructions, Stoke-on-Trent Police (STCA), ref C/PC/14/2/41.

17 Stoke-on-Trent correspondence from CC to HMIC re. increasing number of women, 7 December 1940, 1941, (STCA) ref C/PC/14/2/41.

18 Stoke-on-Trent correspondence from CC to HMIC re. manpower, 24 August 1941 and report to Watch Committee, 13 November 1941, (STCA) ref C/PC/14/2/41.

19 Stoke-on-Trent correspondence from CC to HMIC re. manpower, 15 October 1941 and report to Watch Committee, 13 November 1941, (STCA) ref C/PC/14/2/41.

20 Home Office correspondence to force, 21 November 1941 (STCA) ref C/PC/14/2/41.

21 City of Stoke-on-Trent, details of advertisement of vacancies in WAPC, 3 December 1941 (STCA) ref C/PC/14/2/41.

22 Correspondence from CC to Home Office, 19 September 1942 (STCA) ref C/PC/14/2/41.

23 'Policeman versus Policewomen', *Staffordshire Advertiser*, 20 September 1941.

24 'Opposition to Women Police', *Evening Sentinel*, 17 September 1941.

25 'Newcastle Chief Constable: His views on Women Police', *Staffordshire Sentinel*, 23 June 1943.

26 Staffordshire Police, letter from Chief Constable to Mary Holland, chair of the Burton branch of the NCW, 13 November 1942 (SAS) D3882/1/99.

27 'Newcastle-under-Lyme notes', *Staffordshire Advertiser*, 23 November 1940.

28 'No Policewomen for Newcastle', *Staffordshire Advertiser*, 21 December 1940.

29 'Policeman versus Policewomen', *Staffordshire Advertiser*, 20 September 1941.

30 'Newcastle Council Decides', *Staffordshire Advertiser*, 6 December 1941.

31 Staffordshire Police, letter received from Mary Holland, chair of the Burton Branch of the NCW, 11 August 1942 (SAS) D3882/1/99.

32 Staffordshire Police, letter received from Burton upon Trent, Free Church Federal Council, 5 October 1942 (SAS) D3882/1/99.

33 Staffordshire Police, confidential memo, 29 December 1942 (SAS) D3882/1/99.

34 Staffordshire Police, letters from Burton upon Trent Women's Co-operative Guild, 19 October 1942 and Free Church Women's Council, 10 November 1942, (SAS) D38882/1/99.

35 Staffordshire Police, copy of letter sent to Chief Constable by Mary Holland (no date on it but the reply to this letter is dated 13 November 1942), (SAS) D3882/1/99.

36 Staffordshire Police, letter from Chief Constable H.P. Hunter to Miss Mary Holland, of Burton NCW, 13 November 1942, (SAS) D3882/1/99.

37 'Conquering Litchfield's inadequate resources', *The Mercury*, 16 April 1943.

38 'Newcastle Chief Constable: His views on Women Police', *Staffordshire Sentinel*, 23 June 1943.

39 *Ibid*.

40 Correspondence to the town clerk of Stafford from the named groups, and response of CC, 17 and 21 February 1944, (SAS) ref D/1323/T/12/2.

41 Home Office circular 820, 183/57, 19 February 1942, Stoke-on-Trent archives, (STCA) ref C/PC/14/2/41.

42 Home Office circular 96/1944, 30/3/44, Herefordshire Archives and Records Centre ref A43/10.

43 Tancred, E. (1950) *Women Police 1914–1950* (From the records of the National Council of Women of Great Britain), p.28.

44 Gardener, J. (1992) *Over Here: The GIs in Wartime Britain*, UK: Collins & Brown Ltd, pp.119–25.

45 Staffordshire Police General Order No. 7379, Policewomen – Establishment, duties, pay and allowances, 6 September 1944, (SAS) ref C/PC/1/5/9.

Chapter 7

1 In compiling this chapter, the author wishes to acknowledge the assistance of Simon Dell MBE QCB, Professor Kim Stevenson PhD LLB and Eileen Normington.

2 *Women's Auxiliary Police Corps* (2019) Hampshire Constabulary History Society. Available online at: www.hampshireconstabularyhistory.org.uk/2019/11/11/womens-auxiliary-police-corps/ [accessed July 2021].

3 Appendix to Home Office Circular 820,183/3 (22 August 1939) The National Archives.

4 Interview transcript with Eileen Normington (2016) University of Plymouth '50 Years, 50 Voices'.

5 'More Policewomen Wanted', *Western Morning News*, 13 January 1920, p.8.

6 'Policewoman For Plymouth', *Western Morning News*, 16 September 1937, p.5.

7 'Keen Plymouth Policewoman', *Western Morning News*, 3 July 1943, p.2.

8 Jewell, Roy (n.d.) *Just Another Police Story*, unpublished memoir.

9 Hooper, Winifred E. (2010) unpublished memoirs of Auxiliary Policewoman Winifred Hooper.

10 Nominal Roll Entry for WPC 314 Eileen Normington, South West Police Heritage Collections Trust.

11 *Daily Mirror*, 30 September 1948, p.8.

12 Nominal Roll Entry for WPC 314 Eileen Normington, South West Police Heritage Collections Trust.

13 Dell, Simon (2016) *The Fair Arm of the Law*, Tavistock: South West Police Heritage Collections Trust, pp.5–6.

14 Hooper, unpublished memoir.

15 Unpublished memoirs of Winifred Hooper, *c*.1990.

16 Somervell, Donald, Message from the Secretary of State [of the Home Office] to part-time Members of the Women's Auxiliary Police Corps (June 1945), Whitehall: The Home Office.

17 *The Mirror*, 20 September 2009.

Chapter 8

Author's note: One could say that Sophie has authored her own story, as much of the information for this chapter has come from letters that she wrote to her sisters in New Zealand between 1939 and 1948. I am grateful for the permission given to use this correspondence by Sophie's niece, Juliet Barker of Christchurch, New Zealand.

1   Cooke, Iris (1955) (unattributed) 'A young Policeman smiled at Me'.
2   *Timaru Herald*, 1 July 1933, p.3.
3   Alloway, Sophie, letter to her sisters, 12 September 1939.
4   Alloway, Sophie, letter to her sisters, 11 June 1940.
5   Alloway, Sophie, letter to her sisters, July 1945.
6   *Daily Mail*, 8 February 1946.
7   *Evening Standard*, 23 November 1955.
8   *The Chronicle*, 12 August 1975.

Chapter 9
1   Service Record, Jessie Alexander, Nottinghamshire Archives Office (NAO).
2   Application For Appointment in the Nottingham City Police Force: Jessie Green Alexander, NAO.
3   *Ibid.*
4   *Ibid.*
5   *Ibid.*
6   Andrews, Tom (2020) *The Greatest Policeman? A Biography of Capt. Athelstan Popkess CBE OStJ: Chief Constable of Nottingham City Police 1923–1959*, London: Blue Lamp Books.
7   Popkess, Athelstan (1 September 1939) 'Letter to Town Clerk DOS/WK. Wtch. 36', The John Wing Collection: Nottingham City Women's Auxiliary Police Corps (possession of Tom Andrews).
8   'Nottingham City Policewomen', The John Wing Collection: Nottingham Police Volume 14 (possession of Tom Andrews).
9   Brooks, Frank (16 May 1924) Report to Committee on Women Police, The National Archives T 162/53/2.
10   *Nottingham Journal*, 3 October 1938, p.5.
11   *Daily Mail*, 3 October 1938, additional details courtesy of Susan Godward, granddaughter of May and Charles Richardson, private correspondence with Tom Andrews.
12   Andrews, *The Greatest Policeman?*, pp.107–09.
13   Service Record, Jessie Alexander, NAO.
14   Andrews, *The Greatest Policeman?*, p.125.
15   Phillips, Robert and Andrews, Tom (2015) *100 Years of Women in Policing*, Nottingham: Nottinghamshire Police, p.26.
16   *Nottingham Evening Post*, 14 February 1946.
17   'Nottingham City Policewomen', The John Wing Collection: Volume 14.
18   Service Record, Ethel Davies, NAO.
19   Brook, Frank Lt Col (1928) letter to Royal Commission on Police Powers and Procedure, TNA HO 73/121, HO 73/122, HO 73/123.
20   Nottingham City Police Annual Report 1920, NAO.
21   Nottingham City Police Annual Report 1921, NAO.
22   Brooks Report to Committee on Women Police.
23   'Nottingham City Policewomen', The John Wing Collection: Volume 14.
24   Phillips and Andrews, *100 Years of Women in Policing*, p.26.
25   *Ibid.*, p.26.

26   *Ibid.*, p.38.
27   *Nottingham Evening Post & News*, 1 February 1966.
28   Phillips and Andrews, *100 Years of Women in Policing*, p.43.
29   *Ibid.*, p.38.
30   'Nottingham City Policewomen', The John Wing Collection: Volume 14.
31   *Nottingham Guardian Journal*, 10 July 1958.
32   Phillips and Andrews, *100 Years of Women in Policing*, p.23.
33   *Ibid.*
34   *London Gazette*, 31 May 1963.
35   Service Record, Jessie Alexander, NAO.
36   Minutes of the Watch Committee, 12 January 1966, NAO.
37   Phillips and Andrews, *100 Years of Women in Policing*, p.28.
38   Andrews, *The Greatest Policeman?*

Chapter 10

1   Andy George, President NBPA (National Black Police Association).
2   'Sislin Fay Allen obituary', *The Times*, 21 July 2021.
3   *The Guardian*, 2 January 1968, p.2.
4   *Black History Month Magazine 2015*, available online at: www.blackhisto-rymonth.org.uk/article/section/bhm-firsts/sislin-fay-allen-britains-first-black-policewoman/ [accessed June 2022].
5   Greenhow, Raymond (2018) *Britain's First Black Policeman: The Life of John Kent a Policeman in Cumberland 1835–1846*, Cumbria: Bookcase.
6   'Sislin Fay Allen Obituary', *The Times*, 21 July 2021.
7   *The Times*, 27 April 1968.
8   *Black History Month Magazine 2015*.
9   *The Guardian*, 29 April 1968, p.1.
10   *Black History Month Magazine 2015*.
11   *Ibid.*
12   Smith, Clare (2019) 'Elegance with Authority: Norman Hartnell's Designs for the Uniform of Metropolitan Police Women', *Journal of the British Police History Collector Club*, **4**.
13   *Black History Month Magazine 2015*.
14   'Sislin Fay Allen: Britain's first black policewoman', *The Independent*, 15 July 2021.
15   Virdi, Gurpal & Raval, Purnima (2021) 'Celebrating Diversity in the Met: Purnima Raval and Karpal Kaur Sandhu', *Journal of the Police History Society*, **35**, pp.29–34.
16   'Meet Britain's first ever black policewoman', *Sky News*, 28 October 2020. Available online at: www.youtube.com/watch?v=CJ5f-DBZJDM [accessed June 2022].
17   Workforce data report June 2022, Metropolitan Police, available online at: www.met.police.uk/sd/stats-and-data/met/workforce-data-report/ [accessed June 2022].
18   Phillips, Noel (29 October 2020) 'Black History Month: What it was like for Sislin Fay Allen, Britain's first black policewoman', *Sky News Online*, available at: news.sky.com/story/black-history-month-what-it-was-like-for-sislin-fay-allen-britains-first-black-policewoman-12115248 [accessed June 2022].

19   *Ibid.*
20   *Ibid.*
21   *Ibid.*
22   Metropolitan Police statement, cited in 'Sislin Fay Allen: Britain's first black policewoman dies aged 83' (6 July 2021) *BBC News*, available online at: www.bbc.co.uk/news/uk-england-london-57742700 [accessed June 2022].

Chapter 11

1   Heidensohn, F. & Brown, J. (2012) 'From Juliet to Jane: Women Police in TV Cop Shows, Reality, Rank and Careers' in Peay, J. & Newburn, T. (eds) *Policing: Politics, Culture and Control*, London: Bloomsbury, pp.111–34.
2   Jardine, Vanessa (2023) *LGBT+ History Month*, DCC Vanessa Jardine blog available online at: lgbt.police.uk/blog-lgbt-hm23-dcc-vanessa-jardine/ [accessed May 2023].
3   Wyles, Lilian (1952) *A Woman at Scotland Yard: Reflections on the Struggles and Achievements of Thirty Years in the Metropolitan Police*, London: Faber, p.102.
4   Wyles, *A Woman at Scotland Yard*, p.118.
5   *Ibid.*
6   *Ibid.*, p.252.
7   Heidensohn, F. (2008) 'Gender and Policing' in Newburn, Tim (ed.) *Handbook of Policing*, pp.642–65.
8   Lock, Joan (2014) *The British Policewoman: Her Story*, London: Robert Hale, p.199.
9   Interview with Ethel Bush, *The Job*, 10 September 1971.
10   *Uprising* (2021), BBC, directed by Sir Steve McQueen and James Rogan.
11   'The Brixton Riots 40 Years On – A Watershed Moment for Race Relations', *The Guardian*, 11 April 2021.
12   Malton, J. & Mulholland, H. (2022) *The Real Prime Suspect. From the Beat to the Screen. My Life as a Female Detective*, London: Endeavour.
13   *Vishal* Podcast Series, BBC Sounds, 17 April 2023.
14   'Police reopen Vishal Mehotra murder case after missing link to paedophile ring', *The Times*, 12 May 2023.
15   Letter from the Commissioner of the Metropolitan Police to the Home Secretary, 18 October 1918, The National Archives, MEPO 2/2671.
16   'Sir Robert Mark – Obituary', Duncan Campbell, *The Guardian*, 1 October 2010.
17   *Bent Coppers: Crossing the Line of Duty* (2021), BBC, directed by Todd Austin.
18   Sirmons, Julie (2021) *A Rumination on DCI Jane Tennison* available online at: crimereads.com/a-rumination-on-dci-jane-tennison/ [accessed May 2023].
19   Heidensohn & Brown (2012) 'From Juliet to Jane'.
20   Bowling, B., Reiner, R. & Sheptycki, J. (2010) *The Politics of the Police*, 4th Edition, p.178, citing the work of Fitzgerald et al. (2002) *Policing For London*.
21   Lambert, A., 'DCI Jane Tennison? Yes, that was me', *The Independent*, 14 June 1993.
22   Felitti, V.J. et al. (1998) 'Relationship of childhood abuse and household dysfunction to many of the leading causes of death in adults. The Adverse Childhood Experiences (ACE) Study', *American Journal of Preventive Medicine*, 14(4), pp.245–58.

23 Sirmons – *A Rumination on DCI Jane Tennison*.

24 Casey, Baroness (2023) *Final Report: An independent review into the standards of behaviour and internal culture of the Metropolitan Police Service*, London.

25 Malton, J., 'The misogyny of David Carrick lives on', *The Guardian*, 7 February 2023.

26 Malton, J., 'Follow the crowd or stand out', available online at: www.youtube.com/watch?v=O18s9M3-SRs [accessed May 2023].

Chapter 12

1 The majority of this article comes from interviews conducted with Sue Fish in 2020 and 2021 for which the author is immensely grateful. Any quotes not otherwise attributed are from Sue.

2 *The Daily Mail*, 17 November 2012.

3 *BBC News*, 16 November 2012, available online at: www.bbc.co.uk/news/uk-england-nottinghamshire-20366806 [accessed November 2021].

4 *The Nottingham Post*, 31 May 2021.

5 Fellstrom, Carl (2010) *Hoods: The Gangs of Nottingham. A study in Organised Crime*, Lancashire: Milo Books.

6 *The Guardian*, 13 October 2021.

7 *Evening Standard*, 1 October 2021.

8 Nottingham Citizens (2014) 'No place for hate commission for hate', available online at: d3n8a8pro7vhmx.cloudfront.net/newcitizens/pages/1065attachments/original/1469204592/A-CITIZENS-COMMISSION-NO-PLACE-FOR-HATE.pdf?1469204592 [accessed February 2022].

9 *Daily Mail*, 13 July 2016.

10 *The Mirror*, 13 July 2016.

11 *The Sun*, 13 July 2016.

12 *iNews*, 18 June 2020, available online at: inews.co.uk/culture/page-3-why-end-stop-no-more-the-sun-models-topless-how-explained-449587 [accessed November 2021].

13 Mullany, Louise & Trickett, Loretta (2018) *Misogyny Hate Crime Evaluation Report*, available online at: irep.ntu.ac.uk/id/eprint/45247/1/1506540_Trickett.pdf [accessed February 2022].

14 *The Guardian*, 13 October 2021.

15 Sherman, Lawrence (1998) 'Evidence-Based Policing', *Ideas in American Policing Series*, Washington DC: Police Foundation.

16 Fish, Sue, 'Policing misogyny as a hate crime – the Nottinghamshire Police experience', Zempi, I. & Smith J. (eds) (2021) *Misogyny as Hate Crime*, London: Routledge.

17 Allport, Gordon (1954) *The Nature of Prejudice*, Addison-Wesley.

18 *The Guardian*, 13 November 2020; *Belfast Telegraph*, 4 July 2008.

19 UK Government (2021) *Revised Prevent duty guidance: for England and Wales*, available online at: www.gov.uk/government/publications/prevent-duty-guidance/revised-prevent-duty-guidance-for-england-and-wales [accessed December 2021].

20 *BBC News*, 9 July 2020, available online at: www.bbc.co.uk/news/newsbeat-53269751 [as accessed November 2021].

21 Fellstrom, Carl (2010) *Hoods*, p.149.

22 *The Guardian*, 23 October 2000, p.3.

23 *Sunday Telegraph*, 13 March 2005, p.1.

24 Association of Chief Police Officers and National Centre for Policing Excellence (2006) *Murder Investigation Manual*, Bedfordshire: Centrex.

25 Fellstrom, *Hoods*, *passim*.

26 *The Mirror*, 14 March 2010.

27 *The Independent*, 13 October 2005.

28 *The Independent*, 11 August 2004.

29 Home Office, *Police Workforce England and Wales as at 31st March 2020*, 2nd Edition, p.35, available online at: assets.publishing.service.gov.uk/government/uploads/system/uploads/attachment_data/file/955182/police-workforce-mar20-hosb2020.pdf [accessed December 2021].

30 Whiteley, Jennifer et al. (2013) 'The Impact of Menopausal Symptoms on Quality of Life, Productivity, and Economic Outcomes', *Journal of Women's Health*, **22**(11), pp.983–90.

31 Home Office Police Workforce.

32 *Nottingham Post*, 30 January 2018.

33 *Ibid*.

34 Nottinghamshire Police, *PS199 Menopause Policy Version 1.2*, available online at: www.nottinghamshire.police.uk/sites/default/files/documents/files/PS_199_Menopause_Policy_2016_1.2_FINAL.pdf [accessed December 2021].

35 'Award for Menopause Pioneer', *Police Professional*, 17 May 2017, available online at: www.policeprofessional.com/news/national-award-for-menopause-pioneer-2/ [accessed December 2021].

36 Casey, Gerard (2020) *After #MeToo: Feminism, Patriarchy, Toxic Masculinity and Sundry Cultural Delights*, Exeter: Imprint Academic.

37 *The Sun*, 28 January 2018.

38 *Daily Mail*, 27 January 2018.

39 *The Express*, 29 January 2018.

40 *The Guardian*, 13 October 2021.

41 *Sky News*, 'How Sarah Everard's Killer Was Caught', available online at: news.sky.com/story/sarah-everard-murder-how-killer-policeman-wayne-couzens-was-caught-and-the-lengths-he-went-to-cover-up-his-crime-12419714 [accessed December 2021].

42 *The Times*, 5 February 2022, p.24.

Chapter 13

1 While many women who have a sexual orientation to other women do not mind being called lesbian, some prefer the term gay. And younger women in same sex relationships sometimes call themselves queer instead of lesbian or gay. The language used to describe same-sex orientation is changeable with generations. Terms that may be offensive to one person will be used by another.

2 To 'come out' means to tell people you are gay or lesbian, and this process is a continuing one that might occur every time a person enters a new workplace or social situation.

3   'London's highest ranking police officer quietly comes out', *Gay Star News*, 19 April 2017.

4   For example, the Metropolitan Police file in The National Archives on the Caravan Club, 81 Endell St, London WC1 refers to a disorderly house, with male prostitutes, lesbians and 'coloured' people. The National Archives, MEPO 3/758.

5   TNA/AIR 2/ 13859 'Treatment of Immorality – Procedure in Connection with Immorality'. The file contains discussion and policies and procedures regarding lesbianism/homosexuality and cases of homosexuality between airwomen – members of the WAAF and WRAF – between 1945–68.

6   Purvis, June (1995) '"Deeds, not words": the daily lives of militant suffragettes in Edwardian Britain', *Women's Studies International Forum*, **18**(2), pp.91–101. Mary Allen joined the WSPU, the Suffragette organisation led by Mrs Pankhurst, about 1907 (Boyd (2013) p.23).

7   Boyd (2013) p.44.

8   Clifford Williams (2018) 'From Imprisonment to Patrol: The role of some suffragettes in the development of women policing', *Journal of the Police History Society*, **32**, pp.53–56: 'None of the suffragettes were welcomed at the end of the war when some police forces, including the Metropolitan Police, established their first full time women police sections' (p.54). The less militant suffragists of the former NUWSS (National Union of Women's Suffrage Societies) who had no criminal record or record of militant suffragist activity might have been acceptable, though.

9   Jackson (2014) p.167. Nevil Macready, Commissioner of the Metropolitan Police 1918–20, preferred recruits from the National Council of Women (formerly known as the NUWW (National Union of Women Workers)).

10   Marion Sandover lived with Elizabeth Tonra at 46 St Paul's Road, Gloucester. Electoral registers show Marion Sandover with Elizabeth Tonra (1928 and 1947) and in 1965 with Joan E. Furley. Elizabeth Tonra died in 1959, age 73. Gloucestershire Constabulary historian Sue Webb informed me that Elizabeth 'Tonra was a good Catholic so I am sure that lesbianism would not have been spoken about'.

11   In the West Midlands from 1917–31, half of the female officers in the Women's Department who had served or were serving were unmarried. After the ban in 1931, it wasn't until the 1950s that another married woman was recruited, although there was a relaxation in some forces; for example, in Wolverhampton a female officer got married and stayed on during the war. Brazier and Rice (2017) *A Fair Cop 1917–2017 Celebrating 100 Years of Policewomen in the West Midlands*, Birmingham: West Midlands Police, p.58.

12   Martin Stallion (2021) '"Not so elementary my dear Watson". The deeds and deceptions of a Colchester policewoman', *Journal of the Police History Society*, **35**, pp.56–59. Dorothy Watson married David 'Jock' Miller in 1937. Both were serving in Colchester Borough Police at the time but went to London to marry and kept it quiet from the police in Colchester.

13   See Williams, Clifford (2017) 'Women policing the area of Avon and Somerset Constabulary, 1916–1945', *Journal of the Police History Society*, **31**, pp.50–55.

14 Phillips, Robert and Andrews, Tom (2015) *100 Years of Women in Policing*, Nottinghamshire: Nottinghamshire Police, pp.9–11.
15 Brazier and Rice, *A Fair Cop*, p.98.
16 Lock (2014) *The British Policewoman: Her Story*, London: Robert Hale, p.205.
17 *Ibid.*, p.188.
18 Brazier and Rice, *A Fair Cop*, p.127.
19 *Ibid.*, p.127.
20 *Ibid.*, p.128.
21 Brazier and Rice, *A Fair Cop*, p.128 quotes this article. The author has not been able to see the original and it does not seem to have been collected by the Lesbian and Gay News Archives at the Bishopsgate Institute. An article with a similar title, 'Love without Men', appeared in the *News of the World*, 9 November 1969.
22 www.wmpeelers.com/post/if-only-someone-had-talked-to-me West Midlands Police Museum website [accessed 10 March 2022].
23 Hunt, Lee (19 April 1991) 'When I "came out"', *The Police Review*.
24 *Prime Suspect* was a hugely successful television series first released by Granada Television in 1991.
25 Correspondence to the author, March 2022. Jackie prefers to be known as gay rather than as lesbian. She states she was openly gay in 1981 when she was on the Flying Squad. This makes her one of the first openly gay police officers. Her memoirs, *The Real Prime Suspect*, were published in August 2022 by Endeavour.
26 'Lesbian leads police recruitment drive', *Daily Mail*, 12 December 1994.
27 Burke (1993) *Coming Out of the Blue*, London: Cassell, p.vii.
28 Halford, Alison (1993) *No Way Up the Greasy Pole*, London: Constable and Company.
29 'Discrimination case hears of "shock" police officer's language', *The Pink Paper*, 24 May 1992.
30 In July 1992, Halford withdrew her case as Merseyside withdrew their disciplinary charges against her after the two parties agreed an out of court settlement. Halford claimed it as a victory and was medically retired from the police.
31 Halford, *No Way Up the Greasy Pole*, p.156.
32 Burke, *Coming Out of the Blue*, pp.97–98.
33 *Ibid.*, pp.110–11.
34 *Ibid.*, p.152.
35 *Ibid.*, p.150.
36 *Ibid.*, p.142.
37 en.wikipedia.org/wiki/Between_the_Lines_(TV_series) [accessed 23 March 2022].
38 *Diva*, June 1995, Issue 8, p.9.
39 'A Suitable Job for a Lesbian?', *Diva*, October 1997, Issue 22, pp.22–24.
40 Sam Greatrex served in Hampshire Constabulary 1994–2000. She was forced to retire because of injuries. Greatrex recalled in 2022 how some police officers on the Isle of Wight refused to patrol with her because she was lesbian, and how letters were intercepted and her home watched for evidence of being lesbian (communication to author).
41 *Diva*, October 1997, Issue 22, pp.22–24.

42 Bourne, Stephen, 'One PC missing from The Bill', *The Stage*, 20 April 1995. Also reported in *Gay Times*, May 1995. In *Diva*, Issue 8, p.9, it is estimated that about fifty women were in LAGPA in 1995.

43 See Burke, *Coming Out of the Blue*, p.227.

44 Brazier and Rice, *A Fair Cop*, pp.151–52.

45 In 2014 Bourner became the first chair of the WMP Police Museum Committee.

46 ACPO (Association of Chief Police Officers) endorsed a policing charter drawn up by the National Advisory Group – 'Policing Lesbian and Gay Communities', *Police Review*, 5 December 1997.

47 Hampshire Constabulary established liaison officers in 1996. Initially they were called Community Contact Officers. Later they were renamed Lesbian and Gay Liaison Officers (LAGLO). Of course, you did not have to be gay or lesbian to be a LAGLO and many were not.

48 *Daily Mirror*, 16 December 1998.

49 *Sunday Life*, 1 August 1999.

50 'Partnership policing' refers to the development of good working relations and combined approaches to tackling crime and disorder between different agencies, such as social services, health authorities and local government. The Crime and Disorder Act 1998 placed a statutory duty on a number of agencies to work in partnership to reduce crime and disorder.

51 Now the term transgender is used, which covers more than transsexuals. There are different interpretations of what the word encompasses.

52 The Stephen Lawrence Inquiry: Report of an Inquiry by Sir William Macpherson. Ref: Cm 4262 (1999) London: The Stationery Office.

53 'South Yorkshire: Repeat of gay paper advert causes outcry', *Police Review*, 22 August 1997. Years earlier, in 1983, and after he had retired as Chief Constable, John Alderson spoke of the advantages of recruiting some homosexual officers, *Police Review*, 4 February 1983. Sussex Police were the first police organisation to advertise in the gay press. They advertised in the *Pink Paper* in May 1995.

54 See Williams, Clifford (2016) *A History of Women Policing Hampshire and the Isle of Wight 2015–2016*, Hampshire: Hampshire Constabulary History Society.

55 'Lesbian triangle "led to murder bid"', *The Guardian*, 1 March 2001.

56 LAGPA itself folded in 2014 (by which time it was called the Gay Police Association (GPA)). It was replaced by the National LGBT+ Police Network (launched in 2015).

57 Whiting and Fry were also responsible for much of the training and education about lesbian, gay and bisexual communities which was provided for police and staff in the Hampshire Constabulary.

58 It is now a cliché to see police officers marching at a Pride event. And perhaps with such a reduction in visible police presence on the streets it is time for forces to stop marching at Pride events. The point has been made.

59 Jones and Williams (2013) pp.191–92.

60 Brazier and Rice, *A Fair Cop*, p.148.

61 'One in 26 Avon and Somerset Police officers identify as gay or lesbian', *Somerset County Gazette*, 26 February 2022. Lee Broadstock of the National LGBT+ Police Network kindly provided the author with the full data set. This showed the

percentage of police officers identifying as bisexual or gay/lesbian in thirty-nine police forces. No data was available for four police forces. The percentage identifying as gay or lesbian in the forces with data varied from 2.9 per cent (Dyfed-Powys) to 8.7 per cent (West Yorkshire). The percentage identifying as bisexual varied from 0.8 per cent (Dyfed-Powys and Suffolk) to 4.6 per cent (West Yorkshire). The figures for Cumbria were so high it is doubtful that they were completed accurately. The figures generally have to be treated with caution as they are based on a self-declaration. The author is not aware of any published data on the percentage of women who identify as lesbian/gay in any police force.

62 *Sunday Telegraph*, 13 February 2022, reported that the prosecution rate for violent offences was just 5.4 per cent in 2021 and the rate for theft was 4.3 per cent. These are rock bottom figures. The same paper reported on a survey that showed more than 1 in 10 members of the public would no longer bother reporting a burglary or mugging, and that 4 in 10 would not bother to report other crime.

Chapter 14

1   Clare, Pauline, 'An Ambition Fulfilled', *Lancashire Constabulary Journal*, Summer 1995, p.5.

2   Gibbons, Sarah, 'Prime Candidate', *Police Review*, **103**(5323) 23 June 1995, p.15.

3   Clare, 'An Ambition Fulfilled', p.5.

4   Judge, Tony (1995) 'Prospects for Pauline', *Police*, **27**(11), p.24.

5   *Ibid.*, p.24; Lancashire Constabulary (1966) *Annual Report for 1965*, p.6.

6   Clare, 'An Ambition Fulfilled', p.5.

7   Judge, 'Prospects for Pauline', p.25.

8   'Police Chief Clare collects reward', *Ormskirk Advertiser*, 23 May 1991, p.3.

Chapter 15: Roll of Honour

1   The women police numbers are taken from the following publications: England and Wales and Scotland – H.M. Inspectors of Constabulary (HMIC) Reports for 1939, 1945, 1946, 1960, 1975, 1976 HMSO. Northern Ireland – Cameron, Margaret (1993) *The Women in Green – Royal Ulster Constabulary's Policewomen 1943–1993*, RUC Historical Society. Railway Police – Appleby, Pauline (1995) *Force on the Move*, Malvern: Images Pub. Ltd, pp.140–41 (for 1942); British Transport Commission Police, Chief Constable's Report for 1960 and 1975.

2   HM Chief Inspector of Constabulary Annual Report 1994/95, HMSO.

INDEX

The History Press
The destination for history
www.thehistorypress.co.uk